Gold, Frankincense,

The Whole Jesus:

Biblical Truths for Christian Education

Dr. James R. Heyman

California Baptist University

Dedication

This book is thankfully and humbly dedicated first and foremost to our One Teacher, the Lord Jesus Himself (Matthew 23:10). For if there is anything good in this work, it comes necessarily from Him Whose grace is sufficient (2 Corinthians 12:8-10)! For, as I have written, reread, rewritten, and edited this book, I have often to my surprise been deeply convicted, challenged, and inspired myself by what is in it. I reverently, therefore, take this as an obvious sign of the fact that there must be much less of me and much more of Him and His word and therefore His Spirit also herein! All praise be unto Him! May this book, thusly, be a blessing and an honor and a glory to His mercy and grace.

I also humbly dedicate the book to my devoted family, my wife, our five children, their spouses, and the seven grandchildren; may it also be a blessing to them.

And then to all those with whom I have had the privilege of co-laboring in Christian education over the past four decades, much of God's grace to and through you to me and others is herein. A debt of gratitude is also owed to California Baptist University for the half time sabbatical upon which most of this was originally written in Markleeville, California in the Sierra Nevada's and in Nes Harim, in the Judean Hills, of Israel.

And finally to the Holy Spirit, the Anointer of any truly anointed education or of an, in any way, good book about education, may You have the glory that is Your due!

Gold, Frankincense, and Myrrh - The Whole Jesus: Biblical Truths for Christian Education

Introduction: Why Did Jesus Ask so Many Questions, When He Had All the Answers?

This book is full of questions; in faith, hope, and love it also humbly attempts to offer some possible answers which are purposefully and unashamedly founded upon scriptural truth. The questions and the tentative answers herein come from decades of seeking out through the Spirit just what the Lord's heart for education is. They also humbly come from the mercy and grace of the Holy Spirit, from following the call of Jesus, from personal Bible study, from the anointed teachings and challenges of many other believers, from personal experience laboring creatively and experimenting zealously in the field of Christian education over four decades, from working with other Godly Christians in 22 years of K-12 Christian school leadership in three different states, from raising with my wife five children one of whom has Downs Syndrome, from 11 years of founding and teaching and learning within a unique, university level, master's program specifically designed for Christian school leaders and educators which is now entering its ninth cohort at California Baptist University's Metcalf Graduate School of Education, and from the thoughtful and inspired ruminations and writings of many of my students thereof.

But why are there so many questions? I truly and humbly trust that, by following the Lord Jesus' own example, the questions themselves are very valuable. Consider that, by the testimony of the Gospels, Jesus asked many challenging and controversial questions of many people. Some questions He initiated, and some He asked in response to others' statements or others' questions of Him.

If, however, He already knew the answers and our thoughts, why did He ask these questions anyway? Could it be that His purpose in asking these questions has always been and still is to get us to think deeply and to look carefully and honestly inside our own spirits and our own hearts and our own minds so that we might let Him change them? As well, through His questions, does not Jesus graciously reveal Himself to us and the way of salvation, truth, and life?

Jesus' questions were and are anything but random or inconsequential; they are always careful and purposeful and deeply meaningful. He always asks the right questions because He knows it is good for us to meditate and chew upon meaningful questions in order to find the right answers. Good questions can bring about true convictions; they stick around in our hearts and minds and spirits until we answer them; they focus us on the true target, if we let them.

So I have herein prayerfully and humbly and passionately tried to ask the questions I think Jesus would ask about education in our times, believing the Holy Spirit in you and in me will teach and bless us both, as we ponder these questions together. Asking the right questions, asking good and meaningful questions, is half the battle. Without the right questions, without good questions, it is much more difficult to find the right answers!

So asking good questions is a good thing; and it is also, by the way, very Jewish, no? So the King of the Jews, Jesus, is pretty good at it! Is He not?

Luke 10:25-28 And behold, a certain lawyer stood up and tested Him, saying, "Teacher, what should I do to inherit eternal life?"

He said to him, "What is written in the law? What is your reading of it?"

So he answered and said, "'You shall love the Lord your God with all your heart, with all your soul, with all your strength, and with all your mind,' and 'your neighbor as yourself.'"

And He said to him, "You have answered rightly; do this and you will live."

Notice that Jesus here purposefully and masterfully turns a general and hypothetical question, first of all, back to the scripture by asking His own, two, pointed questions, and then, moreover, not just to the scripture but also to our understanding or reading of it. Put into that context by Jesus' careful, counter questions, the lawyer comes up with the right answer, though the rest of the encounter and the parable of the Good Samaritan that follows show that he lacked the right understanding or right reading of the right answer.

The first question of Jesus, pointing him in the right direction, got him half way there. But the lawyer did not really answer the Lord's second question. Instead, the lawyer asked another, self-justifying question of his own in return, to which Jesus gave him the parable that followed and also thus gave him the opportunity to finish the right answer.

Furthermore Jesus' following parable itself ends with another question regarding who was a true neighbor to the robbed and beaten man left by the side of the road! We see here one example out of many of the power of good questions, and the good answers to which they can lead, and how Jesus uses them to shine light into our hearts and minds and spirits.

Matthew 22:29 Jesus answered and said unto them, Ye do err, not knowing the scriptures, nor the power of God. (King James Version)

In order to get things right and not be in error, be it in education or in anything else, we should humbly do at least three things by the guidance of the Holy Spirit: a) ask and hear the questions Jesus would and does ask us, b) know the scriptures, and c) know and walk in the power of the Living God to which the questions and the scriptures point. May our answers to His possible, educational questions, our way of reading and understanding the scripture, and our doing of His word in the power of His Spirit lead us to life in all our educational endeavors and in life itself!

The focus of this book is to search the scriptures and to listen to the Spirit in order to find the power of God as it applies to the crucial questions of truth in Christian education and thus to be a refocusing help to those of us who would lead in any way in this wonderful, God ordained ministry. I truly believe, as we are lead by the Spirit to ponder God's potential questions and God's truthful answers to these questions, we can become even more of a blessing to many and an honor and a glory to our Lord. May we search our hearts and minds and spirits for His questions and for His answers. He is still asking; are we listening?!

Genesis 1:1 In the beginning God created . . .

Serving Him by Serving You,

Dr. Jim Heyman

Associate Professor of Education, California Baptist University, Riverside, California

Program Director, Master of Science in Education, Educational Leadership for Faith-Based Schools

http://www.calbaptist.edu/fbsleadership   jheyman@calbaptist.edu

All scriptures herein are NKJ except where noted; the bolding of words within scriptures is done by this author for topical emphasis.

Chapter 1: Whose Idea is Christian Education Anyway?

Why is this, a Crucial Question?

What difference does it make whose idea Christian education is? Did a group of Godly parents come up with the idea and then try to convince a local church or civil government to support them? Did some Godly children innocently ask for it? Perhaps some dis-spirited teachers, stuck in a Godless and/or pagan education system, dreamed of it? Or maybe an inspired pastor or church board or denomination thought it would be a good idea and the right thing to do or a good way to nourish children and/or affect the larger culture in a Godly way? Perhaps even a civil government here and there in history saw its real and righteous advantages and potential blessings? Or maybe a founding individual or a group of individuals struck out in faith to do it in order to bless God and children and families?

These have actually all been true, and they have also all come and gone with the vagaries of spiritual and cultural and governmental changes, with the arrival and passing of gifted and inspired individuals, and with the sands and winds of history in various places. The problem is that people and cultures and governments and their commitments come and go; but the Word of the Lord and His purposes stand forever! Could it be that in the beginning, the middle, and the end, Christian education was, is, and always will be God's idea and His heart, and that He doesn't change His mind or His heart or His purposes?!

So why is this important? Well, if a Christian education is God's idea and His heart, we are all then responsible to Him for our reaction to His idea and to His heart. Albert Greene (1998) says that the purpose of the whole creation is for God to reveal Himself to us through it and for us to use it to respond back to God and our neighbor in faith, hope, and love. The point is that God, not us, is the initiator and sustainer of Christian education. It is His idea, it comes from His heart, and He is purposeful about it! We choose to either obey or not.

Genesis 1:1 In the beginning God created . . .

Isaiah 48:7b I am the Lord your God who **teaches** what is best for you, who directs the way you should go.

Psalm 25:8-9 Good and upright is the Lord; therefore He **teaches** sinners in the way. The humble He guides in justice, and the humble He **teaches** his way.

Matthew 23:10 And do not be called teachers; for One is your **Teacher**, the Christ.

John 13:13-15 You call Me **Teacher** and Lord, and you say well, for *so* I am. If I then, *your* Lord and **Teacher**, have washed your feet, you also ought to wash one another's feet. For I have given you an example, that you should do as I have done to you.

John 14:26a But the Helper, the Holy Spirit, whom the Father will send in My name, He will **teach** you all things.

Colossians 2:2b-3 . . . to the knowledge of the mystery of God, both of the Father and of Christ, in whom are hidden **all** the treasures of wisdom and knowledge.

What example did Jesus leave us about teaching and learning? Did He say that a Christian education was our idea or His idea? Who should be and actually is *the* real **teacher** in any true education? "The Lord our God who teaches" is how the Heavenly Father identifies Himself. Our "One Teacher" is how God the Son identifies Himself. And God the Holy Spirit is also identified as the One who "teaches us all things." So who are we to think that education, teaching and learning, of any kind, is our idea and our providence to do with as we wish, with or without God? "For One is your **Teacher**, the Christ;" that is Jesus talking about Himself! The Trinity teaches; God teaches!

The lie is that, if we thought it up, then education is ours, to do with it or not as we please. For instance to whom do the NEA (National Education Association) union sophisticates think education belongs, and how has this affected what they think it is or is not or should be? The same question must be asked of the various state legislatures or the federal government or the civil courts or the mandatorily tax supported universities. However, if education is God's idea, His heart, His providence, what are the implications regarding what it should be, how it should be done, why it is important, and what its targeted outcomes ought to be?

 Do even we, as Christian educators in Christian schools, acknowledge Jesus as *the* "One Teacher" and *the* treasure of all wisdom and knowledge in our classrooms, curricula, daily lesson content, faculty rooms, methodologies, school and student policies, administrative offices, athletic fields, arts programs, parent meetings, and board rooms?

How is this done, and what happens if it is or is not done? What kind of education did Jesus die and rise again to give us? Who are the humble to whom it is offered? Can Christian education help us wash each other's feet and thus help clean up our walks with God? Why is the only time Jesus Himself specifically mentions being an example to us tied directly to being a teacher and to teaching by example?

Good answers to these good questions can be found, but only if we first acknowledge that our learning and our teaching, what we call education, belongs to God. It is His initiative, His idea, His heart, His purpose. It is His providence to teach. We dare not try to steal education from Him or ignore or take indifferently a truly Christian education as though it is not important to Him. He died on the cross and rose again to give it to us.

It is, therefore, the faith, hope, and love of this book to humbly seek His good questions and good answers, not ours, about His idea, His heart, His purpose: a truly Christian education. Education belongs to God. God teaches. All others are either humble imitators and servants or prideful imposters, corruptors, and thieves. This is our foundation. If we do not get this right, whatever we build is destined to fall.

Suffering and Christian Education

Luke 18:16   But Jesus called them unto him, and said, "Suffer little children to come unto me, and forbid them not: for of such is the kingdom of God." KJV

I have for years wondered at the suffering referred to here by our Lord. Through over 30 years in the Christian school, educational ministry on every level of it from kindergarten to graduate school, I have seen and experienced plenty of suffering. But why should we be surprised that an education centered on Jesus involves suffering? Is this not a part of the calling, suffering to allow students to come unto Jesus?

Isaiah 53:3   He is despised and rejected by men, a Man of sorrows and acquainted with grief.

Hebrews 12:2   Looking unto Jesus, the author and finisher of our faith, who for the joy that was set before Him endured the cross, despising the shame, and has sat down at the right hand of the throne of God.

And what was the joy set before Him but our salvation, the living way that He opens unto us by His suffering, sorrow, and endurance! Are we so suffering to allow students to come unto Him?

So, then, who was a child in Hebrew culture, the ones for whom Jesus wants us to suffer in order to allow them to come to Him and forbid them not? The basic answer physically is anyone from conception to 12 years old. At twelve, after bar or bat mitzvah, one becomes a son or a daughter of the law, old enough to read the scripture and to understand through them right from wrong and to be responsible for one's own choices, to understand for oneself. We can witness, for instance, Jesus at twelve in the temple in Jerusalem for the first time, discussing theology with the elders of the nation on an equal footing. We recognize this particular age span as covering pre-school, preschool, and elementary school if we think as contemporary educators.

Of course there is, however, another and crucial dimension to this idea; spiritually we all must become child like in our faith to enter the Kingdom. All of us who receive the Lord start out as re-born children in the Kingdom at any physical age, becoming like a little child all over again. Are we then willing to suffer for both the physical and the spiritually reborn children in order for them to come unto Jesus in their education and thus in the forming of their world views, their cosmologies, their theologies, and their views of reality and life? Or do we forbid them this yearning from the heart of Jesus because we are unwilling to suffer for it?

1 Peter 2:21 For to this you were called, because Christ also suffered for us, leaving us an example, that you should follow His steps.

2 Timothy 1:8-9 Therefore do not be ashamed of the testimony of our Lord, nor of me His prisoner, but share with me in the sufferings for the gospel according to the power of God, [9] who has saved us and called *us* with a holy calling, not according to our works, but according to His own purpose and grace which was given to us in Christ Jesus before time began . . .

If, therefore, we are allowing the physical and spiritual youth this great privilege, then how is this suffering done? Is there economic suffering? Is there social suffering? Is their personal suffering? Are there spiritual attacks? Do others resent this choice because it bothers their conscience? Do we unfairly pay double for education or do we gain a fraction for a salary that could be had elsewhere? Do we give up a second income to stay home and home school or require a second salary to make ends meet to pay tuition? Do some pastors resent the money and time families spend on Christian education and jealously question the validity of our obedient and Godly choice? Do adults selfishly feel they are being short changed? In what do we invest?

Truthfully, our time, effort, money, faith, hope, love, and lives can be invested in things that pass away or in just ourselves or in God through the youth, our own and others' youth, whose eternal reward is just that, eternal. The one thing you can take to heaven and eternity with you is people, not things or earthly power, pleasure, or fame!

And what happens if this suffering is not done? If no one will suffer for the youth to come unto Jesus in the fullness of their lives and training, what happens to them? Why can the present culture and even parts of the institutional church be such an obstacle? Anyone familiar with Christian education in the last 50 years in America knows that many church people have not embraced it, even have opposed or scorned it, rather than supported it. To those who have embraced it, this opposition has been a great angst and even down-right puzzling. While the Gallup Poll has shown for decades that a large majority of American parents would choose for their children a Christian or faith-based education if it did not cost them double through tuition beyond their already heavy, civil, educational, mandatory, tax burden and while despite the obvious decline of the spiritual and moral state of American youth and the American family, many clearly have been unwilling to suffer for the children to come unto Jesus in their education, hoping a God-less education would do or not caring enough to choose rightly.

On the other hand, if one combines the number of people choosing various forms of Christian school education with those who have pursued Christian home schooling, the number is quite large, despite the unjust obstacles, of those who are suffering for children to come unto Jesus in the formation of their thinking, learning, believing, and behaving, in their education. However, even if education is God's idea, His heart, and yet if many other Christians have not chosen to suffer for the children's sakes, who ends up suffering the most but the youth themselves? And all youth are tomorrow's adults whose choices will form tomorrow's culture.

In the twenty-eighth chapter of Matthew, the resurrected Jesus gives all Christians the Great Commission to go and to make disciples, to baptize, and **to teach them**.

<u>Matthew 28:20</u> Teaching them to observe all things whatsoever I have commanded you: and, lo, I am with you always, even unto the end of the age. Amen.

<u>Deuteronomy 4:9</u> Only be careful, and watch yourselves closely so that you do not forget the things your eyes have seen or let them slip from your heart as long as you live. **Teach them** to your children and to their children after them.

Our One Teacher has not changed and will not change His commission to us as believers in Him. And, if we do not or will not disciple our own children in their education, their baptism, their teaching and learning, how can or will we disciple the nations?

Unfortunately civil, supposedly secular education in most nations, including our own, has chosen to outlaw *teaching all things Jesus has commanded us,* forbidding the youth to come unto Him in their learning. What is clear is that Jesus is the issue!

Yet we must also ask, in Christian education itself, are our staff and our whole curricula and policies geared to enabling our students to observe and obey all the things Jesus has commanded us **even to the end of the age**? Or do we use the trials and testings and lures of the end of the age as an excuse to dodge our obedience to do so? *All things Jesus has commanded* are definitely powerful and comprehensive in word and in deed. Even if we see the corruption of this age of sin exploding all around us and pulling from within us, Jesus' commission to us stands firm to the end. This is the humble, attempted target of this book, teaching and learning Jesus' commands regarding education, even to the end of this age.

Whose School is it?

Yet this target begs a corollary question to the one with which we started. First we asked: whose idea is Christian education? Now we ask: whose school, then, is it?

To whom does each Christian school belong? In a culture built on property rights, ownership is an important question. In our minds, whoever owns the school calls the shots, has the rights, sets the course! So who owns a Christian school? We might say a church or a denomination owns a school or an independent board of directors, a parent co-op, a private person or company, some other 501C3 non-profit entity, maybe a home schooling parent, or even an unusual civil government. Perhaps a bank really owns it!

This is, however, looking at ownership from our perspective, but what is God's perspective? Whose blood purchased a Christian education for us? We may be stewards, but who is the real owner? The foundation of this book is that education is God's idea and that Christian schools belong to Him in so far as they are truly Christian schools. The cattle on a thousand hills are His! The universe is His creation. The whole cosmos is sustained by Him! These truths about educational providence, suffering, commission, and ownership set a perspective that is both liberating and captivating, but also definitely humbling. How we answer these questions in our own hearts and in the convictions of our minds and spirits makes a huge difference in how we go about the ministries in which He has called us and placed us. May God stir up our convictions, forgive our misgivings, and deliver us in His mercy and grace from evil to His honor and glory regarding Christian education.

Matthew 9:36 But when He saw the multitudes, He was moved with compassion for them, because they were weary and scattered, like sheep having no shepherd.

Luke 11:23 "He who is not with Me is against Me, and he who does not gather with Me scatters."

Luke 13:34 O Jerusalem, Jerusalem, the one who kills the prophets and stones those who are sent to her! How often I wanted to gather your children together, as a hen gathers her brood under her wings, but you were not willing!

Chapter 2: What is Christian Education?

<u>Genesis 1:26a</u> Then God said, "Let **Us** make man in **Our image**, according to **Our likeness** . . .

How do we mirror God's plural (**Us** and **Our**), triune **"image"** and **"likeness"**? If God is a triune God, three in one, and we are made in His image and likeness, plural and one, how do we mirror this **"image"** and **"likeness"**? In Christian education we often talk a great deal about educating the whole child, the image bearer of God (e.g. Van Brummelen, 2002; Graham, 2003), but what really is this whole **"image"** and **"likeness"**?

This question has become such an important topic that even ASCD (Association for Supervision and Curriculum Development), a giant, supposedly secular mouthpiece regarding American, civil education and curriculum and leadership, has launched a huge, contemporary campaign trying to give a deceptive and Godless spin to the idea of educating the whole child but completely without reference to or dependence upon God or His image in us. Is this possible?

<u>1 Thessalonians 5:23</u> Now may the God of peace Himself sanctify you **completely**; and may your **whole spirit**, **soul**, and **body** be preserved blameless at the coming of our Lord Jesus Christ.

Semantics

This above scripture points us to some important, possible answers concerning the whole student. But first we should look at the obvious concerning what Christian education is. When we call our school Christian or our education Christian or even our church Christian, what do we literally mean? The meaning of the word *Christian* is clearly given in the two original languages of scripture, but we use its English version so often, we can frequently forget its plain semantics.

Christian means more than just Christ-like, though this idea is so immensely profound in itself. The English word is derived from the Greek word, transliterated in English, *Christos,* which is itself a translation of the Hebrew word, מָשִׁיחַ, transliterated in English, as *Mashiach* or Messiah. Both of these words in their native tongues, the Hebrew *Mashiach* and the Greek *Christos,* literally mean *anointed.* This is also part of Jesus' transliterated, Hebrew title, *Yeshua H'Mashiach,* in English, Jesus, the Christ, and literally in Hebrew, Savior, the Anointed One, or put another way around, God's anointed Savior or Jehovah's anointed Savior.

The point is, thusly, such and such Christian school, therefore, is really proclaiming itself to be such and such **anointed** school. This can and should have many levels of meaning for us. For one, it should be a school that follows in everything the true Anointed One, God's anointed Savior, Jesus, the Christ. Another is that it is a school that functions under God's anointing in everything it is and does and says. Or a third would be a school where the Holy Spirit, Who does the anointing, does the teaching and enables the learning. Of course all three of these definitions and probably potentially many more are part of the same truth. The point being, the very name, whether referring to a type of school or a type of education or a type of teaching or a type of curriculum is deeply spiritual and centered upon the **anointing** of the Spirit of God in the name and power of Jesus, our Anointed Savior through the same Holy Spirit.

John 14:26a But the Helper, the Holy Spirit, whom the Father will send in My name, He will teach you all things.

The Whole Student

Now let us return to the afore-quoted, Thessalonians, complete sanctification scripture.

1 Thessalonians 5:23 Now may the God of peace Himself sanctify you **completely**; and may your **whole spirit**, **soul**, and **body** be preserved blameless at the coming of our Lord Jesus Christ.

Accordingly, one very clear way from the scripture, then, that we mirror the triune image and likeness of "the God of peace" is that we have by His creation: a spirit, a soul, and a body.

This is the *complete* and *whole* us; we are made in three parts which are also one, made spirit, soul, and body. Interestingly the spirit comes first; it must be right, born again in God, for the rest to be right. The soul then includes our minds and our emotions and our wills and follows the spirit. The body, which comes last, includes our physical needs, drives, and pleasures which need to follow the spirit as well.

Contemporary, supposedly secular education clearly aims at training the body, the mind, the emotions, and the will, but it also clearly supposedly ignores the spirit, either as though it does not even exist or as though it is irrelevant to life or as though it is just too convicting or confounding to discuss or more sinisterly as though what is happening therein is being purposefully hidden. Contemporary civil education therefore now strives to be supposedly spiritless or at least neutral among spirits; though in doing so, it actually and inexorbitantly becomes full of all kinds of false and thus evil and ungodly spirits, as there are no spiritual vacuums in the creation from God's perspective.

Again, as Greene (1998) aptly points out, this Holy Spirit denying education leads to serving a host of idols instead of serving the one true God.

This is a clear line of demarcation between so called, secular education and true, Christian education. Christian education clearly calls upon and is identified with the **anointing** of a named Holy Spirit, that of God Almighty, the Creator and Sustainer of the universe, who was and is and always will be manifest to us in Jesus, The Anointed One. The other pretends to be spiritless or neutral, while actually thus inviting in a host of God denying spirits, summed up by what scripture calls the spirit of anti-Christ. There is, again, no neutral ground in the spirit; that is a myth and a lie of supposed secularism. Thus the secular claim of neutrality is, in the Spirit, impossible and a ruse of the Devil, the father of all lies and liars!

Luke 11:23 "He who is not with Me is against Me, and he who does not gather with Me scatters."

So using this Thessalonians, three parts in one perspective, Christian educators should be fundamentally compelled to ask the definingly important question, how does one, first and foremost, educate a student's spirit and only then, as well, his or her soul and body? And how does this relate to a school as an **anointed** school or an education as an **anointed** education? Do we dare try to present a Spiritless education, a supposedly secular one with a few prayers, in the name of Jesus, The Anointed One, and call it a Christian education!? Is this reaching the whole student?

Conversely, when we allow our children to be educated in schools that deny or obfuscate the existence and/or the importance of their students' spirits, as well as the existence and the importance of God and His Son and the Holy Spirit as *the* Teacher, and thus attempt to adequately and only educate students' disconnected souls and bodies in the flesh, what happens? What are the disasters and the fruit of a supposedly spiritless education; and this even if it is a religious one? Can one sanctify only the soul and the body without the spirit? Would this be reaching the whole child the way Jesus wants us to reach the whole child, the whole student, the whole person? And, of course, worse than this, what about an education that educates either openly or deceptively in another spirit than the Holy Spirit? What is the fruit of this? Are these issues about which Jesus, God's **anointed** One, is deeply concerned?

And what are the victories and blessings and challenges of a truly Holy Spirit centered and Holy Spirit filled education that does reach to the whole student, spirit, soul, and body in everything the student learns and does and becomes? These are the two sides of another great divide, the all important, anointing divide. Under whose anointing are we functioning in our teaching and learning, in our education?

John 4:22-24 You worship what you do not know; we know what we worship, for salvation is of the Jews. But the hour is coming, and now is, when the true worshipers will worship the Father **in spirit and truth**; for the Father is seeking such to worship Him. **God *is* Spirit** and those who worship Him must worship in spirit and truth.

Do we prioritize, balance, and integrate the education of our students' spirits, souls, and bodies in Christian schools the way Jesus would and the way He wants us to? How do you speak to, reach, and educate a youth's, a student's, spirit? What does this have to do with truth and worship and our Heavenly Father, Who is Spirit!?

For instance, it is said of John the Baptist that:

Luke 1:80a So the child grew and became **strong in spirit** . . .

And of Jesus also:

Luke 2:40 And the child grew and became **strong in spirit**, filled with wisdom; and the grace of God was upon Him.

Of course half the battle is recognizing the reality of the Spirit in education in the first place. Everything in our supposedly secularized culture works to remove the Holy Spirit, the Spirit of the Lord, the Spirit of Truth, the Spirit of the Living God, from our lives and particularly from our education and from our teaching and learning and then to replace it solely with supposedly spiritless, human only, knowledge from the flesh, from the soul and from the body only.

If the truth be told, far too much of what goes on even in Christian schools takes place only on the level of the soul and the body and de-Spirited, worldly, knowledge-only acquisition. The battle to wrench the soul and the body away from the Spirit of the Lord is ever present in our God-denying-ignoring culture. Even clearly seeing the battle is a powerful step in the right direction. God is Spirit; therefore a Spiritless education is a Godless education, and a Godless education opens the door to ungodly spirits, pagan spirits, and demonic spirits and is an abomination to the God who teaches. Witness, for instance, how Halloween and Earth Day and soon to come Sexual Liberation Day are celebrated in our supposedly secular, mandatorily tax funded, civil schools, but Christmas and Easter are now outlawed. All foul spirits, witches, warlocks, and the perverse are welcome, but not the Holy Spirit or anything truly wholesome. And Thanksgiving has nothing to do with God! Again Jesus is the issue.

In Luke 11:24-26 and Matthew 12:43-45, Jesus makes it clear that an empty house not filled with the Holy Spirit, even if swept clean and put in order, soon becomes inhabited with many worse, foul spirits!

Ephesians 6:12 For we do not wrestle against flesh and blood, but against principalities, against powers, against the rulers of the darkness of this age, against **spiritual** hosts of wickedness in the heavenly places. Therefore take up the whole armor of God, that you may be able to withstand in the evil day, and having done all, to stand.

An anointed education, a Christian education, cannot ignore the spirits of the students or of the teachers, or of the curricula, or the spiritual warfare that engulfs us and them, or the teaching of the Holy Spirit and still be true to its name! It is a wrestling match in the spirit, and one that we cannot just wish away or ignore as not relevant or pretend that it is not there.

Remember, however, we have the One who has the Spirit without measure on our side, seated at the right hand of God, the Creator and Sustainer of the universe, ever interceding for us if we are on His side and He is inside of us! Growing and strengthening students' spirits in the Holy Spirit should be the heart and be the identifier of Christian education, anointed education! Should not having our students become **strong in spirit** be our major and central goal? If it was good enough for John the Baptist and Jesus, why would it not be for us?

John 16:13 However, when He, the Spirit of **truth**, has come, He will guide you into **all truth**; for He will not speak on His own authority, but whatever He hears He will speak; and He will tell you things to come.

So in whose authority do we speak and teach and learn? An anointed school, an anointed education, speaks in the authority of God, through the authority and anointing of the Spirit of Truth, the Holy Spirit of God. It is not your truth or my truth or someone else's truth nor is it knowledge in the absence of truth but rather God's eternal Truth from which we derive our authority to speak and to teach and to learn Christianly. God is the author of Christian education, an education anointed in His Spirit and truth.

John 14:26a But the Helper, the Holy Spirit, whom the Father will send in My name, He will **teach** you **all thing**s.

What are "**all things**" or "**all truth**?" One might ask, can the Holy Spirit teach chemistry or history or mathematics or language? But a better question to ask is can chemistry or history or mathematics or language be truly taught without the Holy Spirit? A spiritual education includes all things and all truth taught spiritually! God, not man, nor a meaningless universe, creates chemistry, history, mathematics, and language through the Spirit! If they are His continuous creations, ought He not to be best to teach them to us through His Spirit?!

Hebrews 12:2 Looking unto Jesus, the author and finisher of our faith, who for the joy that was set before Him endured the cross, despising the shame, and has sat down at the right hand of the throne of God.

Can an anointed education, then, a Christian education, be too spiritual? We cannot just talk about Jesus all day long; or rather can we? If, as C. S. Lewis (1955) wrote, the whole creation is Jesus (Aslan) singing to us in the Spirit, what else is there to talk about?

Again, as Albert Greene (1998) so aptly points out, echoing Romans 1, when we split the creation from the Creator, we end up worshipping Mother Nature, the materialistic, false god of meaningless, random, and purposeless chance. God's creation is a huge part of our curriculum. Furthermore, if our education looks unto Jesus, our faith also is not only authored, it is eventually finished, completed in what we learn in Him! Thus education that looks unto Jesus allows Him to author and finish our faith through the Spirit and changes the way we see everything, including the creation which He continuously sustains (Greene, 1998).

1 John 2:26-28 These things I have written to you concerning those who *try to* deceive you. But the anointing which you have received from Him abides in you, and you do not need that anyone teach you; but as the same anointing teaches you concerning all things, and is true, and is not a lie, and just as it has taught you, you will abide in Him. And now, little children, abide in Him, that when He appears, we may have confidence and not be ashamed before Him at His coming.

So, again, who then is our real teacher in an anointed school "**concerning all things**?" How does our education, our teaching and learning, reflect this? Are we learning collaboratively under the anointing of the Spirit of God, Who "is true?" True education, then, is collaboration between the Holy Spirit and our spirits, souls, and bodies, not merely God-less collaboration among God-denying people in the flesh. Can we see this Godly collaboration in our daily lessons, in the way we invite the Holy Spirit to shape our own and our students' view of reality and our view of our subject matters, in our spirits, souls, and bodies? How actively does the Holy Spirit teach in our schools in everything that we teach and learn, in our worldview, our cosmology, our theology, and our philosophy and our practical, everyday living? Is He invited, recognized, identified, followed, acknowledged, obeyed, appreciated, and made preeminent? Is He the real and apparent, head teacher whom we dare not offend with lies or with Spirit-less, worldly and pagan curricula? Do we allow Him to truly integrate all our lessons and activities in spirit, soul, and body? How much do we humbly let Him do this in the nuts and bolts of every one of our daily lessons and activities? Or do we, on our own, just teach lifeless and Spiritless, human knowledge in our prideful, disconnected, and rebellious flesh?

The Connection between the Spirit and the Heart

Proverbs 15:13 A merry heart makes a cheerful countenance, but by sorrow of the heart the **spirit** is **broken**.

Proverbs 17:22 A merry heart does good, like medicine, but a **broken spirit** dries the bones.

Proverbs 18:14 The **spirit** of a man will sustain him in sickness, but who can bear a **broken spirit**?

Luke 4:18 "The **Spirit** of the LORD is upon Me, because He has **anointed** Me to preach the gospel to the poor; He has sent Me to heal the **broken** hearted, to proclaim liberty to the captives and recovery of sight to the blind, to set at liberty those who are oppressed."

There is a definite connection between the heart and the spirit, so it follows that an anointed education aims at the heart and the spirit as well as the mind, the emotions, and the will. These scriptures highlight how important it is in education to guard the spirit and thus the heart from which Jesus says our life issues and vice versa. Does our education carefully nurture and guard our students' spirits?

Luke 4:18 above is part of Jesus' own mission statement quoting from Isaiah (more on this later). It is a spiritual mission. He is essentially saying the Holy Spirit has *Messiah-ed* Him, anointed Him, Christened Him. He is talking about spiritual poverty, spiritual brokenness, spiritual captivity, spiritual blindness, and spiritual oppression, all of which also have soulful and physical manifestations. *The* Teacher has a spiritual education in mind and in heart for us, and it begins with the Spirit of the Lord's **anointing!** True Christian education heals the spirit and the heart and thus blesses the soul and body as well! Is this what our mission and our curricula are all about? How do all of our daily lessons and activities do this?

Acts 10:38 . . . how God **anointed** Jesus of Nazareth with the Holy Spirit and with power, who went about doing good and healing all who were oppressed by the devil, for God was with Him.

Education in the Spirit or the Flesh

John 3:1-12   There was a man of the Pharisees named Nicodemus, a ruler of the Jews. This man came to Jesus by night and said, "Rabbi, we know that You are a teacher come from God; for no one can do these signs that You do unless God is with him."

Jesus answered and said to him, "Most assuredly, I say to you, unless one is born again, he cannot see the kingdom of God."

Nicodemus said to Him, "How can a man be born when he is old? Can he enter a second time into his mother's womb and be born?"

Jesus answered and said to him, "Most assuredly I say to you, unless one is born of water and the **Spirit**, he cannot enter the kingdom of God. That which is born of the flesh is flesh, and that which is born of the Spirit is spirit. Do not marvel that I said to you, 'You must be born again.' The wind blows where it wishes, and you hear the sound of it, but cannot tell where it comes from and where it goes. So is everyone born of the Spirit."

Nicodemus answered and said to Him, "How can these things be?"

Jesus answered and said to him, "Are you the teacher of Israel, and do not know these things? Most assuredly I say to you, We speak what We know and testify what We have seen, and you do not receive Our witness. I have told you earthly things and you do not believe, how will you believe if I tell you heavenly things."

Jesus makes it very clear that "**the teacher**" of Israel was seeing, and thus also surely only teaching and learning, in the flesh and not in the Spirit. The Trinity's (*We, Our*) witness was in the Spirit, and being born of the Spirit in one's spirit was the only way to see God's Kingdom and to be in it. Nicodemus asked a question in the flesh; Jesus answered him in the Spirit. The education Jesus offers, even to *the* teacher of Israel, is a spiritual one, an anointed one, a Christian one! He was speaking to the whole Nicodemus and especially to his spirit! And the scripture later suggests to us that Nicodemus was eventually born again because of it! His spirit heard Him!

Luke 9:51-56 Now it came to pass, when the time had come for Him to be received up, that He steadfastly set His face to go to Jerusalem, and sent messengers before His face. And as they went, they entered a village of the Samaritans, to prepare for Him. But they did not receive Him, because His face was set for the journey to Jerusalem. And when His disciples James and John saw this, they said, "Lord, do you want us to command fire to come down from heaven and consume them, just as Elijah did?"

But He turned and rebuked them, and said, "You do not know what **manner of spirit** you are of. For the Son of Man did not come to destroy men's lives but to save them." And they went to another village.

Here we see Jesus addressing the **"manner of spirit"** of His own disciples. Again, the education Jesus offers, even to His own disciples, is a spiritual one, an anointed one, a Christian one! He was speaking to the whole disciple and especially to their spirits! We also see here, by the way, the danger of their merely soulful knowledge, even of the Bible!

It is not that all of this is easy. There are reasons why, dealing only with knowledge, we slip comfortably into trying to teach to and from just the soul and the body. They are less like the wind, seemingly easier to pin down. It is interesting to note that the Hebrew word for *breath* and *wind*, transliterated as *ruach* in English, is also the word for *spirit* in Hebrew! This double meaning could not have been lost on Nicodemus. No breath, no Spirit, no life!

Speaking to a student's spirit is similar to trying to address a student's heart attitude. "What attitude?" is the normal soulish or fleshly response. But an anointed education cannot ignore the manner of spirit, the manner of heart attitude, because they make the lesson whole, as well as the student, learning from the lesson, whole!

Hebrews 4:12 For the word of God is living and powerful, and sharper than any two-edged sword, piercing even to the division of soul and spirit, and of joints and marrow, and is a discerner of the thoughts and intents of the heart.

So how do you teach a student's spirit, how to you give to him or to her an anointed education, a Christian education, a spiritual education? The Word of God is part of the answer. As Frank Gaebelein (1954) made clear over a half century ago, Christian education hinges upon the Holy Spirit in teachers who are saturated in God's Word in all their thinking, their lives, their teaching and deeds, their spirit and especially their understanding of their subject matters.

As seen above, it is often difficult to discern the spirit from the soul. Supposedly secular educators miss this distinction completely. The very essence of Christian education, however, makes these intents of the heart and spirit both crucial and paramount. They are joint and rich in substance [marrow]. The marrow produces the blood, and our life is in our blood!

Making the connections between the spirit and the soul as well as discerning the difference and finally submitting to the preeminence of the Spirit are what an anointed education, a Christian education, is on any level of education.

Yet one must live and teach in and through the word of God and the Spirit of God and the power of God, and, as well, the word of God and the Spirit of God and the power of God must live and teach in and through us, to do it. A spiritual education must be spiritual! And that by no means, means that it is impractical; that is a lie of Satan and assumes that the whole universe is not upheld and sustained by God's Spirit. John Dewey is wrong, and Jesus is right! God, not nature sustains us.

Mercy, grace, faith, hope, love, purity, wholesomeness, beauty, wisdom, understanding, humility, righteousness, and justice, all of which the Bible constantly teaches, are matters of the spirit, of the heart attitude, and matters of their manifestations in both word and deed. One cannot truly reach or attain or enliven them only in the soul and the body. This is what makes a Christian education Christian, it is anointed, it is of the Spirit in our spirit, and it is taught by the Holy Spirit. This is how, through a truly Christian education, God can sanctify the whole student, spirit, soul, and body, even to the end of the age! We are three, but we are also one. To divide ourselves wounds and destroys us; it breaks our oneness, our wholeness, our wholesomeness. To unite ourselves, spirit, soul, and body to and in God, brings healing and eternal life! This is why the concept of spiritual integration looms so large in Christian education.

Galatians 5:22 But the fruit of the Spirit is love, joy, peace, longsuffering, kindness, goodness, faithfulness, gentleness, self-control.

So education is God's idea, His heart, His initiative, His providence, it belongs to Him; and Christian education is an anointed education, a Spirit centered, directed, and filled education that sanctifies the whole or complete student, spirit, soul, and body.

An anointed education cannot be too Spiritual by definition, and it cannot in a living manner integrate too much of God's Word. For the creation is God's created, spoken, and sustained word; the Bible is God's written, inspired, and holy word; the person of Jesus is God's Living Word; and the Holy Spirit is God's ever present word. Seen in the Spirit, their integration is a Christian education.

Colossians 1:9-10 For this reason we also, since the day we heard it, do not cease to pray for you, and to ask that you may be filled with the knowledge of His will **in all wisdom and spiritual understanding;** [10] that you may walk worthy of the Lord, fully pleasing *Him,* being fruitful in every good work and increasing in the knowledge of God;

Therefore, how we answer the question, what is Christian education, in our own spirits, hearts, minds, and convictions makes a huge difference in how we go about the ministries in which He has called and placed us. May God stir up our convictions, forgive our misgivings, and deliver us in His mercy and grace from evil to His honor and glory.

1 Corinthians 2:11-16 For what man knows the things of a man except the spirit of the man which is in him? Even so no one knows the things of God except the Spirit of God. 12 Now we have received, not the spirit of the world, but the Spirit who is from God, that we might know the things that have been freely given to us by God. 13 These things we also speak, not in words which man's wisdom teaches but which the Holy Spirit teaches, comparing spiritual things with spiritual. 14 But the natural man does not receive the things of the Spirit of God, for they are foolishness to him; nor can he know *them,* because they are spiritually discerned. 15 But he who is spiritual judges all things, yet he himself is *rightly* judged by no one. 16 For *"who has known the mind of the LORD that he may instruct Him?"* But we have the mind of Christ.

There is such a thing as "the spirit of the world," though supposedly secular education deceitfully tries to deny it. In the Spirit of God "we have the mind of Christ;" not that we can instruct God but rather in order to be instructed by Him through His anointing! We should be beyond man's wisdom to God's wisdom. We should be functioning in a realm where natural man cannot see. Do we see this happening in our Christian, anointed schools?

As a concluding example of this entire topic of defining Christian education as anointed education in the Spirit, please consider Mary, the hand maiden of the Lord.

Luke 1:46-47   And Mary said: "My soul magnifies the Lord, and my spirit has rejoiced in God my Savior."

May we give our students an education that leads them to magnify the Lord in their souls, that is in their minds, emotions, and wills, **and** having also already taught their spirits to rejoice in God their Savior! For the first is impossible without the second! The second *had* already happened, so the first could! So we have John the Baptist, Jesus, and Mary as examples for us! May it be said of our students, as it was with Daniel:

Daniel 5:14   I have heard of you, that the Spirit of God is in you, and that light and understanding and excellent wisdom are found in you.

Again the later cannot happen without the former!

1 Corinthians 2:5   . . . that your faith should not be in the wisdom of men but in the power of God.

Deuteronomy 6:5   You shall love the LORD your God with all your heart, with all your soul, and with all your strength.

Heart, soul, and strength are the Old Testament, parallel statement of the Thessalonians' spirit, soul, and body. Let us educate the whole student!

Job 32:8   But *there is* a spirit in man, and the breath of the Almighty gives him understanding.

Isaiah 45:19b   I, the LORD, speak the truth; I declare what is right. (TNIV)

Chapter 3: Is Education Only About Knowledge As the Supposed Secularists Believe?

"Knowledge is **the** outcome of learning," (Anita Woolfolk, *Educational Psychology*, 2005, p. 229, emphasis mine). Pick up any educational psychology textbook used in the nation's universities to train teachers, and you will get this same theme: education, teaching and learning, they are all about knowledge. *The* outcome is not a slip of the tongue; it is a clear, intentional, philosophical and theological position. It sounds so reasonable, rather innocent and obvious; but is it really? How much have we lost that this sounds so true to our modern or post-modern ears?

The Pre-eminence of Knowledge or Truth

Our time has been called the information age, and in the information age, is not knowledge king or perhaps even dictator? As reasonable as this sounds to our contemporary ears, what then are the roles of truth, faith, wisdom, hope, love, beauty, humility, purity, faithfulness, understanding, justice, and righteousness in educational or learning outcomes? What of the fruits of the Spirit: love, joy, peace, longsuffering, kindness, goodness, faithfulness, gentleness, self-control? Should they also be *outcomes of learning*? Or have these all been pushed to the curb? Where would Jesus rate them as learning outcomes alongside just knowledge? Is knowledge **the** outcome of learning in His eyes?

Here we reach another crucial, demarcation line, another great divide: outcomes. Is education all about just knowledge or all about truth and all that comes with truth such as faith, wisdom, hope, love, beauty, humility, purity, faithfulness, understanding, justice, righteousness and the fruits of the Spirit: love, joy, peace, longsuffering, kindness, goodness, faithfulness, gentleness, self-control?

<u>3 John 4</u> I have no greater joy than to hear that my children walk in truth.

One can walk in knowledge without walking in faith, or wisdom, hope, love, beauty, humility, purity, faithfulness, understanding, justice, or righteousness; but one cannot walk in truth without also walking in faith, or wisdom, or hope, or love, or beauty, or humility, or purity, or faithfulness, or understanding, or justice, or righteousness or the fruits of the Spirit: love, joy, peace, longsuffering, kindness, goodness, faithfulness, gentleness, self-control. Consider that Satan has knowledge that he walks in, but he does not walk in truth, nor faith, wisdom, hope, love, beauty, humility, purity, faithfulness, understanding, justice, nor righteousness!

This is not to disparage knowledge.

Proverbs 10:14a Wise people store up knowledge.

It is a matter of preeminence, of focus, of values, and of emphasis and of reverse exclusion. In an anointed education knowledge is not **the** outcome of learning; it is **an** outcome of learning, and a secondary one at that. It is not an idol unto itself possessed and worshiped by the supposedly best and brightest among us, the intellectual elites. In fact knowledge without truth is very dangerous as was made abundantly clear in the Garden of Eden. Should knowledge, then, have preeminence in Christian education as it does in supposedly secular education? Do we get trapped into just doing knowledge; perhaps even only doing just knowledge, but just doing it better?

When discussing Godly outcomes, Frank Gaebelein (1954), echoing Cervantes, said that all truth is God's truth; but what does this mean? For one it means that, if something is true, it must be of God because God is truth. Jesus does not just walk in the truth, He is the Truth.

John 14:6 Jesus said to him, "I am the way, the truth, and the life. No one comes to the Father except through Me."

One of our charges in Christian education, anointed, spiritual education, is to be a true witness; and to be a Godly witness we must tell the truth, the whole truth, and nothing but the truth, so help us God, and this with our hand on and in the Bible!

This kind of education cannot be just about knowledge, not even primarily about knowledge; for this is a lie and not the truth. However, if you step into many Christian school lessons, you will most often find them to be primarily if not exclusively about dispensing knowledge, just like the tax supported school down the road. This should not be so. If it is so, is the Holy Spirit, the Spirit of truth, the Teacher? Do we make sure our teachers and thus our students understand the truth of their subject matter as well as they understand the knowledge concerning it? Are we teaching a Christian, an anointed way of life?

Again to paraphrase Albert Greene (1998), civil schools or what one can call Caesar's schools prefer knowledge only, what he calls meaningless facts. They do this because knowledge does not require a response. It is supposedly neutral or dead information about a random, meaningless universe. It is simply a tool to be used as one selfishly wishes.

Truth on the other hand requires action; it is alive, it is a Person, it is an anointed way of life. Children whose education does not inspire nor require a response tend to become passive and cynical, demanding their rights. Children whose education does inspire and require a response should become active, personal, and hopeful, engaging their responsibilities. Again this is not to disparage knowledge. It is important, but it loses its meaning when it is separated from truth and taught and learned in isolation as an end in itself, as an idol of the supposedly best and brightest. Or worse yet, when knowledge is united to lies instead of truth, its true meaning is twisted, and it becomes completely distorted and destructive, a tool of the enemy.

This leads to Herbert Spencer's famous curricular question from two centuries ago: What knowledge is most worth knowing?

John 17:3 And this is eternal life, that they may **know You**, the only true God, and Jesus Christ whom You have sent.

Colossians 1:10 . . . that you may walk worthy of the Lord, fully pleasing Him, being fruitful in every good work and increasing in the **knowledge of God**

Colossians 3:16a Let the word of Christ dwell in you richly as you teach and admonish one another with all wisdom . . .

John 17:17 Sanctify them by the truth, your word is truth.

John 6:45 It is written in the prophets. They will be taught by God. Everyone who listens to the Father and learns from Him comes to me.

Those who are taught by, listen to, and learn from God come to Jesus!

Knowledge of God is the most important knowledge anyone can have; it is the knowledge most worth knowing. Moreover, again, God can be known in at least four ways. He reveals Himself to us in His continuous creation, the world and the universe; He reveals Himself to us in His written word, the Bible; He reveals Himself to us in the Living Word, Jesus, His Son; and He reveals Himself to us in His ever-present word, the Holy Spirit, speaking into our spirits if and only if we are humble enough to accept the Truth as preeminent through the Spirit.

The Knowledge Explosion

We also live in what is called the knowledge explosion. Curricularists in particular are overwhelmed by it. Aristotle wrote an only two volume encyclopedia that had all the known knowledge of his day in it. No such thing of a giant library full of volumes could exist today, even in a single subject area. There is no human alive who knows even a fraction of what is known cumulatively at this point in history.

Daniel 12:4 But you, Daniel, shut up the words, and seal the book until the time of the end; many shall run to and fro, and knowledge shall increase.

This knowledge explosion via telecommunications and electronic webs and computers and multitudinous forms of travel and the sheer size of the human population has not caught God by surprise. He both authors it and foretold it. He also prophetically ties it to the time of the end, or the end times. Keeping this knowledge explosion from replacing or trivializing or minimizing truth and its imminent and transcendent value in our times is one of our greatest challenges. Many wonderful, Christian education writers have focused on the integration of truth and faith with learning as a key to truly Christian education. The explosion of knowledge can overwhelm our time and our efforts from this crucial task, if we let it. We should not, if truth is truly preeminent!

Ephesians 4:15 but, **speaking** the **truth** in **love**, [we] may grow up in all things into Him who is the head — Christ —

Example in the Courts

The fusion or integration of truth and knowledge is something that scares supposedly secular educators. Presently, Des Starr, a Christian school superintendent and a graduate of the CBU, masters program in Educational Leadership for Faith-Based Schools, has run into full battle with the University of California over the issue of Christian integration of faith and learning. Because Calvary Chapel Christian School of Murietta, California has made a valiant effort to found the knowledge in its courses upon Biblical truth and this within an anointed and spiritual and Biblical perspective, the humanists and materialists who control the California state universities have declared war on them. Why? Because the university's entrenched, supposedly secular, humanist and materialist religion is being challenged and threatened by the Truth, Jesus, Whom they have made an outlaw and an enemy at the university!

Although this legal issue has presently gone poorly, it is well worth our time to examine this crucial case within the context of truths for a truly Christian education. Contrast can verily sharpen focus. The case also points out the clear prejudice, injustice, and spiritual blindness of those who oppose truly, Godly education in the supposedly secularized, tax funded, state university establishment which again unfortunately oversees the training of most of the teachers in this nation, even perhaps a majority of those working in Christian schools!

The matter concerns state university approval of high school courses for university entrance requirements and thus whether or not a state university education, funded by all of our taxes, would or would not be a feasible option for a student graduating from any particular kind of high school. It is framed by the university as an issue of proper rigor and preparation regarding high school coursework. The reality is competing religions and what is and what is not politically, philosophically, theologically, and religiously correct in their eyes. The tax funded, state university's argument is basically that learning from a Christian and Biblical, faith perspective is by its very nature and definition inferior to learning from a Godless, materialist, humanist, and supposedly secular perspective and is therefore unacceptable preparation without question. It is a frontal attack on Christian high schools that take their anointed and Biblically integrated education seriously. It is therefore clearly prejudicial: spiritually, religiously, and politically, and thus an obvious freedom of religion, legal issue.

For instance, courses taught from an African American perspective, a gay-lesbian, transgender perspective, an American Indian perspective, a Hindu perspective, in fact any perspective you can possibly imagine are approved; but not a Christian and Biblical perspective. This is clearly unjust, especially considering that Christians, who easily out-number any of the above mentioned minority groups, support the existence of these same universities by civil law with their taxes and massive governmental debt and wanton borrowing. But these supposed secularists are not interested in justice or fairness but rather promoting their Godless religion, materialistic humanism, which abhors the Gospel Truth. As a graduate in philosophy from UC Berkeley, I personally know whereof I speak!

Oddly enough by singling out Christ, they are unwittingly paying Him a giant, if backhanded, compliment; He alone is different from all the others. Believing anything else is not on par with believing in Jesus! This unwitting compliment and truth does not, however, excuse their gross injustice, religious bigotry, and therefore tax thievery.

Finally their spiritual blindness is evident. Their argument has nothing to do with reality. The students who have entered the university from this particular school and these particular kinds of curricula in question, which they have purposely singled out, have done perfectly well at the university and in fact better than the average university student there. Their judgment is not based on clear evidence nor reality, but simply on prejudice and perhaps blind guilt and even spiritual hatred and contempt. It is their learned and scholarly opinion without any basis in reality which is the definition of prejudice. The truth is they disdain Christianity and Christians. They should be pitied for the mean and foolish state of their souls, but they should also be brought to justice for the damage they are doing to the youth of the nation with our tax dollars. They are of a different anointing, and the anointing of the Truth scares them and convicts them and angers them. They sit in the seat of the scornful and mock those who do not share their Godless religion. Of course Caesar never has been a true friend of Jesus but, at best, has held a temporary relationship for his convenience for his ends.

The university's persecution and perspective won in the lower courts. Next the case went all the way to the federal, U.S. Supreme Court where the court unfortunately refused to hear the case letting the lower court's negative ruling stand.

As a matter of truth, justice, and religious freedom this case is shocking and deserves all of our prayers and intercession for the apostasy of our nation. Why should the state universities take everyone's taxes but refuse an education to some, and a very sizable minority at that; and this from a university that supposedly champions minority rights? As it turns out, only their chosen minorities count! It is unclear at this point in what kinds of persecutions the University of California will now feel free to engage. This war will rage until the Lord's return. Courses may need to be designed from multiple perspectives to circumvent this court ruling in California by appealing to their diversity idol. Then we can teach the superiority of the Christian perspective.

1 Corinthians 8:1-3 Now concerning things offered to idols: We know that we all have knowledge. Knowledge puffs up, but love edifies. And, if anyone thinks that he knows anything, he knows nothing yet as he ought to know. But if anyone loves God, this one is known by Him.

And speaking to Caesar's representative, Pontius Pilate,

John 18:37 Jesus answered, "You are right in saying I am a king. In fact, for this reason I was born, and for this I came into the world, to testify to the truth. Everyone on the side of truth listens to me."

Accordingly, if in education we are on the side of knowledge only without and/or against truth, will we ever listen to Jesus, the King of Truth? Or conversely, can those who refuse to listen to Jesus be on the side of truth? Knowledge is clearly connected with puffed up pride; truth is connected with spiritual humility and love. What should a Christian education emphasize? Can we humble ourselves enough to teach truth pre-eminently?

The Inside and Outside of the Cup

Matthew 23:26 Blind Pharisee, first cleanse the inside of the cup and dish, that the outside of them may be clean also.

This may hit the heart of the difference between an education centered on knowledge only or one centered on truth and knowledge, that is, knowledge saturated in, founded upon, and embedded and redeemed within the truth.

The blind Pharisees, as an example of whom Jesus called false teachers, had plenty of knowledge, the fact of which they were very quick to point out to everyone; what they lacked was truth and wisdom and thus the love of God. Knowledge then, metaphorically, can only clean the outside of the cup, the appearance, high test scores, neatly dressed students, etc., but not the inside, the reality, the substance of one's life. It is the Truth, Jesus, who can clean the inside, the heart, the motive, the will through the rebirth of the Spirit and then the knowledge comes with it.

Anointed education is all about truth; it should as well be all about the inside of the cup such that, then, the knowledge part regarding the outside will come easily and through the right context as an added benefit but not as an idol unto itself. Anointed education, Christian education, comes from the Spirit of Truth which enables knowledge to be meaningful. Truth has preeminence and knowledge follows it, not the other way around! Truth requires humility, but knowledge puffs up which is probably why the God-rejecting, lost humanists prefer it!

Colossians 1:18 And He is the head of the body, the church, who is the beginning, the firstborn from the dead, that in all things He may have the preeminence.

Therefore we must look inside our classrooms and inside our lessons and activities and inside our policies and see what the balance is and what the connections are and where the preeminence is between truth and knowledge.

An education supposedly only about knowledge or worse yet about knowledge and God-denying, implicit or explicit, lies can be found anywhere down the road and usually and unfortunately paid for by our taxes. An education that has knowledge secondary to and saturated in, founded upon, and embedded and redeemed within the truth and all that the truth brings, such as faith, wisdom, hope, love, beauty, humility, purity, faithfulness, understanding, justice, and righteousness, can only be found in an anointed school, a Christian school, large or small, in a building or a home, where someone suffers to bring the youth unto Jesus, the Truth, in all their learning and in all their lessons and activities.

How we answer the question, is education only or even primarily about knowledge, in our own spirits, hearts, and convictions and practices makes a huge difference in how we go about the ministries in which He has called and placed us. May God stir up our convictions, forgive our misgivings, and deliver us in His mercy and grace from evil to His honor and glory. Is Truth really preeminent in our education, in our daily lessons, in how our students spend their time and energy?

Isaiah 59:4 No one calls for justice, nor does *any* plead for truth. They trust in empty words and speak lies; they conceive evil and bring forth iniquity.
May the prophet's lament and accusation, which can be easily made of modern, Godless and supposedly secular education, never apply to education in the name of Jesus, Who is the Truth!

Malachi 3:6a "For I *am* the LORD, I do not change;"

Knowledge changes daily; truth is eternal. We can easily fall into the knowledge trap, placing it above faith and truth and belief and wisdom. This is where Adam and Eve stumbled; Satan tempted them with knowledge not truth. Finally regarding these matters let us consider the contrast of Zacharias and Mary at the first coming of our Lord.

Luke 1:18 And Zacharias said to the angel, "How shall I **know** this? For I am an old man, and my wife is well advanced in years."

When Archangel Gabriel came straight from God's throne to tell Zacharias, who was by testimony a righteous priest and a descendent of Abraham no less, that he should rejoice because God was answering his prayers through the birth of his son, John the Baptist, in his old age, Zacharias looked to *knowing* instead of *believing* the plain truth in front of him and the faith for which it called. As a result he became deaf and dumb until the prophecy came to pass and he finally obeyed, naming the Baptist, John.

When Mary, however, was faced by the same Gabriel, the outcome was faith and believing instead of just knowing. This was attested to by none other than Zacharias' own wife, Elizabeth, when Mary, pregnant with Jesus, later visited her in the Judean Hills.

Luke 1:45 Blessed *is* she who **believed**, for there will be a fulfillment of those things which were told her from the Lord."

May Christian education believe truth, receive it, obey it, walk in it, and make it preeminent to knowledge in all its daily lessons and thus in its mission; there is a greater blessing waiting here!

Psalm 33:4   For the word of the LORD is right, and all His work is done in truth.

John 17:17   Sanctify them by Your truth. Your word is truth.

John 1:17   For the law was given through Moses, but grace and truth came through Jesus Christ.

Psalm 15: 1-2   "LORD, who may dwell in your sanctuary? Who may live on your holy hill? He whose walk is blameless and who does what is righteous, who speaks the truth from his heart."

Luke 9:26   For whoever is ashamed of Me and My words, of him the Son of Man will be ashamed when He comes in His own glory, and in His Father's, and of the holy angels.

Chapter 4: To Whom Do the Children Belong, Jesus or Caesar?

<u>Matthew 22:21b</u>   And He said to them, "Render therefore to Caesar the things that are Caesar's, and to God the things that are God's."

<u>Psalm 127:3</u>   Behold, children are a **heritage** from the **LORD**, the fruit of the womb is a reward.

How did Caesar become the educator of America's children? The simple answer is that the civil governments of America had a long partnership with Christianity and the church through the founding and building of the nation. In this context the Gospel was a part of civil life and civil education. Even into the late middle of the last century, civil schools had student chaplains, Godly Thanksgiving, Christmas, and Easter celebrations, prayer, scripture reading, invocations and benedictions spoken in the Spirit and in the name of Jesus, Christian baccalaureates lead by school administrators who were publicly professing Christians, and the Lord's Prayer and the Ten Commandments on the school walls.

Americans raised after the 1960s Supreme Court decisions, those now 55 and younger, have no concept of this and, because of constant state university, media, and NEA and ACLU propaganda, even find it both difficult to believe or hard to understand. Once Caesar got control of the children and, through enormous civil taxation, the vast majority of the American people's education monies, however, he broke the longstanding partnership. So eventually we as a Christian people unfortunately got used to Caesar as a supposed friend of Jesus being in charge of the youth, but was this partnership in accordance with the Judeo/Christian scripture in the first place? To whom do the children truly belong, themselves, their parents, the civil state, or God?

Is the Coup of Caesar Scriptural?

According to scripture, is the education of the children a legitimate role of the supposedly secular, civil government? To reward the good and punish the evildoer and to bear the sword, to execute civil justice, and to keep order and even to build the roads, provide currency, or carry the mail does not mean raising the children.

Scripture in Romans and elsewhere recognizes the right and duty of the civil government to keep civil order and to defend the nation from attack and to mete out civil justice to criminals, but the Bible nowhere suggests the civil government should be the educator of our youth. Bluntly, this is not God's idea!

Scripture does clearly and often, on the other hand, charge fathers, families, the synagogue or temple, the church, and the believing community with this responsibility. Biblically the children belong to God first, the family as primary stewards second, and the church third, and not Caesar or the civil state. The state is supposed to serve the people, not the people serve the state. In our spiritual freedom and responsibility the people educate the state, not the other way around. Sovereignty lies with God and the people, not with the state. So long as it stays within God's prescribed boundaries, the civil state's authority is to be respected.

Philippians 3:20 But our citizenship is in heaven. And we eagerly await a Savior from there, the Lord Jesus Christ.

Most, younger Americans have lost sight of why the founders believed in *limited government*. It was not that they were for anarchy or license; it was because they saw King Jesus as their ultimate authority and the rightful Governor of human affairs and individual conscience. The civil government's authority was thus clearly limited. The people's Christian conscience was the steward of the good life, not the civil state which was to be the servant of a free people.

Our secularized society now thinks that if the civil government does not control everything, who will? With God out of the picture, the state must take control of everything or there will be anarchy! To the founding fathers there was a higher and more important authority from which the civil government derived its limited duties and authority.

This higher authority was not the civil government itself, nor even the will of the people, but rather the sovereignty of God. God gave limited authority to the civil government, and the civil government could not give or take further authority to or from God. It was *In God We Trust*, not government!

Mark 9:37 Whoever welcomes one of these little children in my name welcomes me; and whoever welcomes me does not welcome me but the one who sent me.

What is the converse of this truth spoken by Jesus? If schools do not welcome youth in the name of Jesus, they do not welcome Jesus; and, if they do not welcome Jesus, they do not welcome God. This is a very clear and accurate description of tax funded, civil schools in America in the present generation. God is an outlaw; He is not welcome, nor is Jesus, nor the Holy Spirit, the Spirit of Truth! This is not limited government!

Romans 1:21 For although they knew God, they neither glorified him as God nor gave thanks to him, but their thinking became futile and their foolish hearts were darkened.

A Purposefully Forgotten History

A very brief history of God, Caesar, the church, and Satan in American education ought to be helpful at this point. In the beginning of the founding of modern America, the Puritans founded their own Christian schools, and they passed *The Old Deluder Act* in their civil colony, in which act they stated that they believed God had made them stewards. The act stated that schools must be supported to teach children to read and write for the purpose that the children could understand the scriptures and thus foil the plots of Satan, the Old Deluder, in order to raise up the next generation to live Godly lives in their own and in succeeding generations as well (Hunkins & Ornstein, 2004). Throughout the colonies both private church schools and civil schools were mostly Christian in substance using the Bible as a primary text.

In fact most public or common schools were so Protestant that Catholics felt compelled to start their own private school systems at considerable expense. This was done, not because the civil schools were too secular, but because they were too Protestant. The Catholics feared the common schools would make their children into Protestants not secularists!

This is how the writers of the constitution and our early Presidents and statesmen and jurists were well educated. But the partnership began to unravel. President Thomas Jefferson, who literally cut out the parts of his Bible that he did not like and published his self-edited version, pushed the land grant colleges and civil public schools in all the new territories and states. Land was set aside and given free to the civil schools and universities as well as mandatory tax monies.

With the land and the mandatory, tax money support, Caesar began to dominate education. What most contemporaries have willfully forgotten is that the vast majority of even these civil schools from their inception all the way through the middle of the last century were essentially Christian. They regularly prayed and asked for God's anointing and honored the Bible and Jesus. The populous would never have supported them otherwise.

The dominance of the McGuffey's Readers in public education in the late 1800s and early 1900s well proves this point. While the population of the nation was 76 million in 1900 (Source: Population Estimates Program, Population Division, U.S. Census Bureau Internet Release Date: April 11, 2000), Hunkins and Ornstein (2004) estimate that 120 million of McGuffey's five Readers were sold between 1836 and 1920. That is almost two for every man, women, and child! It was America's textbook!

> What McGuffey did was to combine the virtues of the Protestant faith with those of rural America – patriotism, heroism, hard work, diligence, and virtuous living. The tone was moral, religious, capitalistic, and pro-American; the selections of American literature included orations by George Washington, Patrick Henry, Benjamin Franklin, and Daniel Webster. Through his Readers, McGuffey taught several generations of Americans. … So vivid and timeless his patriotism and faith in American institutions – home, work, church, and nationhood …. (Hunkins & Ornstein, 2004, p. 67)

Looking at a table of contents, one finds selections that include whole passages of scripture, sermons from famous American preachers and statesmen, lectures on moral issues, and excerpts from Christian literature. Actual selection examples for part of one Reader's table of contents include: *Scripture Lesson, Procrastination, Thirsting after Righteousness, Satan and Death at the Gate of Hell, Thoughts in a Place of Public Worship, The Miser, True Wisdom, Christian Hymn of Triumph, from "The Martyr of Antioch", The Gods of the Heathen, The Fall of Babylon, The Better Land, The Proverbs of Solomon, Comfort ye my People, and America – National Hymn* **(McGuffey, 1889).** This was largely public education in America.

The Supposedly Secular Humanists

It was American public education until the likes of John Dewey and other supposedly secular humanists came on board as progressivists pushing God hating Marx, Freud, Nietzsche, and especially Darwin. Dewey helped write and signed the original Humanist Manifesto (Sellars, 1933). Many contemporary Christians have never read it, much to their detriment; for they then wrestle blindly against this principality and even unwittingly often buy into its doctrines and teachings without examining its source.

Humanist Manifesto I

The Manifesto is a product of many minds. It was designed to represent a developing point of view, not a new creed. The individuals whose signatures appear would, had they been writing individual statements, have stated the propositions in differing terms. The importance of the document is that more than thirty men have come to general agreement on matters of final concern and that these men are undoubtedly representative of a large number who are forging a new philosophy out of the materials of the modern world.

— Raymond B. Bragg (1933)

The time has come for widespread recognition of the radical changes in religious beliefs throughout the modern world. The time is past for mere revision of traditional attitudes. Science and economic change have disrupted the old beliefs. Religions the world over are under the necessity of coming to terms with new conditions created by a vastly increased knowledge and experience. In every field of human activity, the vital movement is now in the direction of a candid and explicit humanism. In order that religious humanism may be better understood we, the undersigned, desire to make certain affirmations which we believe the facts of our contemporary life demonstrate.

There is great danger of a final, and we believe fatal, identification of the word religion with doctrines and methods which have lost their significance and which are powerless to solve the problem of human living in the Twentieth Century. Religions have always been means for realizing the highest values of life. Their end has been accomplished through the interpretation of the total environing situation (theology or world view), the sense of values resulting there from (goal or ideal), and the technique (cult), established for realizing the satisfactory life. A change in any of these factors results in alteration of the outward forms of religion. This fact explains the changefulness of religions through the centuries. But through all changes religion itself remains constant in its quest for abiding values, an inseparable feature of human life.

Today man's larger understanding of the universe, his scientific achievements, and deeper appreciation of brotherhood, have created a situation which requires a new statement of the means and purposes of religion. Such a vital, fearless, and frank religion capable of furnishing adequate social goals and personal satisfactions may appear to many people as a complete break with the past. While this age does owe a vast debt to the traditional religions, it is none the less obvious that any religion that can hope to be a synthesizing and dynamic force for today must be shaped for the needs of this age. To establish such a religion is a major necessity of the present. It is a responsibility which rests upon this generation. We therefore affirm the following:

FIRST: Religious humanists regard the universe as self-existing and not created.

SECOND: Humanism believes that man is a part of nature and that he has emerged as a result of a continuous process.

THIRD: Holding an organic view of life, humanists find that the traditional dualism of mind and body must be rejected.

FOURTH: Humanism recognizes that man's religious culture and civilization, as clearly depicted by anthropology and history, are the product of a gradual development due to his interaction with his natural environment and with his social heritage. The individual born into a particular culture is largely molded by that culture.

FIFTH: Humanism asserts that the nature of the universe depicted by modern science makes unacceptable any supernatural or cosmic guarantees of human values. Obviously humanism does not deny the possibility of realities as yet undiscovered, but it does insist that the way to determine the existence and value of any and all realities is by means of intelligent inquiry and by the assessment of their relations to human needs. Religion must formulate its hopes and plans in the light of the scientific spirit and method.

SIXTH: We are convinced that the time has passed for theism, deism, modernism, and the several varieties of "new thought".

SEVENTH: Religion consists of those actions, purposes, and experiences which are humanly significant. Nothing human is alien to the religious. It includes labor, art, science, philosophy, love, friendship, recreation — all that is in its degree expressive of intelligently satisfying human living. The distinction between the sacred and the secular can no longer be maintained.

EIGHTH: Religious Humanism considers the complete realization of human personality to be the end of man's life and seeks its development and fulfillment in the here and now. This is the explanation of the humanist's social passion.

NINTH: In the place of the old attitudes involved in worship and prayer the humanist finds his religious emotions expressed in a heightened sense of personal life and in a cooperative effort to promote social well-being.

TENTH: It follows that there will be no uniquely religious emotions and attitudes of the kind hitherto associated with belief in the supernatural.

ELEVENTH: Man will learn to face the crises of life in terms of his knowledge of their naturalness and probability. Reasonable and manly attitudes will be fostered by education and supported by custom. We assume that humanism will take the path of social and mental hygiene and discourage sentimental and unreal hopes and wishful thinking.

TWELFTH: Believing that religion must work increasingly for joy in living, religious humanists aim to foster the creative in man and to encourage achievements that add to the satisfactions of life.

THIRTEENTH: Religious humanism maintains that all associations and institutions exist for the fulfillment of human life. The intelligent evaluation, transformation, control, and direction of such associations and institutions with a view to the enhancement of human life is the purpose and program of humanism. Certainly religious institutions, their ritualistic forms, ecclesiastical methods, and communal activities must be reconstituted as rapidly as experience allows, in order to function effectively in the modern world.

FOURTEENTH: The humanists are firmly convinced that existing acquisitive and profit-motivated society has shown itself to be inadequate and that a radical change in methods, controls, and motives must be instituted. A socialized and cooperative economic order must be established to the end that the equitable distribution of the means of life be possible. The goal of humanism is a free universal society in which people voluntarily and intelligently cooperate for the common good. Humanists demand a shared life in a shared world.

FIFTEENTH AND LAST: We assert that humanism will: (a) affirm life rather than deny it; (b) seek to elicit the possibilities of life, not flee from them; and (c) endeavour to establish the conditions of a satisfactory life for all, not merely for the few. By this positive morale and intention humanism will be guided, and from this perspective and alignment the techniques and efforts of humanism will flow.

So stand the theses of religious humanism. Though we consider the religious forms and ideas of our fathers no longer adequate, the quest for the good life is still the central task for mankind. Man is at last becoming aware that he alone is responsible for the realization of the world of his dreams, that he has within himself the power for its achievement. He must set intelligence and will to the task.

EDITOR'S NOTE: There were 34 signers of this document, including Anton J. Carlson, **John Dewey**, John H. Dietrich, **R. Lester Mondale**, Charles Francis Potter, Curtis W. Reese, and Edwin H. Wilson.] Copyright © 1973 by the American Humanist Association

If this was the first time you have read this historic document, perhaps you should read it again, several times, slowly. It is pretty much the Bible of the present, tax funded, state universities in America, not to mention most private universities and teachers unions, and so called progressives throughout our culture, etc. An entire book could be written about the lies and deceptions of these ideas and false teachings.

First, however, some other observations are also important. These humanists and their new religion and *matters of final concern* have essentially won the battle for tax funded education from kindergarten to graduate school in America and elsewhere. Many Christians trying to be progressive or socially acceptable or politically correct have unwittingly or cowardly bought into many of these anti-Biblical lies. Finally, the Anti-Christ will agree with most of what is written therein but take it to its next logical step, worship of himself as Satan incarnate. If you do not know your enemy, he has a distinct advantage over you. We need to open our eyes!

Now go back and read it again and then take another look at the selections from McGuffey's Reader which was once the main curriculum for tax funded, K-8 schools in America. Unfortunately you will not find this fact about McGuffey's historical importance in most of your textbooks which are by and large published by these similar thinking and believing, supposedly secular humanists functioning under the religious, humanistic re-visioning of history!

Now I offer some very brief but obviously incomplete comments on the substance of this manifesto. The prologue makes clear that Godless and Spiritless materialism is its foundation in complete agreement with **God hating Marx, Freud, Nietzsche, and especially Darwin**, its guiding lights. There is only matter and no spirit. Consider this in the light of Chapter 2 herein in this book or look at this blasphemous teaching through the eyes of Jesus.

The introduction makes it clear that Christianity should be literally trashed, which Caesar's schools, K through postgraduate, have now successfully done. Supposedly scientific fact should replace revealed truth from God. Man needs to make his own Spiritless religion. Temporal personal satisfaction and temporal social goals should be our highest values and only legitimate (or legal) ends. Gone is glorifying or pleasing God or enjoying redeemed fellowship with God and with our neighbour through the rebirth of the Spirit of God by faith. This is the modern birth place of the Godless, self esteem idol, personal and collective.

Finally the introduction asserts that the humanists are out to establish a new religion. Here there is finally some honesty; if only the Supreme Court had read this or admitted to its reality instead of pretending that secularism is supposedly neutral spiritually! What the humanists do not understand is that the Bible prophesies that this religion that begins by worshipping man and materialism will end up worshipping Satan, fallen man's most cruel master. The snake in the garden did not say worship me, he said worship yourself first!

FIRST: Call God a lie and a liar. A dead, meaningless, random universe is self-existent matter, time, and space, and thus life itself is a chance accident thereof. Of course this cheapens life, and thus euthanasia, abortion, and eugenics become reasonable. As life started as an accident, it will probably end as an accident! The premise is to steal the creation from the Creator and give it to Mother Nature; thus our interaction with a self existent Mother Nature is how we create for ourselves all possible meaning a la Nietzsche and modern and postmodern existentialists.

SECOND: Accidental, Darwinian evolution created man, not God, and therefore man is just an animal which will evolve into something else. Eugenics and selective breeding are the logical next step. The apostate, pagan, occult, and murderous Nazis understood this quite well!

THIRD: Organic is code for material or body only, no spirit or even soul as anything independent of the flesh. There is no dualism of mind and body because the mind is only body, a bunch of random, chemical reactions governed by a meaningless, natural world and the magic wand of the survival of the fittest which also came about by mere chance. This is modern scientism as dead, supposed knowledge in the flesh without any truth in the Spirit.

FOURTH: God did not create man; man created God as a cultural crutch. Humanist anthropology precedes theology. We are God, the only creators we know of in the universe.

FIFTH: Values have no spiritual reality. Religion must be based on science, a creation solely of the random human intellect. Following Nietzsche and the snake in the garden, we create good and evil as we please. The one with the most power, technique, and will is the one who decides what is temporarily right or wrong.

SIXTH: God is neither present nor even past nor future. Thus Jesus is, therefore, a fraud and so is His return.

SEVENTH: Following Freud, no unredeemed human activity is unrighteous or alien. The supposedly secular is sacred without spiritual rebirth. The flesh is holy and all its desires and perversions are sacred.

EIGHTH: Man's chief end is not to glorify God but rather to realize himself, his unredeemed, fallen, human personality. Self-ism rules. Find Abraham Maslow as a center piece of educational psychology in nearly every American school of education. Self-centered, personal satisfaction and self-aggrandizing, social passion replace holiness and accountability before God. Human personality replaces Godly character. Witness our celebrity culture.

NINTH: Worship is wrong, and prayer is useless. How truly sad is this when their followers will end up worshipping Satan, another created being, to their eternal demise.

TENTH: There is no supernatural. The Spirit does not exist. One cannot be moved by the Spirit. Again this means Jesus could not be the Messiah, the anointed One, our Savior.

ELEVENTH: Human knowledge, not God's Truth, will solve all our problems. Meaningless, self existing matter and random probability is all there is. Reason alone, without faith, is valuable. Education will be their tool! Mental health, i.e. politically correct thinking, replaces spiritual health and prophetic hope. Psychiatry rules.

TWELFTH: Religion should promote the joys of unredeemed creativity and fallen self satisfaction. Live for today and personal self and social self only. Ignore eternity.

THIRTEENTH: All associations and institutions including the church must be taken over and remade as humanistic! Humanists must bring everything under their control. Does this not include Christian schools and universities? What about all churches and para-church organizations? Do we really believe their intentions?

FOURTEENTH: Following God-hating Marx, capitalism must be replaced by socialism. There is no honorable competition, only cooperation, even cooperation with evil. All is moral equivalence. The enlightened humanist state should control the means of production and the means of distribution and replace personal responsibility, charity, and integrity. This is pure, Godless, Marxist doctrine. Individuals and nations will be swallowed up by a universal society ruled by purely unredeemed, human means and ends, the one world government prophesied in Revelations as Mystery Babylon.

FIFTEENTH: Their belief is that progressive humanism will affirm life, its possibilities, and satisfactions for all; but Freud, Marx, Nietzsche, and Darwin have lead to the opposite: rampant sexual immorality and the ensuing, mass scale abortion and STDs and the destruction of the faithful, nuclear and extended family; oppression and totalitarianism by a self appointed elite in the name of economic and social justice; existential meaninglessness and power hungry despair; and personal and social, rationalized animalism by individuals and nation states. Humanism results from techniques not truth, cunning propaganda not wisdom, deceptive skill not character!

The conclusion reasserts that religion is nothing but human ideas that need to be changed. Man is alone in his quest for the good life in the here and now. God has nothing to say to us. We thank only ourselves! Now carefully notice John Dewey's signature, yet even Christian universities teach his educational ideas! The Mondale is Fritz Mondale's grandfather. Fritz was the Democratic nominee for U.S. President who ran against Ronald Reagan.

Looking at what has happened to the public, tax funded education of American youth and our youths' subsequent demoralization and spiritual emptiness, ignorance, and corruption, one sees the clear fingerprints of the Godless, progressive humanists and, especially in education, of John Dewey, all being manipulated by the father of liars and murderers, Satan, who rebels against and opposes God at every turn. These are strong words, but check your spirit to see if they are true!

The 1960s Supreme Court decisions, illegally legislating from the bench, simply codified this manifesto into law using the technique of changing society through the unconstitutional, court fiat of the atheist intelligentsia and through the utility of Caesar's schools aimed at our youth.

They unwittingly also, however, spurred the re-emergence of Protestant, private schools and home schooling as an exercise of sacrifice and conscience and faith and freedom. Of course, one must ask what has happened to America's majority, public culture subsequent to locking Jesus outside of the tax-funded schools? When Jesus is viewed as an outlaw, Satan's minions become in-laws.

Hosea 8:4 They set up kings, but not by Me; They made princes, but I did not acknowledge *them*. From their silver and gold they made idols for themselves — that they might be cut off.

What is even sadder is that the younger generations of youth and even college students are ignorant of all of this because their history has come from these very same people and from their philosophies and hidden theologies via the tax funded schools and universities, the NEA collaborating, textbook publishers, and the corrupted, self-serving, Godless media. The humanists' techniques of focusing on taking over Caesar's and the culture's institutions have worked, and clearly education and even the church was their stated, key objective.

The First Amendment

These techniques have been patently unjust, but this is a war of faiths, so progressive humanists feel justified in trying to discredit and disenfranchise Christianity and Christ every where they can and by any means; it is their manifesto! We are their enemy; do we understand the spirits behind them?

What the first amendment really means and how it has been purposefully misinterpreted is a clear example of using dishonest and unjust *technique* to attack truth. The First Amendment of our constitution has been so warped from the intentions of the founders and writers of the constitution that it now does the opposite of that for which it was meant and is even constantly misquoted in popular, progressive, humanist culture. I have heard former President Bill Clinton while President and Walter Cronkite, a generational voice of TV news, among many others publicly misquote it. In fact, so has our public consciousness been twisted that, if I misquote it here for you as I do for my university students, you probably will not be able to discern it. So here goes, a misquoted First Amendment: *Congress shall make no law regarding the establishment of religion nor prohibiting the free exercise thereof.*

This is what our present culture, undermined by the purposeful deceit of progressive, humanist religion, thinks the First Amendment says. Did you catch the misquote?

The difference between public myth and historical reality is the article *the.* The true version (you can look it up for yourself) uses *an,* instead. Check the back of your history book if they bother to actually print it. You may be tempted to say, *the, an,* what is the big deal? Well, *the,* as an indefinite article, sets the government at odds with religion in general and thus leads to the *separation of church and state* myth.

Moreover, if you ask contemporary university students if *separation of church and state* is in the constitution, they will say yes. If you ask where, they will give you a puzzled look. Our public consciousness has been purposefully twisted. The *separation clause* is not a clause at all; it was manufactured whole cloth by the Supreme Court from a personal letter of again Thomas Jefferson and was never a part of any of our founding government documents. And it became law by illegally legislating it from the judicial bench by the 1960s Supreme Court in complete opposition to the constitution using purposefully deceitful, progressive, humanist **technique**!

What the founders and writers really meant by the First Amendment is made clear in the context of their times. Several of the original thirteen states, including Virginia where "doubting" Thomas Jefferson was Governor, had state, Christian denominations to which all their citizens paid taxes. They were, therefore, obviously not for the separation of Christianity and government.

They choose *an* establishment instead of *the* establishment precisely because they did not wish a war over the choice of a federal, Christian denomination. They did not choose *the* establishment because they supported Christianity in general and did not want the government to be against religion nor devoid of Christianity; thus the *free exercise thereof*. This is plain history to anyone with an open mind. Even doubting Jefferson as the U.S. President authorized using the federal government, congressional buildings in Washington DC for Christian church services on Sundays which he attended! Our government has been and is still being twisted by those exercising religious warfare in the form of progressive, humanist **technique**.

Even the Illegal Court Ruling Has Been Twisted

Moreover, even what the Supreme Court unconstitutionally but actually said (and how Caesar's schools ignore even this) has been twisted by the general, deceitful, religious humanist and progressivist consciousness that pervades our public arenas. Nord and Haynes (1998), writing for the secular ASCD, make it clear that even the content of the illegal, bench legislation of the Supreme Court has been twisted and not followed. What the Supreme Court in essence said was that tax funded, government schools must remain neutral among religions and also neutral between religion and non-religion. Even this grievous and impossible error found nowhere in the constitution is not what practice has become. To remain neutral among religions, which is of course impossible, tax funded education has basically removed Christian religion from the curriculum accept perhaps as ancient history or ancient literature and become distinctly favorable to so-called non-religion while being hostile to religious voices, especially Christian ones. This is a complete corruption of both the original constitution and the unconstitutional legislation of the Supreme Court. It is also the realization of humanist, Godless, progressivist, religious faith masquerading as supposedly neutral secularism.

Suppression of Victories

And furthermore the NEA and ACLU keep any righteous, legal victories from being used through the threat of expensive, law suits.

This is even more unjust in that both these humanist institutions are supported directly or indirectly by our tax dollars; **some technique**! By the way, Jesus denying John Dewey was also a founding member of both the NEA and the ACLU!

For instance, how many know that the Federal Supreme Court has ruled that handicapped students who attend faith-based schools have the right to the same tax funded, in classroom aids, including skilled personnel and technology, that they would have in a public school (see Zobrest v. Catalina Foothills School District (Supreme Court Case No. 92-94), 1993)? Why then did not this happen routinely all across America? The short answer is ignorance, hostility, greed, religious warfare, and the legal and financial backing of the tax funded NEA and ACLU. The vast majority of school districts under the counsel of the NEA and the ACLU literally dared one to litigate their refusal to obey the Supreme Court; their overwhelming, tax funded resources against your personal resources and limited time! Then Congress passed a law making this court ruling of no avail.

The aggressive, anti-Christian monopoly of tax funded, public universities, where the vast majority of educators are trained, only makes the situation worse. The combination of a generally self indulgent and lukewarm church and of the supremacy of the God-hating philosophies of Marx, Freud, Nietzsche, and Darwin in public, tax-funded education means that those who want a truly Christian education in our times need to look past tax funded education, even though they are unjustly and heavily taxed to support it without any real choice. Public, government controlled, education costs our citizens about a trillion dollars a year, that is $1,000,000,000,000. It is not *free* public education! Thus we must ask if Caesar wishes to be worshipped in place of Jesus? Any serious student of history and the Bible knows the answer.

Romans 1:16-32 For I am not ashamed of the gospel of Christ, for it is the power of God to salvation for everyone who believes, for the Jew first and also for the Greek. For in it the righteousness of God is revealed from faith to faith; as it is written, *"The just shall live by faith."* For the wrath of God is revealed from heaven against all ungodliness and unrighteousness of men, who suppress the truth in unrighteousness, because what may be known of God is manifest in them, for God has shown *it* to them. For since the creation of the world His invisible *attributes* are clearly seen, being understood by the things that are made, *even* His eternal power and Godhead, so that they are without excuse, because, although they knew God, they did not glorify *Him* as God, nor were thankful, but became futile in their thoughts, and their foolish hearts were darkened.

Professing to be wise, they became fools, and changed the glory of the incorruptible God into an image made like corruptible man—and birds and four-footed animals and creeping things. Therefore God also gave them up to uncleanness, in the lusts of their hearts, to dishonor their bodies among themselves, who exchanged the truth of God for the lie, and worshiped and served the creature rather than the Creator, who is blessed forever. Amen. For this reason God gave them up to vile passions. For even their women exchanged the natural use for what is against nature. Likewise also the men, leaving the natural use of the woman, burned in their lust for one another, men with men committing what is shameful, and receiving in themselves the penalty of their error which was due. And even as they did not like to retain God in *their* knowledge, God gave them over to a debased mind, to do those things which are not fitting; being filled with all unrighteousness, sexual immorality, wickedness, covetousness, maliciousness; full of envy, murder, strife, deceit, evil-mindedness; *they are* whisperers, backbiters, haters of God, violent, proud, boasters, inventors of evil things, disobedient to parents, undiscerning, untrustworthy, unloving, unforgiving, unmerciful; who, knowing the righteous judgment of God, that those who practice such things are deserving of death, not only do the same but also approve of those who practice them.

That this scripture is addressed to Romans under the authority of Caesar is not just coincidence. Nor is the fact that tax funded, humanist, progressive education in conjunction with the liberal media, courts, and legislatures now see gay/lesbian/transgender "rights" as their *cause célèbre*. When any people turn from God and refuse to recognize or thank Him, the slippery slope begins. Unfortunately our majority, American culture is at a stage where it is ripening quickly.

Proverbs 14:34 Righteousness exalts a nation, but sin is a reproach to any people.

The Importance of Education

So why does it seem that the communists, socialists, atheists, Islamists, Darwinists, secularists, materialists, new-agers, scientists, humanists, progressives and everyone but Christians seem to understand the importance of education as a personal, cultural, and historical force? Will the church as the Body of Christ accept the challenge or be swept away with its eyes closed by the deluge?

Matthew 7:13-14 "Enter by the narrow gate; for wide *is* the gate and broad *is* the way that leads to destruction, and there are many who go in by it. 14 Because narrow *is* the gate and **difficult *is* the way which leads to life**, and there are few who find it."

John 14:6 Jesus said to him, "I am the **way**, the truth, and the life. No one comes to the Father except through Me.

Genesis 33:5 And he lifted his eyes and saw the women and children, and said, "Who *are* these with you?" So he said, "The children whom God has graciously given your servant."

Isaiah 8:16-18 Bind up the testimony, seal the law among my disciples. And I will wait on the LORD, who hides His face from the house of Jacob; and I will hope in Him. **Here am I and the children whom the LORD has given me!** *We are* for signs and wonders in Israel from the LORD of hosts, who dwells in Mount Zion.

So whose children are they? Are there any left who have the courage of the narrow gate and the difficult way to admit that the children belong to God and that He has given them to us as parents as stewards, and not to Caesar as a thief? Look at the modern demagogues of the last century, such as Hitler, Stalin, Mao, and Hirohito; they all declared the civil state's preeminence over children and their education over and above the family and the church. How far have we fallen from, "We hold these truths to be self-evident, that all men are created equal, that they are endowed by their Creator with certain unalienable Rights, that among these are Life, Liberty and the pursuit of Happiness." Holding *truths to be self-evident* and people being *endowed by their Creator* with *unalienable Rights* (ones outside the jurisdiction of limited, civil government) are not contemporary, tax supported, government schools' doctrines! And we have the supposedly secular humanist progressives to thank for this devastation of the truth in our culture!

The Education of Jesus

Perhaps a final question will help us here. How was Jesus Himself educated?

Perhaps His parents could have chosen Caesar's schools while under Roman occupation, which schools would have been clearly supported by their tax dollars to Caesar? There were also Hellenist, Greek schools available; note the New Testament written in Greek by Israelites, even fisherman. He has also been to Egypt as a child. Yet, picture Him again at twelve in the Temple.

Luke 2:46-47 Now so it was *that* after three days they found Him in the temple, sitting in the midst of the teachers, both listening to them and asking them questions. And all who heard Him were astonished at His understanding and answers.

And then the scripture also says,

Luke 2:51-52a Then He went down with them and came to Nazareth, and was subject to them, but His mother kept all these things in her heart. And Jesus increased in wisdom . . .

It appears that Jesus, instead of attending a pagan, occupying, Roman or a liberal Hellenist Greek school, was both home schooled and probably also spent a good deal of time being schooled at the local synagogue where He must have been an avid reader and discusser of the scriptures (His carpenter's family surely did not own a handwritten set of sheepskin scrolls that comprised the Torah, the law and the poets and prophets). And, in so doing and in also being by choice in submission to His parents, He grew in true wisdom (not just knowledge or man's wisdom)!

His parents chose a Christian education, a God anointed education, a Messiah-ed education!! The Holy Spirit was His teacher; and the scriptures and life His primary text. For through His parables, we see that He also obviously had acquired a deep knowledge and understanding of His culture and of God's creation from practical experience, but again always guided through a Biblical lens of eternal truth as well. If this is good enough for Jesus, is it good enough for our children, our youth, and even so in the midst of Caesar's hostile, educational occupation?

Matthew 22:21b And He said to them, "Render therefore to Caesar the things that are Caesar's, and to God the things that are God's."

This is not just about coins or taxes, although the injustice of supposedly secular and progressive humanism's theft of our educational tax monies is surely plain to any who would see. Let Caesar build the roads and keep the peace, and let God educate the youth!

Matthew 23:37 "O Jerusalem, Jerusalem, the one who kills the prophets and stones those who are sent to her! How often I wanted to **gather** your children together, as a hen gathers her chicks under her wings, but you were not willing!"

What is Jesus' heart about the children? Is He willing to turn them over to Caesar and a God-less education? Or does He want to **gather** them together unto Himself? And why would He want to gather them together unto Himself if not to teach them His ways? The question is who is willing?

Luke 11:23 "He who is not with Me is against Me, and he who does not **gather** with Me scatters."

How we answer the question, to whom do the children really belong, in our own spirits, hearts, and convictions makes a huge difference in how we go about the ministries in which He has called and placed us. Do they belong to God or the civil state? Who has preeminence? Are we listening to the Holy Spirit or to the flesh in these matters? God is calling us to suffer for His children, for the difficult way. Do we gather them together unto Caesar or unto Jesus? Are we gathering with Jesus or scattering against Him? May God stir up our convictions, forgive our misgivings, and deliver us in His mercy and grace from evil to His honor and glory.

Psalm 78:1-8 Give ear, O my people, *to* my law; Incline your ears to the words of my mouth. ² I will open my mouth in a parable; I will utter dark sayings of old, ³ Which we have heard and known, And our fathers have told us. ⁴ We will not hide *them* from their children, Telling to the generation to come the praises of the LORD, And His strength and His wonderful works that He has done. ⁵ For He established a testimony in Jacob, And appointed a law in Israel, Which He commanded our fathers, That they should make them known to their children; ⁶ That the generation to come might know *them,* The children *who* would be born, *That* they may arise and declare *them* to their children, ⁷ That they may set their hope in God, And not forget the works of God, But keep His commandments; ⁸ And may not be like their fathers, A stubborn and rebellious generation, A generation *that* did not set its heart aright, And whose spirit was not faithful to God.

Chapter 5: Is Christian Education for Sundays Only: The Death of Dualism?

Cultural schizophrenia, idolatry, double mindedness, and the lukewarm and indulgently indifferent church are a terrible brew of our present culture in which the youth are growing up. Frank Gaebelein (1954), Albert Greene (1998), and Nancy Pearcey (2005) and many others have all clearly warned about the disasters of dualism and the Enlightenment's two-house failure. This dualism is a split of our lives, where our church and spiritual life is held sacred and our public and daily life, including our education outside of Sunday school or even within a Christian school outside of Bible class, is secular and public and where we furthermore find this compromise comfortable and acceptable.

We hold two religions; Christianity on Sunday or in Bible class and materialistic, temporal humanism the rest of the week. By so doing this, we have privatized our faith and supposedly secularized our culture and the lens through which we view most of our lives. The result is that our faith becomes less and less meaningful to our daily lives, and our temporal humanist and materialist culture eats us alive. As we read in the last chapter, the humanists declared that dualism was dead because the supposedly secular has swallowed up the sacred, but in true Christian education it is the sacred that should swallow up the supposedly secular! Our daily lives should become sacraments to the gifts of faith and truth and hope and love which God has so graciously given us.

Christianity and Democracy

Americans are particularly tempted by this dualism. Our civic culture was founded upon an uneasy alliance between Judeo-Christian faith, values, Spirit, truth, and morals along with Greco/Roman, civil democracy and humanistic, scientific reasoning; a metaphoric treaty between Jerusalem and Athens/Rome. We are thus not sure if we worship God and Jesus or democracy and science and worldly power; we often do one on Sunday and the other the rest of the week. But this balance has been shattered; as Jesus said you cannot serve two Gods.

This is one of the reasons Americans do not understand Islam; we keep looking at its followers through our weekly and supposedly secular and humanist perspectives and wondering why its adherents do not just put their religion in a box and get on with modernist or even postmodernist, materialistic humanism in the rest of their lives as their real god. Why have not democracy and capitalism (or socialism for that matter) and science made them more reasonable? Why have not diversity, relativism, and moral equivalency made them more tolerant of everything? Nations, which take their faith seriously, even if a deadly false one, through their entire week and lives, seem unreal to most Americans. Why is this?

It is because Americans, if we have a faith left at all, have been so deeply split in our own lives by dualism that we cannot see from any unified perspective. The Godless philosophies of Darwin, Freud, Marx, Nietzsche, and Dewey have become more meaningful to us than the Godly one of Jesus, especially in everyday education which shapes our practiced world view. You can preach Darwin, Freud, Marx, Nietzsche, and Dewey in the tax funded schools, but not Jesus. Again He is the issue!

As an aside, this is not to disparage democracy. It may be the best form of civil government we can have in this fallen age. The question rather is, what happens when we worship democracy, see it as our savior, as our greatest good, as that which has blessed us instead of God? Why is democracy the greatest good and goal of Caesar's tax-funded, supposedly secular, humanist schools and their last century, false prophets, John Dewey and Ralph Tyler? What about the Kingdom of God, is it a democracy? What should Christian schools teach about democracy? De Tocqueville (2000), the French philosopher, saw clearly that the young America was blessed, not because its democracy made its people good, but because the goodness of its Christian people with their faith in the Lord made its democracy work. The point is that there is nothing inherently holy about democracy. A democracy, including ours, is only as good as the people in it and what they vote for. The spiritual redemption of individual citizens, not democracy, brings about righteous living and the blessings of God within any nation.

Having said this, amongst redeemed people of truth and Christian good will, civil democracy along with the balance of powers of our federalism can promote protection from tyranny and the wisdom of a multitude of good council.

It is not, however, our greatest good; individual spiritual redemption in Jesus is! Democracy as an idol is no substitute for the transforming mercy and grace of Jesus! Again, is it just a coincidence that the Greek, humanist and philosophical elite that glorified democracy were also pro-homosexuality and human slavery? But that is another story.

Christian Education and Dualism

And what about Christian education, has it escaped this pervasive dualistic culture. To the extent that some of our curriculum, as in hopefully Bible class, is seen through spiritual eyes and then the majority of the rest of the curriculum is not or only minimally so, have we not succumbed to this dualism? Do we practice an education where Christianity can only speak to religion; the rest is governed by the materialistic humanists, modern or post-modern philosophies? Truly Christian education is, in fact, the attempt to break this lukewarm miasma and its debilitating compromises and confusing, confounding, and stumbling messages to the youth. Christian education's very premise is that Sunday school along with forty hours of supposedly secular school does not work in fostering truly Christian youth. Discipling youth, building their world view, helping birth and ignite their faith and their spirit, teaching them to walk in the truth and the love of God is a full time process, done best without continuously mixed messages and deceitful humanist technique full of Godless lies.

Deuteronomy 6:6-9 And these words which I command you today shall be in your heart. 7 You shall teach them diligently to your children, and shall talk of them when you sit in your house, when you walk by the way, when you lie down, and when you rise up. 8 You shall bind them as a sign on your hand, and they shall be as frontlets between your eyes. 9 You shall write them on the doorposts of your house and on your gates.

The true Hebrew notion of education is not dualistic, learn some things spiritually and other things supposedly secularly. It focuses on *echad*, oneness, wholeness, and thus also wholesomeness! It is a twenty-four hour, seven day a week kind of education, integrated into a whole that is spiritual and practical and not contradictory.

This education fills our hearts. It is persistent. It guides whatever we do with our hands and the way we see the creation. And it guides us in how we go out into public life and how we come back into private life. It covers everything! Would not Jesus say we have lost our wholesomeness because we have given up on our wholeness, especially in educating our youth? The education of our youth should be whole and wholesome, unified in the Spirit of the Lord.

Psalm 1:1-2 Blessed is the man that walks not in the counsel of the ungodly, nor stands in the way of sinners, nor sits in the seat of the scornful. But his delight is in the law of the Lord; and in His law he meditates day and night.

This blessing is not for the schizophrenic, the idolatrous, the double minded, the dualistic, the self indulgent, the indifferent, or the lukewarm. Godly counsel on Sunday and ungodly and/or Godless counsel all week, the way of the redeemed on Sunday and the way of the sinner the rest of the week, and the thankful on Sunday and the scornful the rest of the week does not work, not if we are trying to grow Godly and blessed youth, meditating on God's ways day and night!

Again, how was Jesus educated? Was he fed constant, mixed messages? There were plenty of Hellenists in Israel after the Greek occupation fought off by the Maccabees. Note the New Testament written in Greek by Jews! Occupying pagan Romans were everywhere. The false Pharisees were abundant. Did He, however, learn anything that was not saturated in truth, faith, the love of God, the Holy Spirit, and wisdom? Look at His parables; how did He come to see every day events? The One who created and sustains all the laws of mathematics, physics, chemistry and biology sees everything spiritually! Could this have anything to do with how He was taught and how He learned and from whom, and what, and how and why? Was knowledge dead and neutral to Him, something to be worshipped as though it were independent of God? Did He think one way on the Sabbath and another way the rest of the week, one way when studying the Bible and another way when studying the creation?

Luke 8:18a Therefore take heed how you hear.

How we answer the question of dualism or the isolation of our spirituality, in our own spirits, hearts, and convictions makes a huge difference in how we go about the ministries in which He has placed us. May God stir up our convictions, forgive our misgivings, and deliver us in His mercy and grace from evil to His honor and glory.

Chapter 6: Can There be a Christian Philosophy Rooted in a Christian Theology?

Albert Greene (1998) answers this crucial question brilliantly. As a philosophy graduate of UC Berkeley in the 1960s myself, I am also personally very familiar with a wide variety of false and worldly philosophies and their terrible and virulent, spiritual, personal, moral, and social effects. It is truly important to understand Godly philosophy because many Christians have written off philosophy all together, thinking they do not have one, or use one, to only then subconsciously and unwittingly adopt worldly ones, much to their detriment.

<u>Colossians 2:6-9</u> As you therefore have received Christ Jesus the Lord, so walk in Him, 7 rooted and built up in Him and established in the faith, as you have been taught, abounding in it with thanksgiving. 8 Beware lest anyone cheat you through philosophy and empty deceit, according to the tradition of men, according to the basic principles of the world, and not **according to Christ**. 9 For in Him dwells all the fullness of the Godhead bodily; 10 and you are complete in Him, who is the head of all principality and power.

The Importance of Philosophy

Why is a Christian philosophy of education so important? Philosophy need not be Godless or a cheat. The word *philosophy* actually means *the love of wisdom*. Should not Christians be lovers of wisdom? Philosophy is all about perspectives on essential questions of reality and life and goodness and beauty and the nature of knowing and the meaning of existence and values.

Everyone uses some perspective on these matters; therefore this is not a question of philosophy or not, but rather which one! Whose wisdom forms the perspectives of our world view, our cosmology, our life view, and our view of reality? This is what philosophy is all about. It is about choosing a way. If one does not see the philosophy which forms one's perspectives, one is in great danger of living by false world views, false cosmologies, living in error.

An un-thought-out philosophy is a philosophy nonetheless, albeit one that most likely leads to confusion and chaos and ineffectiveness. Philosophy guides our ship much more than we realize; that is why it is so important to get it right, to not be cheated by it!

Ephesians 5:15-17   See then that you walk circumspectly, not as fools but as wise, [16] redeeming the time, because the days are evil. [17] Therefore do not be unwise, but understand what the will of the Lord is.

Christians are right to be skeptical of Greek or European or Eastern or American or any philosophies which are based on man's reasoning without God, what is identified by the Holy Spirit in Colossians as "deceitful" and "as according to the tradition of men, according to the basic principles of the world." These are two thousand year old and timeless definitions of supposedly secular humanism and supposedly scientific materialism. But are these the only two sources of wisdom, man's own thoughts about himself and his own understanding of the principles of the material world? What is, "rather", a philosophy "according to Christ?"

Colossians and Ephesians clearly teach to not be fooled or cheated by the deceitful first two types of philosophy (unwise) but rather to follow this other one (wise). What is Jesus' philosophy which is complete and does not short change or cheat? Does Jesus have perspectives on essential questions of reality and life and goodness and beauty and the nature of knowing and the meaning of existence and values? Does He have a systematic or whole, world view and cosmology and a life view that we can live by?

If He is, in fact, the Creator and Sustainer of the universe, the Alpha and Omega, the beginning and the end of time and space as we know it, one would think the answer would definitely be yes! The real question is what is it? False philosophies based only on man's own prideful thinking are deceitful and cheating; they pretend to answer questions they do not answer and thus cheat us, but true philosophy based upon God is a blessing which is filled with truth and real and complete answers, rooted and built up in Jesus!

John 14:6b   I am the way, the truth, and the life.

Greene, Dooyeweerd, and Van Brummelen

Greene (1998), working from the Dutch, Christian philosopher, Herman Dooyeweerd, sees the basis of a philosophy "according to Christ" as focused upon a creation, fall, and redemption, theological or faith paradigm. Understanding the theology of the creation, fall, and redemption gives us the perspectives and wisdom to develop a philosophy "according to Christ." Van Brummelen (2002) adds a fourth paradigm: creation, fall, redemption, and **fulfillment**.

Their point is that everything we are, we teach, and we do in regards to Christian education, ought to agree with, reveal, expound upon, and inculcate the perspectives of these faith paradigms which reveal God to us and call us to repently serve God and our fellow man. This is a true philosophy, a true big picture which frames everything else in the creation and beyond and gives knowledge value and meaning. It is true because it is theologically sound and focused upon Jesus "in whom are hidden all the treasures of wisdom and knowledge."

Are you tempted to think this is too heady? If so, consider Moses, Daniel, and Paul. All were deeply trained at what would have been the graduate university level of their times; and also all were taught directly by the Holy Spirit to understand the differences between worldly or pagan philosophy and Godly philosophy based upon true theology; and all of them have been of great importance in our spiritual history. Furthermore our present culture and thus our schools are rife with the humanist and materialist philosophies of Modernism and Postmodernism, even much of Christian education. What we need, therefore, is a redemptive and transformative philosophy, if we want a truly redemptive and transformative curriculum and learning community built upon it. The curriculum of Caesar's schools is now completely controlled by deceitful philosophies "according to the traditions of men and the basic principles of the world:" humanism and materialism with God and His Spirit as outlaws. Would not Jesus want our curricula to be completely different?

<u>2 Corinthians 10:3-5</u> For though we walk in the flesh, we do not war according to the flesh. 4 For the weapons of our warfare *are* not carnal but mighty in God for pulling down strongholds, 5 casting down arguments and every high thing that exalts itself against the knowledge of God, bringing every thought into captivity to the obedience of Christ.

It is a very legitimate question to ask ourselves, are our teaching and learning and our curricula "bringing every thought into captivity to the obedience of Christ?" Or does most of our education ignore Him and His anointing, as our pagan, dualistic culture teaches us? This is a call to be philosophical soldiers for Christ on the battlefield of our own and our youths' minds and hearts and spirits! Are the cross and our Lord's sacrifice upon it, as the pivot point of the faith paradigms of creation, fall, redemption, and fulfillment, in the foreground of our lessons? Just what philosophies hold sway in our daily lessons and are they **"according to Christ."**

Creation

How thoroughly do we present the perspectives of creation? The propaganda against creation is ever present in our students' lives from the supposedly secular, government schools and universities, to the overwhelming media, to the national parks, and to the textbook, trade book, and literature publishers. How well do we counter it, "casting down arguments and every high thing that exalts itself against the knowledge of God**?"** Do we help our students to see the creation as the creation? Do we speak of and use the vocabulary of the creation as the creation? Do we wonder and awe at the creation as the creation? Do we study the creation as the creation? Do we let the creation always point to the Creator in thanksgiving and worship and in spirit and truth? How whole and wholesome is our own view of the created world and the created universe and all that God sustains within it including our time and space for our benefit? Or do we speak of and worship nature as something separate from God that exists on its own without His sustaining love? Greene rightly calls this idolatry, stealing nature from the Creator! This is a foundational philosophical divide. A wrong turn here lays a foundation for disaster later.

<u>Genesis 1:1</u> In the beginning God created . . .

<u>Hebrews 11:3</u> By **faith** we **understand** that the worlds were framed by the word of God, so that the things which are seen were not made of things which are visible.

Fall

Of course a proper understanding of the creation also requires an understanding of the subsequent fall. Do our teaching and learning and curricula also present the perspectives of the fall and both how evil and sin have marred and distorted the original creation, which God said was good, and how the fall also included ourselves in our spirits, souls, and bodies? For instance, without the perspectives of the fall, we might be tempted to trust our own fallen reasoning above God's reasoning, thus loving self revelation above God's revelation; or we might misunderstand the depravity in the world as caused by just a lack of enlightenment knowledge rather than a work of evil. Knowledge is the supposedly secular humanists' silver bullet. All the people of the world, however, could have several, supposedly secular university degrees, and evil would still run rampant, surely the more so!

Jeremiah 8:9   The wise men are ashamed, they are dismayed and taken. Behold, they have rejected the word of the LORD; so what **wisdom** do they have?

The fall actually begins with Satan and his rebellion in heaven (Prince, 2003). As Jesus testifies,

Luke 10:18   And He said to them, "I saw **Satan fall** like lightning from heaven."

This fall was followed by Adam and Eve's fall when they listened to Satan instead of God. The fall and its effects upon mankind and the creation are Satanic in origin and nature. Like its father, the fall is full of lies and murder. The effects are within us and without us. We live in an age of sin; it distorts and perverts everything. It is centered upon our selfishness and prideful rebellion. What is often missed, however, is that this age of sin is not eternal, but rather temporary. Michael, the archangel over the Jewish people, explained this to humble Daniel,

Daniel 9:24   Seventy weeks are determined for your people and for your holy city, to finish the transgression, **to make an end of sins**, to make reconciliation for iniquity, to bring in everlasting righteousness, to seal up vision and prophecy, and to anoint the Most Holy.

This Old Testament prophecy about the Messiah, the anointed One, Jesus, clearly says there will be "an end of sins." Satan, the author and instigator of evil and sins, will first be locked up and then after one more rebellion eventually cast into the lake of eternal fire. But now we live in an age of spiritual warfare and testing. Do we really teach and learn about the creation, including ourselves as part of it, from this perspective or do we naively believe in supposedly neutral, secular, and natural knowledge and teachers and learners who are all amoral and beyond good and evil to quote Nietzsche (1989)?

If we do not see the creation as being temporarily in bondage to the evil one because of our fall, then its distorted cruelty either speaks falsely to a random, self existent, survival of the fittest or to perhaps a survival of the meanest reality or even to a cruel creator. Trying to make sense out of reality without an understanding of the reality of evil grows all kinds of humanist and materialist hypocrisy, insanity, depravity, meaninglessness, and nonsense. It also masks the spiritual warfare within which every school lesson takes place both for teachers and learners. It is in this context that "casting down arguments and every high thing that exalts itself against the knowledge of God" becomes truly meaningful. If we do not see this in our teaching and learning and in our lessons, it is because our philosophy is false and is out of focus with reality. A Christian education must not be afraid to call what is good, good and what is evil, evil. The fall is real.

Redemption

This awareness of evil and sin and the ever present spiritual warfare against their spiritual perpetrators leads to the third faith paradigm or perspective of a Christian philosophy of education, redemption. Suddenly within the creation and fall context, the Lord's eternal sacrifice on the cross comes into sharp focus and preeminence; it creates the potential for all of the Christian life, including a truly Christian education. Jesus did not come just to cover sins as in the Old Testament; He came to take them away. He defeated Satan for us when we would not, could not, and did not.

By faith we can now stand in God's holy presence solely by the Lord's righteousness and by His sacrificially shed blood and even without the condemnation which we deserve. While the age of sin ripens, Christians can live a redeemed life in its midst in Jesus' mercy and grace as light and salt through His Holy Spirit. Even though the fall is all around us and even in our flesh and souls, we can have His victory in His Spirit.

Through spiritual rebirth in Him and the putting on of His mind and the filling of His Spirit, Jesus has given us the means to overcome, to teach, to learn, and to live from a completely different perspective from the worldliness of secular humanism and secular materialism and their false and deceitful philosophies and corrupted ways of life. Thus a truly anointed education is a redemptive and transformative education, redemptive and transformative in Jesus of spirit, soul, and body. An educational philosophy based in faith and truth upon understanding and appreciating the creation and its Creator, upon admitting to the effects of the fall within us and about us, and upon obeying and enjoying the blessings and grace of redemption and transformation in Jesus is very much different from an educational philosophy based upon fallen, rebellious, self serving, human thought and crass, happenstance materialism based on puffed up, current, and incomplete knowledge. Yet redemption and transformation are not yet completely manifest in us or in the world around us. There remains the fourth dimension of a Christian philosophical paradigm, fulfillment.

Fulfilment

It is a four act play that God has authored, and the first three acts are incomplete without the fourth. Without the promise and fulfillment of the King's return, the Kingdom is never complete. The church is now the Lord's betrothed; yet the wedding and the feast are about to come.

Revelation 19:6-10   And I heard, as it were, the voice of a great multitude, as the sound of many waters and as the sound of mighty thunderings, saying, "Alleluia! For the Lord God Omnipotent reigns! **7** Let us be glad and rejoice and give Him glory, for the marriage of the Lamb has come, and His wife has made herself ready." **8** And to her it was granted to be arrayed in fine linen, clean and bright, for the fine linen is the righteous acts of the saints. **9** Then he said to me,

"Write: 'Blessed *are* those who are called to the marriage supper of the Lamb!'" And he said to me, "These are the true sayings of God." **10** And I fell at his feet to worship him. But he said to me, "See *that you do* not *do that!* I am your fellow servant, and of your brethren who have the testimony of Jesus. Worship God! For the testimony of Jesus is the spirit of prophecy."

We are engaged to Jesus, His promised bride to be. There is a point in history where the true church goes from being His promised to being His mate, His wife, truly one with Him at the marriage super in heaven. At that point we return to earth with Him to reign at His side!

Revelation 19:11-15 Now I saw heaven opened, and behold, a white horse. And He who sat on him was called Faithful and True, and in righteousness He judges and makes war. 12 His eyes were like a flame of fire, and on His head were many crowns. He had a name written that no one knew except Himself. 13 He was clothed with a robe dipped in blood, and His name is called The Word of God. 14 And the armies in heaven, clothed in fine linen, white and clean, followed Him on white horses. 15 Now out of His mouth goes a sharp sword, that with it He should strike the nations. And He Himself will rule them with a rod of iron. He Himself treads the winepress of the fierceness and wrath of Almighty God.

"He Himself" strikes the nations and brings justice and righteousness to earth; and, with His wife following at His side, "He Himself" establishes His Kingdom over all nations. "He Himself" will rule with a rod of iron. Jesus wins!

That Jesus wins is the crown of a Christian philosophy of education. It is not a metaphor but rather reality. The second coming is just as true as the first coming. The second coming is no more of a metaphor than the first coming was! That Jesus wins changes everything. Especially in these last days of sin and testing, if the youth fail to grasp that Jesus wins, they will be lost, swallowed up in the Godlessness and fearfulness of our times. Seeing history and the future through the eyes of humanist materialism is a grim and phony picture indeed, and one that will sacrifice the youth to Mystery Babylon.

A Christian philosophy of education must proclaim fulfillment, must proclaim that Jesus keeps His promise to His betrothed, that, when all else around us and even some of what is in us is unfaithful, He remains faithful and true and that Jesus wins over the evil one, over the evil in this world, and over the fallen flesh in all of us, His children by faith! Jesus wins! He redeems and transforms; and He fulfills! There has never been a time in history when the youth need to understand this more than right now. He wins personally through individual salvation, and He wins corporately in real history through His promised return! Jesus wins!

Creation, fall, redemption, and fulfillment are the faith perspectives, the Christian philosophy, that make Christian education Christian. We ignore them at great peril and expound upon them throughout our teaching and learning to eternal blessing! They put Jesus in the middle of what we are doing! This is Christ-centered education; Jesus as Creator, Jesus as Witness and Testifier to the fall, Jesus as Redeemer and Transformer at the cross and resurrection, and Jesus as victorious Fulfiller in our heavenly wedding and return! These are not metaphors but realities! Are the faith paradigms of creation, fall, redemption, and fulfillment the heart of our teaching, learning, curricula, lessons, and education? Do they saturate everything we learn about God, about ourselves, about our culture, about history, and about the creation? Do they shape our students' philosophies, perspectives on reality and life and goodness and beauty and the nature of knowing and the meaning of existence and values? May God stir up our convictions, forgive our misgivings, and deliver us in His mercy and grace from evil to His honor and glory.

Isaiah 11:2 The Spirit of the LORD shall rest upon Him, The Spirit of wisdom and understanding, The Spirit of counsel and might, The Spirit of knowledge and of the fear of the LORD.

James 3:17 But the wisdom that is from above is first pure, then peaceable, gentle, willing to yield, full of mercy and good fruits, without partiality and without hypocrisy.

Chapter 7: Gold, Frankincense, and Myrrh: The Whole Jesus and Christian Education

Matthew 2:11 And when they had come into the house, they saw the young Child with Mary His mother, and fell down and worshiped Him. And when they had opened their treasures, they presented gifts to Him: gold, frankincense, and myrrh.

Beginnings, names, and gifts are very important in Hebrew culture, the culture through which Jesus chooses to enter this world. They are prophetic, symbolic, and deeply meaningful. Three crucial ministries of Jesus, which symbolically laid out His life's path at His beginning, can be clearly seen in this prophetic scripture, strategically placed at the beginning of the first Gospel account of the New Testament by the Holy Spirit. These ministries, into which we, as educational leaders, teachers, and learners, must also all grow in order to fulfill our callings and to become more and more like Him, can be a further backbone and a focus for important aspects of our Christian education ministries. Moreover they can be amplified as seen through the prism of the three things that remain: faith, hope, and love.

Carefully looking at the three prophetic gifts given by worshipful Wiseman, philosophers if you will, to Jesus as a young child and highlighted by the Holy Spirit in scripture, we can see symbolically and prophetically that Jesus was born to be the King of kings, the Priest of priests, and the Prophet of prophets. He also grew, lived, ministered, died, rose again, will return and reign, and lives forever in these three offices or ministries into which He is also calling us to follow Him. Graham (2003) has come to a similar revelation from examining the spiritual ministries of the Old Testament.

King of kings

Revelation 19:16a And He has on His robe and on His thigh a name written: **KING OF KINGS . . .**

Revelation 4:4 And round about the throne were four and twenty seats: and upon the seats I saw four and twenty elders sitting, clothed in white raiment; and they had on their heads **crowns of gold**.

These are two of many scriptures that can be linked to the Wiseman's first gift of gold, the symbol of kings and kings' crowns. Yet Jesus is not just **a** king; He is **the** King, the **"KING OF KINGS."** He epitomizes kingship. There is no greater king than King Jesus. He is the archetype, the essence, the original; all others are humble imitators or rebellious imposters. Of course a king has a kingdom; and, as the King of kings, His Kingdom is **the** Kingdom of kingdoms! Again all others are either humble imitators or rebellious imposters. As the Christian patriots of the American Revolution once declared in support of minimalist, human government comprised of checks and balances against inevitable, human folly, "We have no king but Jesus!"

John 18:35-37   Pilate answered, "Am I a Jew? Your own nation and the chief priests have delivered You to me. What have You done?" 36 Jesus answered, "My kingdom is not of this world. If My kingdom were of this world, My servants would fight, so that I should not be delivered to the Jews; but **now** My kingdom is not from here."
37 Pilate therefore said to Him, "Are You a king then?"
Jesus answered, "You say *rightly* that I am a king. For this cause I was born, and for this cause I have come into the world, that I should bear witness to the truth. Everyone who is of the truth hears My voice."

The irony is that in Jesus' first coming He wore a crown of thorns not of gold, because His idea of kingship is so vastly different than ours and His kingdom is not **"now"** from here. Furthermore Jesus makes a radical statement in words and deeds about true rulership. He leads from among, not from separate (Gangel, 1997). He exercises His authority to serve, not to lord it over. He is a King who seeks the glory of the Father and the Kingdom of Heaven, not for Himself (McAlpine, 1982). The keys to His Kingship are humility and servanthood, not pride and domination. His motivation is love, not power for self's sake. He is sold out to the Kingdom as a slave to God's cause, a true shepherd, not just a hired hand. He lays down His own life, not others' lives for the Kingdom's glory. He is a living example for us to follow, not just a doctrine or a figurehead or a speechmaker. He teaches these truths and He lives them out, and He expects the members of a school community under His anointing and name to do the same.

He is the King of Kings, born in a humble animal shelter, crucified outside the city, buried in a borrowed tomb. That He will sit on David's throne, a shepherd, a worshiper, a poet, and a warrior king, should also speak to us. He calls us to be kings like Him, servants, shepherds, worshipers, poets, warriors, and examples to the flock.

Priest of priests

<u>**Genesis 14:18**</u>   Then **Melchizedek** king of Salem brought out bread and wine; he was **the** priest of God Most High.

<u>**Hebrews 7:11**</u>   Therefore, if perfection were through the Levitical priesthood (for under it the people received the law), what further need was there that another priest should rise according to the order of **Melchizedek**, and not be called according to the order of Aaron?

<u>**Hebrews 7:17**</u>   For He testifies: "You are a priest forever according to the order of **Melchizedek**."

The second gift of the Wiseman is frankincense which the priests in the temple burned to symbolize intercessory prayer. But again Jesus is not just *a* priest; He is *the* Priest of priests after the order of Melchizedek, "**the** priest of God Most High," not of Aaron, but preceding and also coming after Aaron. In fact, right now as you are reading this, Jesus is seated at the right hand of the Father in heaven interceding for us as the Priest of priests, **the** Priest at God's right hand! He is also, praise God, the Priest who saves to the uttermost as His priesthood is "forever," eternal! He *is* our substitutionary sacrifice, the Lamb of God. He offered and gave Himself for us forever. He epitomizes priesthood. There is no greater priest than Priest Jesus. He is the archetype, the essence, the original; all others are humble imitators or rebellious imposters.

<u>**2 Peter 3:15a**</u> . . . and consider that the longsuffering of our Lord is salvation

A priest brings man to God and God to man through the sacrifice, one of suffering and love and compassion and intercession. Jesus teaches these truths and He lives them out, and He expects the members of a school community under His anointing and name to do the same. He is the Priest of priests, bringing us the mercy, grace, and justice of God. He is the perfect Priest who saves to the uttermost bringing Himself to God as our righteous sacrifice. He calls us to follow Him in this ministry also.

Prophet of prophets

<u>**Luke 24:19**</u>   And He said to them, "What things?" So they said to Him, "The things concerning Jesus of Nazareth, who was a **Prophet mighty** in **deed** and **word** before God and all the people.

Revelation 19:10   And I fell at his feet to worship him. But he said to me, "See *that you do* not *do that!* I am your fellow servant, and of your brethren who have the testimony of Jesus. Worship God! **For the testimony of Jesus is the spirit of prophecy."**

John 19:39   And Nicodemus, who at first came to Jesus by night, also came, bringing a mixture of **myrrh** and aloes, about a hundred pounds.

Myrrh, an embalmer, seems like a very strange gift for a young child; but, as the third gift of the Wiseman, it is clearly prophetic. Jesus came to die for us. In fact He is **the** Prophet of prophets, the Creator and the Fulfiller of all true prophecy, the Redeemer and Restorer and Fulfiller of history. He epitomizes prophet-hood. There is no greater prophet than Prophet Jesus. He is the archetype, the essence, the original; all others are humble imitators or rebellious imposters. This third ministry of our Lord is often overlooked or down played, but Jesus as Prophet is just as important as Jesus as King and Jesus as Priest. His very testimony is "**the spirit of prophecy**;" everything about Him and what He has to say and do is prophetic. And as His brethren we have this same testimony which is the spirit of prophecy! This ministry of Jesus can be partially illustrated by one of Jesus' other titles, Rabbi. "Forty-one times the New Testament calls Jesus teacher. He is not an ordinary teacher, but a rabbi, a religious teacher, the one who indicates the way to God. Jesus, the teacher, invites all to find wisdom. He taught as no one else did; He spoke about God with authority" (McDermott, 1985, p. 3).

A rabbi is a teacher, but he is much more than what we think of as a teacher. He delivers truth and wisdom and righteousness as well as knowledge. He delivers eternal truth, historical truth, community truth, and personal truth. As such he is a prophet as well as a teacher. A rabbi is a ruler (servant-king) in the community, the priest of the community, and the prophetic voice for the community, both collectively and personally. Jesus allowed Himself to be called Rabbi; He is much more than what we call a teacher, a mere dispenser of knowledge. He is the Prophet of prophets, speaking truth both eternally and in the context of time, the Truth of God.

Jesus' ministry as Prophet scares or embarrasses some Christians, but what happens when we try to remove this dimension of the Lord? If we are embarrassed or ashamed of Jesus as Prophet, what happens to Jesus as King or Priest? If we do not trust Jesus as Prophet, can we truly trust Him as King and Priest? If we turn our backs to Jesus as the Prophet of prophets, are there not a host of other, false prophets eagerly waiting in the wings to fill this void in the minds and hearts of our youth and in doing so marring and twisting and usurping Jesus as King and Priest? For instance the lies of Islam hold over a billion people in spiritual bondage while proclaiming Mohamed to be **the one true** prophet, blinding them to Jesus as King and Priest. In fact Jesus has much to say about false prophets and teachers, and hold in mind that His concept of teacher is much deeper than ours.

Matthew 7:15   Beware of **false prophets**, who come to you in sheep's clothing, but inwardly they are ravenous wolves.

Matthew 24:11   Then many **false prophets** will rise up and deceive many.

Matthew 24:24   For false christs and **false prophets** will rise and show great signs and wonders to deceive, if possible, even the elect.

Note that false christs and false prophets are in some way synonymous; they function under an anointing of a spirit other than the Holy Spirit, a spirit of lies, especially in the last days.

Luke 6:26   Woe to you when all men speak well of you, for so did their fathers to the **false prophets**.

2 Peter 2:1   But there were also **false prophets** among the people, even as there will be false teachers among you, who will secretly bring in destructive heresies, even denying the Lord who bought them, and bring on themselves swift destruction.

1 John 4:1-3   Beloved, do not believe every spirit, but test the spirits, whether they are of God; because many **false prophets** have gone out into the world. 2 By this you know the Spirit of God: Every spirit that confesses that Jesus Christ has come in the flesh is of God, 3 and every spirit that does not confess that Jesus Christ has come in the flesh is not of God. And this is the *spirit* of the Antichrist, which you have heard was coming, and is now already in the world.

These scriptures make it clear that it is very important to see Jesus Christ, God's anointed Savior, as come in the flesh, as the true Prophet, otherwise false prophets abound. 1 John 4:1-4 is a Biblical, epistemological test for revealed truth, a way to test the spirit of what is being revealed to you whether in teaching or art or culture or politics or theology, or anything else. God's anointed Savior has come in the flesh and will return in the flesh! Jesus is actually God in the flesh! Jesus was and is all man and all God! The false prophets deny this truth, the mystery of God stepping into His own creation and fixing it, redeeming it, fulfilling it! If it is the revelation of the Holy Spirit, it will testify of Christ and uphold all of the Word of God. If it does not, it is not of God but the Antichrist! How do we teach our learners to listen to the Holy Spirit? Over and over again we must train them in this kind of thinking using the spiritual test God revealed to us and in this kind of listening as well.

Jesus is the one true prophet; gold, frankincense, **and** myrrh. He speaks the truth in eternity and in time about all subjects including history! Do we teach the Bible as true history or merely as Bible stories or human, metaphorical stories? One leads to prophecy, the others to myth! One leads to hope, the others to despair. It is the same as looking at the Bible as Truth or as just knowledge. Jesus teaches these truths and He lives them out, and He expects the members of a school community under His anointing and name to do the same. He calls us to follow Him in this ministry also, even if unbelieving men and women speak poorly and fearfully of us for doing it. Even as Jesus fulfilled so many Biblical prophecies and continues to do so in real history, He expects us to do the same in His Spirit and name.

King, Priest, and Prophet

So how does Jesus function as King, Priest, and Prophet? He does it like a lamb and a lion (more on this later)! He is both innocent compassion and fierce strength! He rules as a servant. He intercedes compassionately as one who has been tempted in every way we have and yet has always overcome victoriously and who offers Himself, not someone else, as our Sacrifice. And He prophesies as the one who knows the beginning from the end and the end from the beginning, the Alpha and the Omega, the Aleph and the Tav, the fulfillment of God's plan, the Creator and Redeemer and Restorer and Fulfiller of history and the creation!

So how then should we, as kings, priests, and prophets in Jesus, walking in the three things that remain, that have staying power, faith, hope, and love, function in Christian schools? We must faithfully, hopefully, and lovingly stand as ambassadors of His Kingdom, representing and ruling in His authority as stewards, and as examples to the flock, occupying in His mercy and grace and diligence as good and faithful servants until He comes back, and we must boldly proclaim the word of truth about our times and eternity. We are to faithfully, hopefully, and lovingly help to bring people to God and God to people interceding in our own brokenness and in the power of His grace for the brokenness of others, exhorting and encouraging from a thankful heart. And we must faithfully, hopefully, and lovingly speak prophetically both in a personal sense and a historical sense, lighting the way forward in these crucial, harvesting, last, tumultuous, and often dark days, serving as an example of hope, sacrifice, and service in the Lord.

This is the whole anointing for the whole educator for the whole student. Ruling faithfully, hopefully, and lovingly as servants, interceding as lambs, and standing up as prophets speaking truth to this generation and culture; how else do we raise up our students to be faithful, hopeful, and loving kings, priests, and prophets in Jesus themselves? He rules in love, He intercedes with compassion, and He reveals with truth, faithfulness, and hope exactly what is real and what is to come. It is Jesus who said,

Luke 6:40 A disciple is not above his teacher, but everyone who is perfectly trained will be **like his teacher.**

Matthew 10:41-42 He who receives a prophet in the name of a prophet shall receive a prophet's reward. And he who receives a righteous man in the name of a righteous man shall receive a righteous man's reward. ⁴² And whoever gives one of these little ones only a cup of cold *water* in the name of a disciple, assuredly, I say to you, he shall by no means lose his reward.

The Passover Lamb

Exodus 12:3 Speak to all the congregation of Israel, saying: 'On the tenth of this month every man shall take for himself a **lamb**, according to the house of his father, a **lamb** for a household.

Isaiah 53:7 He was oppressed and He was afflicted, Yet He opened not His mouth; He was led as a **lamb** to the slaughter, and as a sheep before its shearers is silent, So He opened not His mouth.

Mark 14:12   Now on the first day of Unleavened Bread, when they killed the Passover **lamb**, His disciples said to Him, "Where do you want us to go and prepare, that You may eat the Passover?"

John 1:29   The next day John saw Jesus coming toward him, and said, "Behold! The **Lamb** of God who takes away the sin of the world!

1 Corinthians 5:7   Therefore purge out the old leaven, that you may be a new lump, since you truly are unleavened. For indeed **Christ**, **our Passover,** was sacrificed for us.

Revelation 5:12   . . . saying with a loud voice: "Worthy is the **Lamb** who was slain to receive power and riches and wisdom, and strength and honor and glory and blessing!"

When we consider the Pesach and the whole lamb, we should ask, can we only take a little bit of Jesus? Is Bible class enough or an opening or closing prayer while the heart of our other lessons are supposedly secular, or is chapel once a week enough? Can we have Jesus as King or Priest or Prophet, but not all three? The Old Testament, inspired prescriptions of the Pesach, the Passover, are very instructive here.

Exodus 12:3-13a   Speak to all the congregation of Israel, saying: 'On the tenth of this month every man shall take for himself a lamb, according to the house of *his* father, a lamb for a household. 4 And if the household is too small for the lamb, let him and his neighbor next to his house take *it* according to the number of the persons; according to each man's need you shall make your count for the lamb. 5 Your lamb shall be without blemish, a male of the first year. You may take *it* from the sheep or from the goats. 6 Now you shall keep it until the fourteenth day of the same month. Then the whole assembly of the congregation of Israel shall kill it at twilight. 7 And they shall take *some* of the blood and put *it* on the two doorposts and on the lintel of the houses where they eat it. 8 Then they shall eat the flesh on that night; roasted in fire, with unleavened bread *and* with bitter *herbs* they shall eat it. 9 Do not eat it raw, nor boiled at all with water, but roasted in fire — its head with its legs and its entrails. 10 You shall let none of it remain until morning, and what remains of it until morning you shall burn with fire. 11 And thus you shall eat it: *with* a belt on your waist, your sandals on your feet, and your staff in your hand. So you shall eat it in haste. It *is* the LORD's Passover. 12 'For I will pass through the land of Egypt on that night, and will strike all the firstborn in the land of Egypt, both man and beast; and against all the gods of Egypt I will execute judgment: I *am* the LORD. 13 Now the blood shall be a sign for you on the houses where you *are*. And when I see the blood, I will **pass over** you . . .

There is so much here, but for our purposes, note first that the whole lamb was to be eaten, not just part; and that so after the fire. Picture Jesus in Gethsemane or before the Sanhedrin or the Roman scourging or on the cross; trails by fire in deed. The lamb was taken by father, family, and neighbor with humble, plain bread not raised by sin, hypocrisy, or pride and with bitter herbs as a reminder of the deliverance from the wages of sin. It was eaten in haste, ready to leave pagan gods and pagan culture behind, and it was eaten in the face of God's judgment that was to *pass over* us because of the innocent blood of the lamb and our obedience to and faith in it and not our own righteousness. The Passover speaks so clearly of the Kingship and Priesthood of Jesus, and of Jesus as the fulfillment of prophecy, our one true Prophet.

The Whole Jesus

This is the Lamb of God, the whole Lamb of God. Is His blood on the doorposts and lintels of our classrooms and our lessons forming a cross vertically and horizontally? But, furthermore, He is more as Prophet of prophets than just the Lamb of God; He is also the Lion of Judah. When He told Pilot that His Kingdom was "**now** . . . not from here," He clearly implied that someday it would be from here, and that here was Jerusalem!

<u>Acts 1: 6-11</u> Therefore, when they had come together, they asked Him, saying, "Lord, will You at this time restore the kingdom to Israel?" 7 And He said to them, "It is not for you to know times or seasons which the Father has put in His own authority. 8 But you shall receive power when the Holy Spirit has come upon you; and you shall be witnesses to Me in Jerusalem, and in all Judea and Samaria, and to the end of the earth." 9 Now when He had spoken these things, while they watched, He was taken up, and a cloud received Him out of their sight. 10 And while they looked steadfastly toward heaven as He went up, behold, two men stood by them in white apparel, 11 who also said, "Men of Galilee, why do you stand gazing up into heaven? This *same* Jesus, who was taken up from you into heaven, will so come in like manner as you saw Him go into heaven."

We will speak more of Jesus as Lion in subsequent chapters, but here point out that He clearly states that the Father will pick the time of His return "in like manner." The Angels make it clear that, as He went up into the clouds, He will return in the clouds and most likely to the same spot in Israel, the Mount of Olives, where the clouds billow up from the coastal plain quite regularly and spectacularly especially at Passover time and Tabernacles time! In the meantime we are witnesses to the King of kings, the Priest of priests, and the Prophet of prophets!

1 Corinthians 13:13   And now abide **faith, hope, love**, these three; but the greatest of these is **love**.

1 Thessalonians 5:8   But let us who are of the day be sober, putting on the breastplate of **faith** and **love**, and *as* a helmet the **hope** of salvation.

We are called to faithfully, lovingly, and hopefully be kings, priests, and prophets following Him in His schools' ministries and communities! Can you see yourself as a humble, faithful servant-king, a compassionate, loving, faithful and hopeful, interceding priest, and a fearless, hopeful, faithful, and loving prophet speaking the truth in your Christian school ministry? Not as the world defines these ministries, but as Jesus defines them!

He calls us to follow Him. How we see ourselves as kings, priests, and prophets in Him and in our own hearts and convictions and spirits makes a huge difference in how we go about the ministries in which He has placed us. Finally do we see our students as kings, priests, and prophets to be in Jesus? Do the education we offer and the example we set help prepare them to walk in these ministries of Jesus in their generation in all that they learn? Are these outcomes spelled out in our curriculum and our assessments and our mission statements? If not, why not? May God stir up our convictions, forgive our misgivings, and deliver us in His mercy and grace from evil to His honor and glory. Jesus never backed down from being King, Priest, and Prophet, and neither should we in Him!

Chapter 8: Servants and Slaves amongst the Flock: What is Leadership in Christian Education?

Matthew 20:25-28 But Jesus called them to *Himself* and said, "You know that the rulers of the Gentiles lord it over them, and those who are great exercise authority over them. 26 Yet it shall not be so among you; but whoever desires to become great among you, let him be your servant. 27 And whoever desires to be first among you, let him be your slave— 28 just as the Son of Man did not come to be served, but to serve, and to give His life a ransom for many."

What does this have to do with Christian, anointed, school ministry? Perhaps it is only for leaders; but who is not a leader of someone? Are not teachers, leaders? Leadership is a critical function in any body, and it includes everyone! How seriously do we take this clear teaching of our Lord? Note that He "called them to Himself" to deliver this teaching. His words, His deeds, and His very Self are the lesson! "Just as the Son of Man did not come to be served, but to serve, and to give His life a ransom for many." Campbell McAlpine (1982) has said that Jesus is the greatest leader who ever lived, the perfect example of leadership; if this is so, and I believe it is, had we not better listen to Him about leadership rather than to anyone else?

Hebrews 1:1-2 God, who at various times and in various ways spoke in time past to the fathers by the prophets, ² has in these last days spoken to us by *His* Son, whom He has appointed heir of all things, through whom also He made the worlds . . .

As in much of His teaching, Jesus puts forth a contrast between the Godly and the worldly or supposedly secular, here regarding leadership. What is the problem with *lording it over* and *exercising authority over*? Is not this how Christian schools are supposed to do leadership? We must ask did Jesus lord it over the disciples and exercise authority over them? Or did He serve them as a shepherd serves and cares for His sheep? This does not mean that He did not correct them or protect them, or allow them to be foolish or disrespectful or unkind, but it does mean it was a free will relationship built upon certain carefully chosen motives and freely made commitments.

His motive was to love them and help them, not just to boss them around or control or manipulate them. There is no vanity or conceit here, just caring. Jesus was not interested in lording it over them nor simply exercising authority over them; these were neither his methods nor his goals. Is this clear in our school and classroom leadership?

1 Peter 4:10   Each one should use whatever gift he has received to serve others, faithfully administering God's grace in its various forms. NIV

Why a servant? A servant chooses to care for the needs of others before himself or herself. How can I help you is his foremost thought. In whose service are we? This is the key question of motives; is our leadership serving ourselves or God and others? But beyond this Jesus actually took this a step deeper. In the above scripture He not only spoke of leadership as service but also as slavery! What is the difference between a servant and a slave? One can quit and go find work, even service work, elsewhere, but the other is sold out!

1 Corinthians 6:20   For you were bought at a price; therefore glorify God in your body and in your spirit, which are God's.

We are the Lord's slaves. A servant can go find work elsewhere or even go into business for himself. A slave says that he is committed, where else would he go? He belongs to the Master in body and spirit!

Nor did Jesus constantly demand the disciple's thanks; He always pointed their thanksgiving to the Father. He made clear that God was their Benefactor. Although He was their Lord and Teacher, He was also their Friend. Brown nosing and groveling were not requirements of discipleship with Him! He lived among them, not over them.

Luke 22:25-26   And He said to them, "The kings of the Gentiles exercise lordship **over** them, and those who exercise authority **over** them are called 'benefactors.' [26] But not so *among* you; on the contrary, he who is greatest **among** you, let him be as the younger, and he who governs as he who serves."

What kind of leadership does this make? How do we lead in Christian education as servants and slaves "**among**" the flock and yet as Godly kings, priests, and prophets? You may say that this sounds impossible, but it is the example Jesus leaves for us! It is our secular ways of thinking, our wrong philosophies, which stumble us here. The world associates leadership with pride; Jesus bases it on humility!

Philippians 2:5-8 Let this mind be in you which was also in Christ Jesus, 6 who, being in the form of God, did not consider it robbery to be equal with God, 7 but made Himself of **no reputation**, taking the form of a bondservant, *and* coming in the likeness of men. 8 And being found in appearance as a man, He **humbled** Himself and became **obedient** to *the point of* death, even the death of the cross.

The keys here are: **no reputation, humility**, and **obedience**: the mind of Christ, His philosophy of anointed leadership! Are these our goals of leadership in the classroom, in the school administration, on the athletic field, in the board room: to be of no reputation, of humility, and of obedience to the Lord for His glory? How would this make Christian schools different?

Glory, the Heart of the Matter

Campbell McAlpine (1982) gets to the heart of the matter, and it settles around the question of who gets the glory? He beautifully points out that, after Jesus did many of His astounding miracles, those in attendance generally glorified God in heaven for what had taken place. Stop and think about that. Why did they not glorify Jesus instead? What was it about the way Jesus did things or the motive and attitude in which he did them or the source of the power and strength through which He did them that turned people toward the Heavenly Father and not toward Him? How was this so clear to those who were witnesses of His miracles that they should glorify God in heaven? Does this have anything to do with being of **no reputation, humility, and obedience: being a servant and a slave, leading from among?** Why did Jesus always look up when He talked to God in front of other people? What was He modeling for us as a leader? Can we teach our lessons secularly and also do this? Who gets the glory? What a crucial question, what a pivotal example! Thank God for Jesus!

Kenneth Gangel (1997) makes the case in another way; he sees Christian leadership as team leadership *from amongst* the flock. Jesus led from among, not over. He slept on the same ground as His disciples, ate the same food, and walked the same roads. He was so much a part of the group that Judas had to point him out to His arresters. He raised up a team by being a member of it, of no reputation, of humility, and of obedience. Gangel in essence says that the New Testament pattern of leadership is group or body growth and consensus with the Holy Spirit as the acknowledged Leader; it seemed good to the Holy Spirit and us!

What are the implications of this for all the various forms of Christian school leadership from the classroom to the athletic fields to the administration to the board of directors? Does it have anything to do with lording it over and exercising authority over? What will meditating upon the difference between among and over do to our leadership?

1 Peter 5:2-4 Shepherd the flock of God which is **among** you, serving as overseers, not by compulsion but willingly, not for dishonest gain but eagerly; 3 nor as being lords over those entrusted to you, but being examples to the flock; 4 and when the Chief Shepherd appears, you will receive the crown of glory that does not fade away.

There is no better leadership example than Jesus. As leaders, whose reputation is most important to us, whose reputation do we defend and build up at all cost, our own or rather the Lord's? Are we sold out servants of the flock or just hirelings who scatter when trouble comes? Do we lead humbly from among or do we proudly lord it over from above? Do we determine to glorify God by our own Godly example or pride ourselves in exercising authority using do as I say but not as I do? Is our leadership example that of Jesus?

Followership

John 5:19 Then Jesus answered and said to them, "Most assuredly, I say to you, **the Son can do nothing of Himself**, but what He sees the Father do; for whatever He does, the Son also does in like manner."

John 8:28 Then Jesus said to them, "When you lift up the Son of Man, then you will know that I am He, and that I do **nothing of Myself**; but as My Father taught Me, I speak these things.

Jesus, Himself, shows us that true leadership is based on true followership. The leader who is truly a follower of Jesus does "**nothing of Himself**" and is therefore in turn someone who is safe to follow. Jesus not only taught this truth but did it even to the cross. This example was not lost upon His disciples, whom He asked to follow Him. Do we teach followership as a key to learning leadership? Jesus did! In the Body of Christ everyone is a follower and a leader. How we see ourselves as leaders and followers in Him and in our own hearts and convictions and spirits makes a huge difference in how we go about the ministries in which He has placed us.

An Example Regarding Prayer

Luke 11:1a   Now it came to pass, as He was praying in a certain place, when He ceased, *that* one of His disciples said to Him, "Lord, teach us to pray . . ."

Jesus led by example. He followed God in prayer, and His disciples, seeing His example, wanted to follow Him in prayer! A whole book could be written on prayer and leadership; if Jesus is our perfect example of followership and leadership, however, it should be obvious that praying from among the flock as servant, slave, example, king, priest, prophet, and shepherd is a must for leaders in Christian education. Leaders should be praying without ceasing; openly talking to God in front of the flock as they go about their ministry just as Jesus did but also spending time away in private prayer just as Jesus did also! This is just one example of many that could be pointed out of how Jesus led by example from among; and others, seeing the example and its fruit, asked to be taught how to follow.

Opportunity and Responsibility

A word about opportunity and responsibility in regards to leadership in Christian schools is in order. One of the great opportunities and thus responsibilities of private, Christian school leadership whether in the board room, the office, the playing field, or the classroom, is the freedom to be creative. There are not giant bureaucracies to be moved, nor usually union rules to encumber, nor overly burdensome state laws with which to wrangle. There is a refreshing chance to be creative and responsive under the authority of the Lord and the through the oversight of the board of directors. A private school can be nimble on its feet. It does not have to do things the way everyone else does just because everyone else does it that way.

Of course, as well, there are fewer safety nets for ill contrived decisions. We have the opportunity to creatively stand with Jesus, yet in the world we often stand more alone.

Therefore this freedom brings with it great responsibility. Just because we can, does not mean we should; and just because we do not have to, does not mean we should not. The key is hearing the Lord and using our freedom to follow Him and not just do and say what others do and say because they do and say it. This is a great opportunity and a great responsibility! We should do and say what Jesus does and says!

Matthew 7:13-14 "Enter by the narrow gate; for wide *is* the gate and broad *is* the way that leads to destruction, and there are many who go in by it. 14 Because narrow *is* the gate and difficult *is* the way which leads to life, and there are few who find it . . .

This is the great challenge, opportunity, and responsibility of leadership in private, Christian schools. May we choose creatively and wisely to follow Him because He is very creative and all-wise and definitely different from the ways of the many. The way of the narrow gate may be more lonely or difficult, even trying or scary, but it can be much more creative and exhilarating and fruitful and full of life! The Creator expects us to be creative and responsible in service to Him and to others as we follow our King, Priest, and Prophet, Jesus! Are we brave and faithful enough to use our freedom well or cowardly just to imitate pagan education? Jesus calls us to be of good courage and good will and follow HIM!

Is Jesus a Stakeholder?

Again this is more than a metaphor. Much of contemporary, leadership writing centers, and rightly so, around inclusive or team leadership (e.g. Gangel, 1997). The essence of this idea is that a leader should involve all of the stakeholders in any situation as early and as often as possible in any decision making process. This leads to a multitude of counsel, wisdom, involvement, ownership, and commitment and therefore greatly increases the chances of successful implementation of a better decision. Yet who are stakeholders? Generally they are anyone who has a stake in the effects of the decision to be made. This is leadership from among.

While pondering these ideas, the Holy Spirit impressed upon me that Jesus is the Stakeholder of stakeholders!

This is true of everything but even more so of Christian education in particular. He has bought anointed education with His own blood from the **stakes** driven through His hands and feet! Is He not, then, our preeminent **stakeholder** to be involved as early and as often and as thoroughly as possible in any decision making process, any act of leadership and followership? If He is the Author and Finisher of our faith and if without faith it is impossible to please God, then we only please God when Jesus authors and finishes our decision making regarding anything that has to do with leading and following in His schools!

We could meditate upon the fact that He held the atoms that formed the stakes, the hammer, the spear tip, the thorns, the wood of the cross, even the scourge in existence. How humbling is this? Of what kind of love for us does it speak? Of what kind of joy set before Him does it witness? Who is the ultimate Stakeholder in our schools and the decisions made there by anyone who leads and follows in any capacity? God help us to walk in this truth in any leadership and followership through which we minister in Christian education! Jesus is our preeminent Stakeholder! He is the Stakeholder of all stakeholders! May God stir up our convictions, forgive our misgivings, and deliver us in His mercy and grace from evil to His honor and glory.

Matthew 10:24-25a   A disciple is not above *his* teacher, nor a servant above his master. [25] It is enough for a disciple that he be like his teacher, and a servant like his master.

Chapter 9: Is Pride a Christian School Value?

What does the scripture say about pride and humility? This may seem like an odd topic for a book on Christian education, but it may be one of the most important. In our times, when the supposed secular educationists have made a giant idol and powerful principality out of self-esteem, and, given Jesus' warnings and rebukes to the religious of His day, it is surely curious that humility does not get its honor due, even often in Christian education. Conversely, every modern and/or postmodern, educational psychology text, through which almost all teachers are trained, espouses boldly the great motivational benefits of teaching children to be proud of themselves and proud of their accomplishments and to be enamored with their own self-esteem. Moreover, one can see this false teaching often being lived out in Christian schools as well!

The supposedly secular theory, put succinctly, is that those who do well do so because they have learned to take pride in themselves and in their work and, conversely, that those who do not do well do so because they have not yet learned to take pride in themselves and their work. Therefore it is our job to teach youth to take pride in themselves and their work. Self-esteem is the magic wand of education, or so we have been told.

Psalm 45:4   And in Your majesty ride prosperously because of truth, **humility**, and righteousness; and Your right hand shall teach You awesome things.

Proverbs 15:33   The fear of the LORD is the instruction of wisdom, and before honor is **humility**.

Proverbs 22:4   By **humility** and the fear of the LORD are riches and honor and life.

Zephaniah 2:3   Seek the LORD, all you meek of the earth, who have upheld His justice. Seek righteousness, seek **humility**. It may be that you will be hidden in the day of the LORD's anger.

Acts 20:19   . . . serving the Lord with all **humility**, with many tears and trials . . .

Colossians 3:12   Therefore, as the elect of God, holy and beloved, put on tender mercies, kindness, **humility**, meekness, longsuffering . . .

2 Timothy 2:25 . . . in **humility** correcting those who are in opposition, if God perhaps will grant them repentance, so that they may know the truth . . .

Titus 3:2 . . . to speak evil of no one, to be peaceable, gentle, showing all **humility** to all men

1 Peter 5:5 Likewise you younger people, submit yourselves to your elders. Yes, all of you be submissive to one another, and be clothed with **humility**, for "God resists the proud, but gives grace to the **humble**."

Numbers 12:3 (Now the man Moses was very **humble**, more than all men who were on the face of the earth.)

Deuteronomy 8:2 And you shall remember that the LORD your God led you all the way these forty years in the wilderness, to **humble** you and test you, to know what was in your heart, whether you would keep His commandments or not.

2 Samuel 22:28 You will save the **humble** people; but Your eyes are on the haughty, that You may bring them down.

2 Chronicles 7:14 . . . if My people who are called by My name will **humble** themselves, and pray and seek My face, and turn from their wicked ways, then I will hear from heaven, and will forgive their sin and heal their land.

2 Chronicles 12:6 So the leaders of Israel and the king **humble**d themselves; and they said, "The LORD is righteous."

2 Chronicles 12:12 When he **humble**d himself, the wrath of the LORD turned from him, so as not to destroy him completely; and things also went well in Judah.

2 Chronicles 32:26 Then Hezekiah **humble**d himself for the pride of his heart, he and the inhabitants of Jerusalem, so that the wrath of the LORD did not come upon them in the days of Hezekiah.

Ezra 8:21 Then I proclaimed a fast there at the river of Ahava, that we might **humble** ourselves before our God, to seek from Him the right way for us and our little ones and all our possessions.

Psalm 10:17 LORD, You have heard the desire of the **humble**; You will prepare their heart; You will cause Your ear to hear.

Psalm 18:27 For You will save the **humble** people, but will bring down haughty looks.

Psalm 25:9   The **humble** He guides in justice, and the **humble** He teaches His way.

Psalm 113:6   Who **humble**s Himself to behold the things that are in the heavens and in the earth?

Psalm 149:4   For the LORD takes pleasure in His people; He will beautify the **humble** with salvation.

Proverbs 3:34   Surely He scorns the scornful, but gives grace to the **humble**.

Proverbs 11:2   When pride comes, then comes shame; but with the **humble** is wisdom.

Proverbs 16:19   Better to be of a **humble** spirit with the lowly, than to divide the spoil with the proud.

Proverbs 29:23   A man's pride will bring him low, but the **humble** in spirit will retain honor.

Isaiah 29:19   The **humble** also shall increase their joy in the LORD, and the poor among men shall rejoice in the Holy One of Israel.

Isaiah 57:15   For thus says the High and Lofty One Who inhabits eternity, whose name is Holy: "I dwell in the high and holy place, with him who has a contrite and **humble** spirit, to revive the spirit of the **humble**, and to revive the heart of the contrite ones.

Jeremiah 44:10   They have not been **humble**d, to this day, nor have they feared; they have not walked in My law or in My statutes that I set before you and your fathers.'

Ezekiel 21:26   … thus says the Lord GOD: "Remove the turban, and take off the crown; Nothing shall remain the same. Exalt the **humble**, and **humble** the exalted."

Daniel 10:12   Then he said to me, "Do not fear, Daniel, for from the first day that you set your heart to understand, and to **humble** yourself before your God, your words were heard; and I have come because of your words.

Zephaniah 3:12   I will leave in your midst a meek and **humble** people, and they shall trust in the name of the LORD.

Matthew 18:4   Therefore whoever **humble**s himself as this little child is the greatest in the kingdom of heaven.

Matthew 23:12   And whoever exalts himself will be **humble**d, and he who **humble**s himself will be exalted.

Romans 12:16   Be of the same mind toward one another. Do not set your mind on high things, but associate with the **humble**. Do not be wise in your own opinion.

Philippians 2:1-11   Therefore if *there is* any consolation in Christ, if any comfort of love, if any fellowship of the Spirit, if any affection and mercy, 2 fulfill my joy by being like-minded, having the same love, *being* of one accord, of one mind. 3 *Let* nothing *be done* through selfish ambition or conceit, but in lowliness of mind let each esteem others better than himself. 4 Let each of you look out not only for his own interests, but also for the interests of others. 5 Let this mind be in you which was also in Christ Jesus, 6 who, being in the form of God, did not consider it robbery to be equal with God, 7 **but made Himself of no reputation, taking the form of a bondservant**, *and* coming in the likeness of men. 8 And being found in appearance as a man, He **humbled** Himself and became obedient to *the point of* death, even the death of the cross. 9 Therefore God also has highly exalted Him and given Him the name which is above every name, 10 that at the name of Jesus every knee should bow, of those in heaven, and of those on earth, and of those under the earth, 11 and *that* every tongue should confess that Jesus Christ *is* Lord, to the glory of God the Father.

James 4:6   But He gives more grace. Therefore He says: "God resists the proud, but gives grace to the **humble**."

James 4:10   **Humble** yourselves in the sight of the Lord, and He will lift you up.

Matthew 11:29   Take my yoke upon you and learn from me, for I am gentle and **humble** in heart, and you will find rest for your souls. NIV

And yet we often hear teachers tell students how proud they are of them and/or of their accomplishments or principals tell teachers or staff the same, or coaches their athletes, or board members or parents or students doing likewise about various kinds of talents or accomplishments. We often give or hear speeches about how proud we are of people's achievements, of winning teams, of test scores, of our school's Christian environment or atmosphere, and on and on.

Why is this? Did God ever say He was proud of Jesus? Did Jesus ever say He was proud of the disciples or His mother or His younger brother James, head of the Jerusalem church, His step-father Joseph, His other brother Jude, or His late-born apostle, Paul? Why not? Did the Trinity just selfishly or carelessly forget? Are They too curmudgeonly or proud to do so?

To quote the Bible scholar, Derek Prince (2003, p.61), "I believe it is vitally important for all of us to realize that the first sin in the universe was not murder, nor adultery, but rather *pride.*"

Proverbs 21:4   A high look, and a proud heart, even the lamp of the wicked, is sin. ASV

Proverbs 16:5a   Everyone proud in heart *is* an abomination to the LORD;

Proverbs 8:13   The fear of the LORD *is* to hate evil; **pride** and arrogance and the evil way and the perverse mouth I hate.

Psalm 101:5a   The one who has a haughty look and a **proud** heart, Him I will not endure.

What is Satan's big sin? What caused the religious Pharisees' hypocrisy? What are the connections between humility, thankfulness, and obedience versus pride, envy, and rebellion? The Apostle Paul spoke clearly against boasting; but said, if we must, we should only boast in Jesus and not in ourselves! So who is lurking behind our pride? And why would we want to let him have a foothold in the Lord's schools and the teachers and students thereof?

1 Timothy 3:6 . . . not a novice, lest being puffed up with pride he fall into the *same* condemnation as the devil.

It is powerful to note that, when Jesus instituted communion at His last Passover, He surely used matzos as the bread symbolizing His body to be broken for us. Matzos has no yeast, as in the Feast of Unleavened Bread; but, to be sure it does not raise (puff up), stripes of pierced holes are put in it so any air can escape in baking. You have probably taken communion with matzos before; it is still made the same way and is used as the bread of the Passover. It is symbolic of humility, and it is symbolic of our Lord Jesus. The next day He was striped and pierced for us in utter humility!

Glory and Motivations

The key to all of this is again a question of glory (McAlpine, 1982). Why does God say He will not share His glory with another? To whom should the glory go when something good happens? Did Jesus seek His own glory? Did He seek the glory of His disciples? Was it pride that motivated Jesus to go to the cross, the greatest accomplishment in history and eternity? Was the joy that was set before Him, self-righteous pride or the humble fulfillment of His love for us? Will Jesus brag about the cross in heaven?

James 1:17   Every **good gift** and every **perfect gift** is from above, and comes down from the Father of lights, with whom there is no variation or shadow of turning.

These are not trivial questions, for they go to the bedrock of motivations (McAlpine, 1982). We ask again, is pride a Christian value? Can you find anywhere in the Bible where pride or self esteem is spoken well of or is not spoken against? Therefore does the Holy Spirit cringe when we use pride or self esteem to motivate our Christian youth? Does Satan smile? Why have we so easily and tirelessly fallen into this trap? Why do we tell ourselves that it is just innocent rewarding and good for the youth; they deserve it, have they not earned it? Who are we robbing of His glory when we do this? And what are we teaching the students by our example?

Luke 6:40   A disciple is not above his teacher, but everyone who is perfectly **trained** will be **like his teacher**.

Jesus said that. Let us be challenged by the Lord to replace the heart reality of and the word of *pride* itself with *humility* and the heart reality of and the word of *proud* with *humbled* in our hearts and in our speech. "Well done. How *humbled* I am that you are learning so well, Johnny; let us give God the glory for helping you to be so diligent and for opening your understanding! God is good; isn't He?! He is pleased with your progress. Let us be thankful and humbled by His blessing and favor." Think of the lessons that are learned here by both the teacher and the student!

Do we have a right to be proud of ourselves or our students when it is God Who blesses the students He has put in our care with understanding? Or do we proudly think we are the teacher and not the Holy Spirit? Can we do anything good as teachers or learners without God's anointing? If we are anointed, Christian, teachers and learners and leaders, to whom should the glory go? Again, what are we modeling for the students? Are we following the example of Jesus? Or are we being thieves of God's glory, as if our teaching and our learning of anything good happened separately or independently from Him?

Conversely, why do supposedly secular educators promote self pride and self esteem and ignore Godly humility and God Himself as the path to achievement and success? Should we Christian educators follow their example and do the same? Go back and re-read the scriptures listed earlier in this chapter; meditate on each one of them; then re-read all these questions. Notice how many times truth, righteousness, understanding, honor, joy, wisdom, rest, grace, exaltation, greatness, God's blessing, God's favor, God's care, and salvation itself are associated with humility, and how often and how boldly contrasted with pride as something God hates!

Do we want all of these blessings for ourselves and our students? Do we believe the consistent teaching of the Bible or the constant lies of modern and post-modern, supposedly secular, God-ignoring psychology? This is another great divide in education, the pride versus humility divide, the who gets the glory divide. Is it not Biblically clear who between Jesus and Satan is on which side of this divide; the question is where do we stand in our own hearts and spirits and practice and words and deeds as models for others in these matters? These are not trivial matters to God!

Mark 1:41   Then Jesus, **moved with compassion**, stretched out His hand and touched him, and said to him, "I am willing; be cleansed."

Christian motivation is compassion based, full of humility, willingness, and a desire to glorify God not self.

France and the Dignity Trap

Consider the dignity trap: France's human dignity laws and the pending, akin, American, so-called, hate crimes legislations are good examples. Do you know that it is against the law in France, with the most proudly and avowedly atheistic citizenry on earth, to offend anyone's dignity?

This might even sound good to our modern and postmodern, self-esteeming ears. But, did not someone once have the courage and humility to tell us that we were sinners who needed salvation and a Savior, regardless of offending our foolish dignity by doing so? Whose dignity really counts anyway? How does dignity match up with humility? God's love should make us feel worthwhile but not proud, because we never earned His love and never could.

Romans 5:8 But God demonstrates His own love toward us, in that while we were still sinners, Christ died for us.

We need to protect our students' worth, not their human dignity. If each one of them was the only person on earth, Jesus would have died just for them. That is how much they are worth, the blood of the Lamb of God. But be careful of dignity, for it is soaked in pride, and is an enemy of humility and thus of God! And yet many Christian schools, mimicking supposedly secular schools, have dignity in their mission statements in the place of humility! This should not be.

Humility and Magnifying God

How do we change our hearts, our actions, our understandings, and our vocabularies in the Christian classroom, the faculty room, the administrative offices, parent meetings, awards assemblies, sports fields, and the board rooms regarding pride and humility, and dignity and worth? Simply we make it a priority to humble ourselves and to magnify God's goodness and glory! These two actions always go together. We cannot have one without the other; and, furthermore, the absence of either of them always diminishes the presence of the other. The more proud and dignified we are the less humble and worthy we become! The more we glorify ourselves, the less we glorify God! On the other hand, the more we praise God and humble ourselves, the less we are stumbled by pride and dignity and self esteem.

We can and should express pleasure and honor and reward in a Godly way for goodness and good acts as long as we make it a priority to humble ourselves and to magnify God's goodness and glory in doing so! Whom do we thank for blessings, and what example does this set? "How blessed and pleased I am, Sally, to see your improvement. God has been graciously working through our humble efforts, and we should humbly thank Him for it!"

Why would we be embarrassed to give the glory to Whom it truly belongs? Is this a small matter to God? Think of Herod's example in the New Testament, eaten by worms for trying to steal God's glory. Or ask this question, why is supposedly secular humanism based on pride and not humility? Or is it just by chance that they call it gay pride?

Who gets the glory? Why is this so important? Is the problem that God is a glory hog? I would humbly submit to you that God takes the glory because He knows we cannot handle it without being horribly warped by it. Again, consider the archangel Lucifer, originally unsurpassed in beauty among created beings. God is not hogging the glory; He is humbly protecting us from it. Who of us would leave the glory of heaven to go bear the sins of the rebellious, ungrateful, twisted, proud and fallen and do it in a humble, redemptive act of love? Think of the passion of Christ. Revelations 5 makes it clear that in Heaven or on earth only Jesus is worthy. We should worship God and God only! Humility is admitting that God alone is righteous and we are not, outside of His grace to us, which we can never earn.

Matthew 5:3 "Blessed are the poor in spirit, for theirs is the kingdom of heaven."

So how do the students learn this? How do they learn the infinite and eternal value of humility as opposed to the disaster of pride? How do we promote and exalt humility and not pride in our schools? We humble ourselves before God and ask Him to show us how in everything we do and say! We repent and root the pride out of our own hearts and ask God for a spirit of humility and thankfulness and praise unto Him instead. It is a gift He wants to give us. We must learn to acknowledge, thank, and worship God for what He accomplishes for and through and in us. Then we model this humility because we have it! Like God, we reward humility and not pride. We follow the example of Jesus!

What would happen if your school took a focused year, as a local manifestation of the Body of Christ, to seek out all the ways it could honor humility before God in all that the school is, all that it says, and all that it does? Praise God, would not humility change things for the better?! The example starts from the top, the middle, or the bottom! It starts with any of us following Jesus, Who **humbled** Himself and became obedient to *the point of* death, even the death of the cross.

Mark 8:34 When He had called the people to Himself, with His disciples also, He said to them, "Whoever desires to come after Me, let him deny himself, and take up his cross, and follow Me."

Matthew 10:38   And he who does not take his cross and follow after Me is not worthy of Me.

Critical Thinking Skills

This whole issue of valuing humility instead of pride can be clearly seen at work in the example of one of the chief aims of supposedly secular education: critical thinking skills. It is sad to say that so many Christian educators go right along with this concept as if it were, not only harmless, but a great, Christian idea. Like so many of Satan's ploys, it is a twisted half truth made evil. The Bible clearly calls us to be *discerning*, but where does it call us to be critical? Is being critical a fruit of the Spirit? Do we think Satan may have employed some critical thinking skills when he got a third of the angels to rebel with him against God? Did he use critical thinking skills on Eve and Adam in the garden?

Matthew 10:16   Behold, I send you out as sheep in the midst of wolves. Therefore be wise as serpents and harmless as doves.

In reality, it is pride and fear that make us critical; humility makes us, however, wise, discerning, harmless, and compassionate! Critical thinking skills sound good to our flesh because they appeal to our pride, not to our humility. Critical thinking skills are dependent on our own skills, our own intellectual superiority, and our own ability, in our own foolish self-righteousness, to see other's faults. Discernment, on the other hand, is totally and humbly dependent on God's gracious Spirit, His revelation! Thus these two are miles apart.

Of course we should teach our students to be humbly discerning and wise in the Holy Spirit, but this is a far cry from being pridefully critical! We are humbly dependent on God's teaching in His written Word, the Bible, on His example in His living Word, Jesus Himself, and on His gracious guidance through His ever present Word, the Holy Spirit, for the discernment that leads to walking in His righteousness and wisdom by His mercy and grace. Can we see the difference between critical thinking skills and anointed, Godly discernment, between a prideful self-possession and a gracious gift from above? May God graciously give us the discernment and courage to do so!

Perhaps it would thus be pleasing to God for us to change some our stated aims, goals, and objectives in this light? Just what are we promoting? It is so dangerous to blindly follow the Godless examples of supposedly secular educators instead of being humbly discerning of Godly truth! Thank God for His mercy and grace! Discernment and wisdom are gifts of the Spirit for which we can thank God, not ourselves! These are anointed educational goals, Christian educational goals!

Luke 18: 9-14 Also He spoke this parable to some who trusted in themselves that they were righteous, and despised others: Two men went up to the temple to pray, one a Pharisee and the other a tax collector. The Pharisee stood and prayed thus with himself, "God, I thank You that I am not like other men – extortioners, unjust, adulterers, or even as this tax collector. I fast twice a week; I give tithes of all that I possess." And the tax collector, standing afar off, would not so much as raise his eyes to heaven, but beat his breast, saying, "God, be merciful to me a sinner!" I tell you this man went down to his house justified rather than the other; for everyone who exalts himself will be humbled, and he who humbles himself will be exalted.

Matthew 11:29 Take my yoke upon you and learn from me, for I am gentle and humble in heart, and you will find rest for your souls. NIV

Proverbs 11:2 When pride comes, then comes shame; but with the humble is wisdom.

It is not that we should withhold expressions of pleasure or blessing or encouragement, but our well-done and pleasure statements should always remind us of from where our goodness and faithfulness comes, God's grace, not ourselves! We should truly and generously encourage one another and acknowledge those who work hard among us but in a way that acknowledges our humility before the Lord and His gracious goodness to us not in our pride in ourselves. We should never forget the deadly principality we are playing with when we are tempted to spread pride about. Better to honor humility and to praise God generously!

May God stir up our convictions, forgive our misgivings, and deliver us in His mercy and grace from evil to His honor and glory.

Ecclesiastes 7:8a The patient in spirit is better than the proud in spirit.

Hebrews 5:7-9   . . . who, in the days of His flesh, when He had offered up prayers and supplications, with vehement cries and tears to Him who was able to save Him from death, and was heard because of His godly fear, [8] though He was a Son, *yet* **He learned obedience by the things which He suffered**. [9] And having been perfected, He became the author of eternal salvation to all who obey Him,

I am no theologian, though trained in philosophy, yet it seems obvious that Jesus **learned** regarding obedience and humility versus rebellion and pride; and He did it through suffering. Just what are we modeling and teaching and learning, educating, about humility and pride?

Chapter 10: Mission Statements that Make a Difference

Most schools now have written, mission statements. Their purposes are variously to proclaim beliefs, ideals, and convictions, to enumerate purpose, goals, intentions, faith, and values, to focus the target of their members' efforts, to create an identity, and to keep the main thing the main thing. As already noted in Chapter 2, Jesus' mission statement is found in Luke with Him reading by choice from Isaiah at the public inauguration of His ministry in His hometown synagogue. Here is the first half of it again.

<u>Luke 4:17-21</u> And He was handed the book of the prophet Isaiah. And when He had opened the book, He found the place where it was written:
   18 *"The Spirit of the LORD is upon Me,*
   Because He has anointed Me
   To preach the gospel to the poor;
   He has sent Me to heal the brokenhearted,
   To proclaim liberty to the captives
   And recovery of sight to the blind,
   To set at liberty those who are oppressed;
   19 *To proclaim the acceptable year of the LORD."*

Then He closed the book, and gave *it* back to the attendant and sat down. And the eyes of all who were in the synagogue were fixed on Him. 21 And He began to say to them, "Today this Scripture is fulfilled in your hearing."

Note that Jesus "found" this passage; it was purposeful. Again we point to the literal meaning of Messiah as *anointed* by God and conversely anointed by God as being *Messiah-ed* and their connection to an *anointed* school or education. What does the possible first half of Jesus' mission statement have to do with Christian, Holy Spirit *anointed* schools?

If we are following Jesus, should not our mission and our anointing be such that we make it our first priority to preach the good news of redemption and salvation to the poor and humble in spirit in our midst?

And should not it follow that we heal broken hearts with the truth of God's love both taught and walked, that we proclaim liberty and freedom to those who are in bondage to the sins and false teachings of this present, supposedly secular and pagan culture, and recovery of sight to see reality, the creation, and life as Jesus sees and sustains them, and to proclaim liberty from the oppression of false principalities and evil spiritual powers and their lies that would make us captives, and finally to proclaim the joy of the jubilee of God's willingness to accept us in Jesus' mercy and grace and through His substitutionary sacrifice for our debt of sin in this present age and in eternity?

Do our mission statements speak of these things, or do they rather speak of dignity, self-esteem, intellectual accomplishment, independent thinkers, a Christian atmosphere or environment, critical thinking, and worldly success and change? Does Jesus' anointing have anything to do with ours? Does His mission statement have anything to do with our mission statement? How would Jesus write the mission statements of His schools if we were to let Him?

The Second Half of Jesus' Mission Statement

I mentioned above that this was the *possible* first part of Jesus' mission statement, the part that was "fulfilled in your hearing" that day in the hearing of the people in His hometown synagogue. Is there a second part, yet to be fulfilled, and what might it have to do with Christian education in our times? I cannot prove this idea, but it is very interesting to note that Jesus stopped abruptly, even mid-sentence, in the middle of the Isaiah passage inspired by the Holy Spirit that He was quoting. The whole passage goes like this:

<u>Isaiah 61:1-3</u>
"The Spirit of the Lord GOD *is* upon Me,
Because the LORD has anointed Me
To preach good tidings to the poor;
He has sent Me to heal the brokenhearted,
To proclaim liberty to the captives,
And the opening of the prison to *those who are* bound;
2 To proclaim the acceptable year of the LORD,
And the day o**f vengeance of our God;**
To comfort all who mourn,
3 To console those who mourn in Zion,

To give them beauty for ashes,
The oil of joy for mourning,
The garment of praise for the spirit of heaviness;
That they may be called trees of righteousness,
The planting of the LORD, that He may be glorified."

Why did Jesus not finish the prophecy passage? Was He disowning a part of God's word, which of course He inspired and wrote in the first place, and thus proclaiming only the mercy of God and not also the justice of God? Or could it be a matter of timing? Could it be that the second part of this prophecy, His chosen mission statement, will be fulfilled in His soon, second coming, His return, just as the first part was fulfilled in His first coming? He obviously could not have said that the second half was fulfilled that day in their hearing; is that why He stopped mid sentence?

Strangely in many churches it is not very popular theology these days, but the Book of Revelation, the Revelation of Jesus (Revelations 1:1), is still there at the end of our Bibles. The whole Bible proclaims that there is a day of God's vengeance, of His judgment, even if the supposedly secular humanists and materialists do not believe it, any more than they are thankful for God's day of mercy and grace found in His first substitutionary coming!

Jesus clearly taught that there is a day of judgment coming (e.g. Matthew 24 and Luke 17). There is also a day coming when "all who mourn," and also specifically those who "mourn in Zion," will be comforted! Who mourns the Godlessness, debauchery, unthankfulness, irresponsibility, depravity, wickedness, and injustice of our God-ignoring day but the universal, true church and those truly awaiting their as yet unrecognized Messiah in Zion? Comfort from the rages and from the ravages of this fallen world order and culture is coming for the redeemed and elect! While we struggle with mourning, ashes, and heaviness of spirit at what we now see and experience around us and yes also within us, there are comfort, joy, consolation, beauty, praise, and righteousness coming right around the corner. Both judgment and comfort are near! Look up, not down. We must encourage this generation with this truth! We will see God's mercy and His justice.

The Lamb and the Lion

Metaphorically speaking this comfort and vengeance can be seen in Jesus as Lamb and as Lion.

Revelation 5:4-7 So I wept much, because no one was found worthy to open and read the scroll, or to look at it. 5 But one of the elders said to me, "Do not weep. Behold, the Lion of the tribe of Judah, the Root of David, has prevailed to open the scroll and to loose its seven seals."
6 And I looked, and behold, in the midst of the throne and of the four living creatures, and in the midst of the elders, stood a Lamb as though it had been slain, having seven horns and seven eyes, which are the seven Spirits of God sent out into all the earth. 7 Then He came and took the scroll out of the right hand of Him who sat on the throne.

This scroll, as is clearly seen in the next chapters of Revelation, is God's judgment, His vengeance and His comfort, to refer back to the second half Jesus' prophetic, mission statement from Isaiah. The title of this book which you are reading refers to the whole Jesus and Christian education. Here we are talking about that Prophet ministry that goes along with His King and Priest ministries. Remember that to have God's righteous judgment *Passover* us, we had to take the whole Lamb with His blood on our two door posts and one lintel, all three aspects of Jesus!

Looking again at the above scripture, why is Jesus the only one worthy? Maybe a second question will help us understand: Can you imagine trying to administer God's eternal judgment, His vengeance and His comfort? How badly would we, any one of us, botch it!? How would that power twist us and make hypocrites out of us? How well and fairly would we judge? Or let us ask this question the other way around, who else but Jesus would you trust with this responsibility and power concerning you and your loved ones?

Thank God for Jesus! By the fact that He is the sacrificial Lamb of God, He also has the right to be the Lion of Judah, the root of David, the poet, warrior king through whom God established Israel's kingdom and throne, the one Jesus will sit upon at His return. It is interesting that, while it is true that Jesus was royally blood-descended from David through Mary's genealogy, He is also at the same time from where David came, his "root!" Jesus is the eternal Lamb and the eternal Lion, full sevenfold of the Spirit of God! Jesus is God's mercy and grace to us and shortly God's just judgment, in either vengeance or comfort, to all.

Do we teach the coming judgment, both its righteous vengeance and its merciful comfort, and why or why not, and to what result? Is this a part of our mission statement as it is in the rest of Jesus' mission statement? Do we wish our youth to be spiritually strong? Then let us not give them a lukewarm Gospel with only selected, Sunday school pieces of Jesus. Let us honor Jesus as our Prophet as well as our King and Priest. Give our students the whole Jesus that they may be on the right side of the judgment to come, escaping God's vengeance and inheriting His comfort!

So much is at stake! A weakened Jesus is not enough in these times. Our youth must know the difference between being wheat and being tares, between the gracious comfort for the humble, repentant, and obedient and the just vengeance on the proud, thankless, and rebellious! Another great divide opens up here; those who are wisely ready for the soon coming judgment and those who foolishly are not! We have a great responsibility here to the children of this generation. If Christian education will not speak of these matters, who will?

A Revealed Mission Statement

Now let us look at another question which comes out of the idea of mission statements. Has the Holy Spirit revealed to your school, your community of educational truth seekers, your local, educational manifestation of the Body of Christ, its God given mission statement? Jesus, the Living Word of God, is the word in at least two other ways in the Bible: as s specific word to a specific person or group and as a general and universal word to all people. There is the general Word of eternal and universal truth. And there is a specific Word of that general truth spoken specifically to an individual or group in time and space. The two always agree and come from the same source. This does allow, however, a certain variety of emphasis in the body. But given this truth of variety, does your school's mission statement truly come from both God's general Word of truth and from His specifically, spoken by the Holy Spirit, Word of truth to your school community?   And, if your school's mission statement is really Jesus' mission to you, then is your school's mission statement really your school's true mission? Does the school live out its Godly mission statement?

Furthermore, who should have a mission statement, and again from where should they come? Should not every important endeavor in our school's ministry have a mission statement? And should not these various mission statements align with the school's overall mission which also in turn clearly aligns with Jesus' mission statement? And all these statements, must they not flow out of and align with both the general Word of truth and Jesus' specific Word to your school as a part of His Body, a local manifestation of the Body of Christ in a particular time and place? Or do we instead turn to supposedly secular educators and civil government standards for what our mission ought to look like and contain and include and exclude?

In a later chapter we will discuss the necessity of aligning these anointed, mission statements with our anointed, job descriptions and anointed assessment practices. At this point we should, however, look at two principles Frank Gaebelein took from scripture way back in 1954: 1) does any school activity please God and 2) does it bring God glory?

He proclaimed that all of our activities, and thus by inference all of our mission statements about those activities, must meet these two criteria. It must be clearly shown how and why they please God and how and why they bring Him glory. If they cannot or do not, we should not be doing them!

1 Corinthians 10:31 Therefore, whether you eat or drink, or whatever you do, do **all** to the **glory** of **God**.

Colossians 1:10 . . . that you may walk worthy of the Lord, fully **pleasing** Him, being fruitful in every good work and increasing in the knowledge of **God**;

The assumption is that there are activities that do and/or do not please and glorify God. The former belong in a Christian school and the latter do not!

A Personal Mission Statement

Finally I would ask do you have a personal mission statement, yourself, given to you by God? I am dead sure that He has one for you and that He wants to give it to you and to make it clear to you, both as a specific and a general Word to you! All we need to do is ask and listen with our whole and humbled hearts and spirits.

Jeremiah 29:11 For I know the thoughts that I think toward you, says the LORD, thoughts of peace and not of evil, to give you a future and a hope.

Matthew 7:7 Ask, and it will be given to you; seek, and you will find; knock, and it will be opened to you.

A personal mission statement from the Lord does what an institutional mission statement from the Lord does; it provides focus, strength, faith, hope, love, and a future in Him on a personal level. It is your calling in Him.

As a personal testimony, over forty years ago as a babe in Christ God kept bringing me back, over and over again, and often in very unique and unmistakable ways, to this scripture:

John 21:15-17   So when they had eaten breakfast, Jesus said to Simon Peter, "Simon, *son* of Jonah, do you love Me more than these?"
He said to Him, "Yes, Lord; You know that I love You."
He said to him, "Feed My lambs."
16 He said to him again a second time, "Simon, *son* of Jonah, do you love Me?"
He said to Him, "Yes, Lord; You know that I love You."
He said to him, "Tend My sheep."
17 He said to him the third time, "Simon, *son* of Jonah, do you love Me?" Peter was grieved because He said to him the third time, "Do you love Me?"
And he said to Him, "Lord, You know all things; You know that I love You."
Jesus said to him, "Feed My sheep."

At the time I was in my twenties and a new Christian and headmaster of the lower and middle school campus of Ojai Valley School, a proclaimed, non-sectarian, secular boarding school in Southern California founded in 1911 by progressive educators. I was pondering the scriptures, the meaning of true education, and my life's path having just come out of being a philosophy major at UC Berkeley and what was then called the cradle of the counter culture; and God kept bringing up this scripture to me, many times in many unmistakable ways. It would take a separate book to do justice to what this specific word meant to me then and subsequently over the years. Suffice it to say that I have, by God's merciful prodding and enduring patience, believed it is God's gracious and humbling mission statement to me (and surely to many others as well), His gracious, guiding hand leading me out of my darkness.

Shortly thereafter, I was called into the school's CEO's office and told that the board thought I was doing a great job, and that they wanted to extend to me another year's contract, but that the school was not a Christian school and that I had to stop talking to everyone about Jesus if I wanted to stay. Having a young wife and two of our eventual five children at the time, I was surprised by the answer the Holy Spirit prompted from me, which was simply that, if Jesus had to go, I had to go with Him. It was 1977.

Actually I was dumbfounded by what I had done. I turned down my next year's contract, having no idea where I was going; but God had called me through the above John 21: 15-17 scripture and I knew it. I did not deserve this calling, in fact I was clearly not very fit for it, but He had called me anyway. And His general Word of truth and His specific Word of truth have sustained and guided and encouraged me these forty plus years, as they have step by step unfolded before my eyes though five different, Christian education, leadership ministries, what He had in mind in spite of my unworthiness.

I share this with you not for my own applause but as an encouragement to you and for God's glory. If God could and can use me, He can use anyone! Find God's mission statement to you, that specific word that He speaks directly into your spirit; it is a great blessing. To what He calls, He miraculously enables!

In conclusion, when Jesus said that it was finished on the cross, could He not have had, at least partly, the first part of Isaiah 61 in His mind and heart? Did He not also reiterate this mission statement to John the Baptist's disciples when John inquired through them if He was the One (Matthew 11:4)? Anointed, Godly, Biblically integrated, Holy Spirit directed, mission statements that are made the main thing are a great blessing both to schools, and to each endeavor within a school, and to individuals! If an anointed and Biblical, mission statement was good for Jesus, why not for us who follow Him? He wants to connect to us! He set the example. May God stir up our convictions, forgive our misgivings, and deliver us in His mercy and grace from evil to His honor and glory.

Chapter 11: The Importance of Knowing the Times

The men of Issachar have been quoted by many.

1 Chronicles 12:32 . . . men of Issachar, who understood the times and knew what Israel should do . . .

Accepting Jesus as our Prophet of prophets, why then would the Book of Revelation be so important to this generation both as a statement of epistemology and as a guiding, prophetic light of truth and hope in these perilous, spiritual times? Who is going to define the times for our youth, Jesus or the lost, supposedly secular humanists and materialists and their media and universities?

Revelation 1:1a The Revelation of Jesus Christ, which God gave Him to show His servants—things which must shortly take place.

The Holy Spirit proclaims this last book of the Bible to be "The Revelation of Jesus Christ;" not that all the rest of the Bible's books are not (Luke 24:27); but there is a clear emphasis here. How can we, therefore, skip over this book and claim that we are sharing the whole Jesus with our students in these times?

An Example for Our Times

Revelation 3:14-22 "And to the angel of the church of the Laodiceans write, 'These things says the Amen, the Faithful and True Witness, the Beginning of the creation of God: 15 "I know your works, that you are neither cold nor hot. I could wish you were cold or hot. 16 So then, because you are lukewarm, and neither cold nor hot, I will vomit you out of My mouth. 17 Because you say, 'I am rich, have become wealthy, and have need of nothing'—and do not know that you are wretched, miserable, poor, blind, and naked— 18 I counsel you to buy from Me gold refined in the fire, that you may be rich; and white garments, that you may be clothed, *that* the shame of your nakedness may not be revealed; and anoint your eyes with eye salve, that you may see. 19 As many as I love, I rebuke and chasten. Therefore be zealous and repent. 20 Behold, I stand at the door and knock. If anyone hears My voice and opens the door, I will come in to him and dine with him, and he with Me. 21 To him who overcomes I will grant to sit with Me on My throne, as I also overcame and sat down with My Father on His throne. 22 "He who has an ear, let him hear what the Spirit says to the churches."

The obvious question raised by this scripture is, does this scripture describe well and also therefore accurately apply to our present, 21st century circumstances in America and the world? It is the last of seven specific churches from the first century to be addressed by Jesus from heaven after the resurrection. As this whole, last book in the Bible is prophecy, is it not reasonable to assume these particular churches are also prophetic of more than just themselves, especially because they have all long since disappeared? Many believe this last church of Laodicea is in fact emblematic of our last days, the close of this age. As we look carefully at Jesus' words to this church, please ask the Holy Spirit to help you decide about this for yourself and what this might have to do with successfully ministering to today's youth through evangelism and discipleship in Christian education.

First, Jesus uses three titles to identify Himself to this last church. He uses different titles to identify Himself to each of the other six, preceding churches. So the obvious question is why these titles for this last church, knowing that Jesus does not use words idly or by chance? The first title is "the Amen," a clear reference to the final word. Jesus has the final say on our times, whether or not a God ignoring population and its supposedly secular leaders think so or not! The shock of His second coming will prove it. As many were caught off guard by His first coming, both in timing and manner, will not the same be true even more so of His return?

Next is "the Faithful and True Witness." There is probably no more accurate description of our present culture than *faithlessness or unfaithfulness,* and *false witness.* Unfaithfulness is glorified by this culture, to young lovers, to spouses, to parents, to children, to voters, to politicians, to businesses, to clients and to anyone from which one can steal for self glorification. Look at the casual sex, abortion, one third unwed births, fifty percent divorce rate, fatherless, no one home for children culture; and now ask ourselves why Jesus would identify Himself as "Faithful" to this generation of unfaithfulness?! Consider Wall Street or Major League Baseball or Hollywood or government. Cheating and lack of commitment and lying are epidemic in all avenues of life, but He remains "Faithful."

A "True Witness" declares the truth, the whole truth, and nothing but the truth so help him God with one hand raised to God and another on the Bible! We the people, of all ages in this generation, have turned away from truth, God, and the Bible in the way we live our lives and in the people we elect to make our laws and in our heroes and idols and instead have purposefully listened to, admired, and emulated liars who teach blasphemous doctrines. The whole entertainment industry is based upon this premise as well as most of our tax funded schools and universities and publishers of popular books and textbooks. The politicians, who cheat and lie the most effectively, often win our elections. Businesses cook the books and dare you to try to make them keep their word. We have outlawed truth. Why would Jesus identify Himself as the "True Witness" to this false generation, the witness who always told the truth about God and about us? Because as a culture we no longer take God's Word seriously, we no longer take our own word seriously either!

Last is "the Beginning of the creation of God." Would a culture lost in thankless, God denying, and power hungry Darwinism need this reminder? He specifically uses the word "Beginning" because, if He begins all things, He also ends all things, and even re-begins as He chooses. This statement proclaims not mere chance, nor some magical black box out of which a self existent nature just fell, nor a big bang from which no one knows where or how or why it came into being in the first place exists. This is God beginning and sustaining creation through His Word, Jesus, "so that the things which are seen were not made of things which are visible" (Hebrews 11:3). Only the Holy Spirit could have known two thousand years ago how appropriate this title would be to us now in a culture that blindly uses Darwin and materialistic scientism as an excuse to hide from God! Are these three titles both a general and a specific Word of truth to us now in our times? I would say so! I believe this is a specific Word, the revelation of Jesus, for us now! It is also the eternal and general Word of truth. You will have to decide for yourself how relevant this is to your worldview and cosmology in the here and now.

But He is not done; He is writing to the church within a culture, and He addresses the church's works as an expression of their faith to and within that culture. Preceding churches in the list of seven often had a commendation; not so here. It is not pretty what Jesus sees. One foot in and one foot out, half Christian and half worldly, the Lord lightly on Sunday or whenever and God hating Marx, Freud, Darwin, Nietzsche, and Dewey the rest of the week, or the Lord lightly in Bible class and Marx, Freud, Darwin, Nietzsche, and Dewey in the rest of the curriculum; all this makes Him sick to His stomach! He wishes we would really follow His anointing or stop pretending and await His judgment.

Jesus does not like lukewarm Christianity! And He gives us the reason why, which is that we are basically fooling ourselves with it and headed to destruction, all the while thinking we are "ok", to use modern psycho-babble.

We think we are rich spiritually, having the best of both worlds, wealthy materially, and in need of nothing, ok. Yet He thinks we are "wretched, miserable, poor, blind, and naked." Who is right? Here is another great divide, who is right about us, who is right about our present culture, and who is right about the future, Jesus or the spirit of the anti-Christ already so powerfully at work in our modern and postmodern times?

Being our loving and sacrificial Savior, He has some advice for us. Suffer for the truth tried in the fire, and we will really be spiritually rich. Walk humbly in purity and wholesomeness, and we will not be ashamed. Finally seek His anointing to see reality as it really is, and we will not be blind. If we are feeling rebuked and chastened by this, rejoice; it is a sign He loves us (Hebrews 12:6-7)! And here comes the clincher for our times, repentance and zeal; they are the antidote to lukewarm, compromised blah heading for disaster.

Repentance and Zeal

Do we want to take away our precious Savior's distaste; repent and be zealous! Is there anything our prideful, tolerant, self-esteeming, dignity loving culture hates more than true repentance? Think of the long line of politicians, corporate CEOs, preachers, athletes, entertainers, educators, media personalities, etc in our celebrity culture fumbling with the microphone, trying to look like they are repenting when it is obvious they believe it must have been someone else's fault, they really did not do anything all that wrong, it all depends on what the meaning of *is* is, they are not really to blame, and anyway everyone else does it, even the beloved ex President. Why does this present culture find it so difficult to face reality and to repent, for there is no real zeal for the Lord without true repentance and the true forgiveness it brings? Mercy and grace are very humbling!

<u>Luke 7:40-55</u> And Jesus answered and said to him, "Simon, I have something to say to you."
So he said, "Teacher, say it."
41 "There was a certain creditor who had two debtors. One owed five hundred denarii, and the other fifty. 42 And when they had nothing with which to repay,

he freely forgave them both. Tell Me, therefore, which of them will love him more?"

43 Simon answered and said, "I suppose the *one* whom he forgave more."

And He said to him, "You have rightly judged." 44 Then He turned to the woman and said to Simon, "Do you see this woman? I entered your house; you gave Me no water for My feet, but she has washed My feet with her tears and wiped *them* with the hair of her head. 45 You gave Me no kiss, but this woman has not ceased to kiss My feet since the time I came in. 46 You did not anoint My head with oil, but this woman has anointed My feet with fragrant oil. 47 Therefore I say to you, her sins, *which are* many, are forgiven, for she loved much. But to whom little is forgiven, *the same* loves little."

48 Then He said to her, "Your sins are forgiven."

49 And those who sat at the table with Him began to say to themselves, "Who is this who even forgives sins?"

50 Then He said to the woman, "Your faith has saved you. Go in peace."

Jesus is throwing us a lifeline while we are drowning in our culture going over a cliff, but are we too proud or embarrassed or selfish to repent and be zealous for our Lord and His anointing? Old age has silenced Billy Graham; who therefore now calls the nation to spiritual repentance in Jesus that the culture at large will listen to? The life saving, Laodicean invitation is to "anyone!" He is standing outside! He is locked out by our double mindedness, our foolishness, our unwillingness to take a stand, to suffer for truth, to remain pure, to see by way of His anointing and to repent and be zealous.

But Jesus does not give up; He is faithful and true; He is still knocking on our closed door and calling to us. If we listen, we can still hear His knocking and His voice and choose to open the door, each one of us, one by one. He wants to forgive us, He wants to come in and sup with us, and He wants to re-ignite our faith and our zeal as with the two on the road to Emmaus whose hearts He set on fire at a seemingly hopeless point in history (Luke 24:32)! It is an individual invitation, "anyone."

And our reward for overcoming our own pride and embarrassment and lukewarm, self-serving compromises is to sit with Jesus on His throne in His coming Kingdom, just as He overcame! We need "**an** ear" of our spirit to hear all this; only our two fleshly ears will not do!

So what are the implications of this general and specific Word of truth for our times and for Christian education? How do we teach for **repentance and zeal** in all our lessons? We must model, praise, encourage, and reward it! Do our examples and our curriculum and our school programs help our students to hear His knocking and His voice and then to chose to open the door in all our lessons and subjects and activities and learning and let Him in and break bread with Him? In our times is there anything more important that we could be doing?

Are we producing repentant and zealous over-comers? From whom do we get what we need in our times and how? Where do suffering for the truth, walking in purity and wholesomeness, seeking the vision of Jesus, repentance, and zeal rank in what we are doing, teaching, and learning? "The Amen, the Faithful and True Witness, the Beginning of the creation of God," Jesus is knocking on our school doors, our classroom doors, and our lesson doors; will we hear Him and let Him in? He so desires to sup with us, to break bread with us!

Another Contemporary Lesson from Revelations

If you are ministering to adolescent and teenage youth in Christian schools in our times, here is another teaching from Revelation that should be helpful.

Revelation 9:21   And they did not repent of their murders or their **sorceries** or their sexual immorality or their thefts.

Revelation 18:23b   For your merchants were the great men of the earth, for by your **sorcery** all the nations were deceived.

Revelation 21:8   But the cowardly, unbelieving, abominable, murderers, sexually immoral, **sorcerers**, idolaters, and all liars shall have their part in the lake which burns with fire and brimstone, which is the second death.

The teaching is about drugs, a scourge of our youth, and a world-wide, multi-trillion dollar, illegal business, used by Communists, Islamicists, greed driven gangs, and other evil and immoral God haters to prey upon and rob our youth and fund their evil ways.

Unfortunately this clear teaching in the original Greek of the New Testament is hidden in most modern translations of the Bible. This hidden truth centers around the word translated above as "**sorceries, sorcery, and sorcerers**" (NJKV). The NIV uses the words *magic arts*. The original Greek word is transliterated in English as *pharmakea*. It is a compound word, *pharma* and *kea*. The first word should be obvious as in the cognate, pharmacy; it means drugs. The second word means magic, as in the NKJV translation *sorcery* or the NIV translation *magic arts*.

The clear meaning and translation should be *drug magic* or in the common vernacular just *drug use* to alter your being or the use of drugs for magical or conjuring purposes. This is not medicine; it is potions, the mixture of drugs, magic, and evil spirits in order to get high or loaded or wasted or whatever one calls it, to change or escape reality. In our times, every Christian young person needs to hear this teaching loudly and clearly. They are all tempted by this end times, evil principality. The sociological and criminal and spiritual statistics bear this out.

We could, therefore, re-translate the above three scriptures this way:

Revelation 9:21   And they did not repent of their murders or their **drug use** or their sexual immorality or their thefts.

Revelation 18:23b   For your merchants were the great men of the earth, for by your **drug use (and trafficking)** all the nations were deceived.

Revelation 21:8   But the cowardly, unbelieving, abominable, murderers, sexually immoral, **drug users**, idolaters, and all liars shall have their part in the lake which burns with fire and brimstone, which is the second death.

Our average youth could chew on this version or translation of these scriptures a little more easily and profitably. I first heard this truth by the grace of God from Gene Dawson, the founder of Drug Abuse Prevention Centers, playing pool with him in a garage next door to where I was living when I was considering the claims of the Gospel in the early 1970s.

Let us take a closer look. The 9:21 passage is a list of the big four, end times sins: murder, drug use, sexual immorality, and theft. It does not take much astuteness or awareness of present, world-wide culture to see how all four of these go together. The drug culture obviously is full of murder, sexual immorality, and theft. Ask any honest policeman how much of our culture's murder, sexual immorality, and theft is connected to drugs and vice versa, and be ready for a long talk and some scary facts and figures.

But this leads to the second scripture about **deception**, world-wide deception, verse 18:23. Here the Holy Spirit pins the very nature of drugs as potions, as evil magic, as full of deceiving spirits. The heart of illegal drug use, *pharmakea*, is deception, first of all deceiving oneself and then being deceived by and deceiving those around you. Most youth, pumped up on self-esteem, think they can handle it; it is no big deal; the adults are just trying to spoil our fun! It is just a little pot or speed or ecstasy or whatever. They know better from what they have seen around them, but they lie to themselves. Few start out to become a drug addict or casualty.

But the bigger lie of the supposedly secular and materialist culture is that this is just a *chemical problem* or a *substance abuse problem*. The real and ignored problem, however, is the lying and seducing, deceptive spirits whose unwitting acceptance causes the Spirit of Truth to leave, followed by the loss of conviction, and then the rest of the evil pours in. *Pharmakea* is a spiritual deception. It is a spiritual battle at heart, the Spirit of Truth versus the spirits of deception and of lies that promise pleasure and fun and end up giving death and disease, both spiritual and then physical. The real damage of drug use is therefore spiritual. Do we make sure our youth see the spiritual battle here? Spiritual death and bondage precedes physical death and bondage. And a generation in pain from family disintegration and unfaithfulness and constant bombardment of lies is so vulnerable, looking to ease the pain. We must speak the truth plainly here. Only repentance and faith in the forgiveness, mercy, and grace of Jesus can heal the pain.

The final outcome, verse 21:8, is Hell! God have mercy on the Christian youth and those who are falling prey to this evil! Has your Christian middle or high school or even upper elementary school had this teaching woven throughout their curriculum? In our times, why not? Pharmakea is not medicine; it is a spiritual scourge.

True hope for a hopeless generation will not come from modern makeovers of ancient idols: Mammon, Moloch, Ashteroth, and Baal (Smith, 2006). Jesus made it clear that worshipping money, financial success, possessions, that which is called Mammon, means you will end up hating God (Luke 16:13). Likewise, Moleck was the god of pleasure. Always living to please ourselves, our self esteem, means we rarely please God or truly serve others and miss His blessings which are true pleasures. Ashteroth was the god of sexuality. Disconnected from true, agape love and Godly family commitments within sanctified marriage, it is a disintegrating and cruel and yet shallow master that leads to all kinds of grief and disease of spirit, soul, and body.

And finally Baal was the god intellectualism. We have already seen where prideful thinking devoid of God's truth leads, how knowledge alone puffs up. These gods are unfortunately alive and active in our present culture and form the bedrock of the modern, supposedly secular university. Chuck Smith of Calvary Chapel has excellent teaching on these idols. Part of the ministry of prophecy is to give a better hope! Do our schools unmask these false idols? Do they give a powerful and better hope?

The Second Coming of Jesus

Now let us consider the second coming of Jesus, could there be a timelier topic for our youth? Why would not the second coming be even more miraculous, surprising, profound, and history changing than His first coming? Let us consider the first coming of Christ. We literally count history and time by it, BC and AD.

The second coming will change history and time even more! The first coming was announced by angels, involved a miraculous virgin birth, the arrival of humbled wise men from afar, and had heavenly choirs singing to lowly shepherds, and it confounded the worldly powerful and the religiously deceitful. The second coming moreover involves the miraculous catching up of believers, the opening of graves, a wedding feast in heaven, a final harvest of the earth, fierce judgment on the unrepentant and unbelieving wicked, and the omnipresent return, like lightning all across the sky, of the Lion of Judah riding a white horse with the armies of heaven, His bride and the heavenly hosts, to destroy the world's attack on Zion.

In the first coming Satan was defeated for the faithful, and in the second coming he will be bound and banished for a thousand years. Talk about change! Can you even imagine life with no tempter, no accuser of the brethren, no deceiver, no father of all liars and murderers? In the first coming Jesus ruled in our hearts; in the second coming we will also rule with Him governmentally on the earth. In the first coming Jesus died and rose again to release us from the penalty of our sins; in the second coming He will reign in righteousness and justice over the whole earth with a rod of iron. If we believe in the miracles of the first coming; why would we be ashamed of the miracles of His return?

For the students' sakes, eschatology and prophecy cannot be ignored. There are far too many false prophets who are all too eager to jump in and steal them to false visions of the future that will not come to pass but will nonetheless enslave them. When the truth is not proclaimed, lies rush in. Just as Anna and Simeon lived for the hope of the first coming (Luke 2), this generation needs the hope that is to live for His soon return. Ignorance and attempts at impossible neutrality here are not a blessing but a curse!

Luke 19:44 . . . and level you, and **your children** within you, to the ground; and they will not leave in you one stone upon another, **because you did not know the time of your visitation**.

2 Peter 3:3b-4 … knowing this first: that scoffers will come in the last days, walking according to their own lusts, 4 and saying, "Where is the promise of His coming?"

The issue of **fulfillment**, the fourth paradigm of a Christian philosophy (Van Brummelen, 2002), is paramount for our times. The youth desperately need the hope of His soon return. Those who scorned and scoffed His first coming will regret it for eternity. What of those who scorn and scoff His return? Youth without hope is tragic; Jesus is our hope! Is this a focus of our schools?

This blessed hope of no more sin, of actually ruling as kings and priests with Jesus, our Prophet, our Priest, and our King, here on earth in real time and place is humble medicine in deed to our spirits, souls, and bodies. We must not try to symbolize or falsely spiritualize this away as if it will happen without His return by our own efforts anymore than we can His first coming and the cross and still have the whole Jesus.

Revelation 7:17 . . . for the Lamb who is in the midst of the throne will shepherd them and lead them to living fountains of waters. And God will **wipe away every tear** from their eyes."

The second coming will be even more miraculous, surprising, profound, and history changing than the first! The best is yet to come! We dare not, especially in these spiritually desperate times, be ashamed of His second coming, any more than we dare not be ashamed of His first coming. We must face the times truthfully, and give our youth hope, even if others mock us for this faith just as they did those seeking Him at His first coming!

2 Peter 1:18-21   And we heard this voice which came from heaven when we were with Him on the holy mountain. 19 And so we have the prophetic word confirmed, which you do well to heed as a light that shines in a dark place, until the day dawns and the morning star rises in your hearts; 20 knowing this first, that no prophecy of Scripture is of any private interpretation, 21 for prophecy never came by the will of man, but holy men of God spoke *as they were* moved by the Holy Spirit.

May God stir up our convictions, forgive our misgivings, and deliver us in His mercy and grace from evil to His honor and glory.

Chapter 12: Christian Schools and Fatherhood

Abraham

As our earthly example of a faithful father, why do we have Abraham? God could have chosen anyone to begin His prophetic intervention for mankind! He could have chosen a European, an African, a Chinaman, a Polynesian, a North or South American, or an Eskimo! Instead He chose an Iraqi from Ur of the Chaldeans and made him the first Jew by covenant. The scripture says that the redeemed are now all children of Abraham by faith.

Galatians 3:29   And if you are Christ's, then you are **Abraham**'s seed, and heirs according to the promise.

Why did God so honor and trust this man, and what does this have to do with a Christian education? How important are fathers anyway? Certainly Abraham's faith and faithfulness were key factors in God's selection, but was there more in how his faith and faithfulness were made manifest? His very name means father.

Genesis 18:19   For I have known him, in order that he may command his children and his household after him, that they keep the way of the LORD, to do righteousness and justice, that the LORD may bring to Abraham what He has spoken to him.

It seems one of Abraham's main qualifications along with faith and obedience was his willingness to "command his children and his household after him, that they keep the way of the LORD, to do righteousness and justice!" God knew faithful Abraham would give his family a Godly, anointed education centered upon keeping "the way of the LORD!" No Godless, choose your own truth or way, lock Jesus outside education here, but a spiritual and even handed one focused on keeping both personal righteousness and social justice in "the way of the LORD."

Personal Righteousness and Social Justice

It is fashionable in our times to excuse personal unrighteousness under a cloak of social justice. If I am for the right causes, spreading the wealth around socialism or self-aggrandizing capitalism, green environmentalism, animal rights, criminal rights, or even the Gospel, then the sin of my personal life does not matter, I'm cool. Conversely it is also fashionable in our times to excuse my social injustice, if I keep my personal life somewhat righteous. If I am good and faithful in my personal relationships, a nice guy, and tithe at church, I can be a terror in my social or business practices, greedily abusing, crushing, oppressing, and robbing others for my own benefit. Neither of these examples are God's idea of keeping the "way of the LORD, to do righteousness **and** justice!" This is the whole anointing for the whole person! It is God's call to fathers, both personally and socially. And it is also God's call to Godly education, commanding the children after us in the "way of the LORD, to do righteousness **and** justice!"

Leviticus 19:15 You shall do no injustice in judgment. You shall not be partial to the poor, nor honor the person of the mighty. In righteousness you shall judge your neighbor.

For rich or poor, God's justice is always fair, honest, and unbiased; we are without excuse.

Fatherlessness

So why then is Satan so interested in destroying fatherhood, motherhood, and the family? Looking at our present media culture where fathers are depicted as Homer Simpson cowards, buffoons, and selfish if sentimental fools or the flip as the essence of demented evil but never as a Godly, father that humbly knows and does right from wrong, we see the attempted destruction of a positive manhood under God's headship before our very eyes. Fatherlessness is a hallmark of our times as well as a diminishing of the value of committed, faithful, Godly fathers who stand for something other than selfishness and vanity. Fatherlessness is exploding and destroying our culture.

John 5:19   "Most assuredly, I say to you, the Son can do nothing of Himself, but what He sees the Father do; for whatever He does, the Son also does in like manner."

Have the fathers in the church allowed Caesar to become the official father and mother of us all, including the children through the children's educations? What can Christian schools do to honor faithful fatherhood, motherhood, marriage, and family in a culture where 50 million children have been put to death before they were born as a by-product of the immorality of the so called sexual revolution and where 1/3 of all births are now to unwed men and women and half of the remaining 2/3's of born children lose their families to divorce before they grow up and where all this is mainly being true even within the churched? Do we call fathers first when children have discipline or academic or social needs? What do we purposefully do to honor faithful fatherhood, motherhood, marriage, and family?

Psalm 78:5-7   For He established a testimony in Jacob, and appointed a law in Israel, which He commanded our **fathers**, that they should make them known to their children; [6] That the generation to come might know *them,* the children *who* would be born, *that* they may arise and declare *them* to their children, [7] That they may set their hope in God, and not forget the works of God, but keep His commandments;

The Example of Jesus

Consider the example that Jesus set regarding His Father; do we teach it?

Luke 2:51   Then He went down with them and came to Nazareth, and was subject to them, but His mother kept all these things in her heart. 52 And Jesus increased in wisdom and stature, and in favor with God and men.

Even to His earthly stepfather, Jesus "was subject" by His own choice and this after He had just confounded the teachers of Israel up in the capital with His wisdom and understanding as a twelve year old no less. What a wonderful example He always sets, even at the age of a nascent teenager! Yet His deepest submission was clearly to His Heavenly Father to whom He always showed love, obedience, thankfulness, and faithfulness. What a powerful example! His goal was to glorify His Father, to please Him, and to do His will. He trusted in His Father's goodness, even on the cross. Do we teach this Godly example explicitly?

Do we use this example in the way we by faith appreciate and honor fathers in our school practices, or do we in unbelief accept and expect the Godless stereotypes of our present culture? With the destruction of fatherhood comes the concomitant destruction of motherhood, and Caesar's state and the Godless media end up raising the children. God, the Father, must think fatherhood is pretty important, because it is Who He is!

Who then is responsible for Christian education?

Ephesians 6:4 **Fathers**, do not exasperate your children; instead, bring them up in the training and instruction of the Lord.

The clear and logical converse of this scripture is that, if fathers do not "bring them up in the training and instruction of the Lord," they will in fact exasperate their children. A Godless education will always eventually exasperate our children's lives because lies and Godlessness lead to sin. And where God is an irrelevant outlaw, lies abound. This bringing up is both deeds and words, "the training and instruction of the Lord."

Are we giving fathers leadership in educational choice, policy, discipline, social development, and placement decisions? Are we carefully and purposefully using technology and a constant flow of meaningful information to empower and involve fathers in their children's education? Is there a place for fathers in our activities and curricula and governance?

Deuteronomy 6: 1-9 "Now this *is* the commandment, *and these are* the statutes and judgments which the LORD your God has commanded to teach you, that you may observe *them* in the land which you are crossing over to possess, 2 that you may fear the LORD your God, to keep all His statutes and His commandments which I command you, **you and your son and your grandson, all the days of your life**, and that your days may be prolonged. 3 Therefore hear,

O Israel, and be careful to observe *it,* that it may be well with you, and that you may multiply greatly as **the LORD God of your fathers** has promised you—'a land flowing with milk and honey.'

4 "Hear, O Israel: The LORD our God, the LORD *is* one! 5 You shall love the LORD your God with all your heart, with all your soul, and with all your strength.

6 "And these words which I command you today shall be in your heart. 7 **You shall teach them diligently to your children**, and shall talk of them when you sit in your house, when you walk by the way, when you lie down, and when you rise up. 8 You shall bind them as a sign on your hand, and they shall be as frontlets between your eyes. 9 You shall write them on the doorposts of your house and on your gates.

Is **"diligently"** a part time affair with supposedly secular learning taking up the bulk of our children's time and energy and life? If we pray for fathers to step up to their calling, do we honor them in our practices when they do it? Do we teach our students to love their fathers, to appreciate them, to obey them, and to thank them? Jesus did!

Supporting Marriage and Families

How do we support families and marriages? Do we have the courage to positively intervene when our school families are in trouble? Do we, for instance, understand and teach why God hates divorce?

<u>Malachi 2:10-16</u>   Have we not all one Father? Did not one God create us? Why do we profane the covenant of our fathers by breaking faith with one another? 11 Judah has broken faith. A detestable thing has been committed in Israel and in Jerusalem: Judah has desecrated the sanctuary the LORD loves, by marrying the daughter of a foreign god. 12 As for the man who does this, whoever he may be, may the LORD cut him off from the tents of Jacob —even though he brings offerings to the LORD Almighty. 13 Another thing you do: You flood the LORD's altar with tears. You weep and wail because he no longer pays attention to your offerings or accepts them with pleasure from your hands. 14 You ask, "Why?" It is because the LORD is acting as the witness between you and the wife of your youth, because you have broken faith with her, though she is your partner, the wife of your marriage covenant. 15 Has not the LORD made them one? In flesh and spirit they are his. **And why one? Because he was seeking godly offspring**.

So guard yourself in your spirit, and do not break faith with the wife of your youth. 16 "**I hate divorce**," says the LORD God of Israel, "and I hate a man's covering himself with violence as well as with his garment," says the LORD Almighty. So guard yourself in your spirit, and do not break faith.

How can Christian education help strengthen what remains of faithful fatherhood, motherhood, purity, marriage, and spiritual family values in a faithless, unfaithful, broken, covenant mocking, Spiritless, and violently selfish generation? We can stand up for the truth! A great lie, for instance, of the last two generations is no-fault divorce. We pretend under its legal and spiritual cover that divorce is mainly a private, adult matter of little consequence to anyone else. It is supposedly a good solution to a bad problem. The children will be better off. The marriages of others will not be affected nor the culture. It is an honorable way to make up for poor choices.

Evidently God does not think so. The above scripture clearly implies that God wants faithful, united marriages between believers in order to produce Godly offspring. Even making this clear statement of scripture in our sin compromising times makes many people blanche.

Conversely this does not mean, however, that, if your parents' marriage breaks, you cannot be Godly; but it surely implies that it must be much harder that way, or why would God say what He so clearly says about hating divorce and why? Divorce hurts us all. It hurts the adults, it hurts the children, it hurts the grandchildren, and it hurts the community. It is not no-fault in God's eyes! Do we have the courage to admit this and stand against it in word and deed?

What did Jesus say about why Moses permitted divorce?

<u>Matthew 19:4-8</u> And He answered and said to them, "Have you not read that He who made *them* at the beginning *'made them male and female,'* 5 and said, *'For this reason a man shall leave his father and mother and be joined to his wife, and the two shall become one flesh'*? 6 So then, they are no longer two but one flesh. Therefore what God has joined together, let not man separate."
7 They said to Him, "Why then did Moses command to give a certificate of divorce, and to put her away?"
8 He said to them, "Moses, **because of the hardness of your hearts**, permitted you to divorce your wives, but from the beginning it was not so."

This is not something that our contemporary, live to please yourself culture wants to hear either, even in the churched. Jesus clearly describes the cause of divorce as *hardness of heart*, not no-fault, irreconcilable differences. Do we believe him?

Our heartless culture teaches us to run the other way and say divorce is their personal business and no one else's. That is a lie, especially where the children are concerned but also regarding the community. A culture is nothing but the sum of our individual choices. Can we pretend that our Godly interventions do not matter? We are not our brother's keeper, are we? How do we as Christian schools honor and encourage faithfulness and tenderness of heart?

Furthermore do we encourage children to have a voice in these matters? The Godless culture makes the children silent bystanders and victims, when it is their family that dies; children get divorced just like adults do, despite all the broken promises of the adults! Yet do we teach in a way so as to encourage their voice in these matters; children will almost universally say no to divorce. It was adults, not children, who passed the so called, no-fault, divorce laws (Wallerstein, Lewis, & Blakeslee, 2000).

Christian schools must stand up for Godly, faithful, united marriages and for the voices of the children in the matter of their families' futures. None of our practices should divide but always unite and encourage families. We should be purposeful about softening hearts.

I have personally counseled Christian school youth to get off the sidelines and clearly speak to their parents about their own desires for their family to survive and stay together and seen positive results and miracles. Adults often delude themselves that the children do not care; and, when confronted with the opposite truth, often reconsider their selfish, hard-hearted intentions and actions. Children who dare to speak the truth in love can often soften hearts!

3 John 1:4 I have no greater joy than to hear that my children **walk** in **truth**.

The one thing we can take to heaven with us is not our material possessions or our social status or our earthly accomplishments or pleasures, but rather our children, people!

In a culture that has destroyed vertical relationships, we must stand up for them. Our horizontal culture makes friends more important than families. Our peers are all that counts, and then we wonder why we suffer so deeply from blind, peer pressure. This lack of vertical relationships breeds a wisdomless and irresponsible culture, with the blind leading the blind and both of them falling into a ditch.

Teenagers are especially vulnerable to this. We need to strengthen the ultimate vertical relationship with God the Father throughout our schools, but also we need to strengthen the vertical relationships between our students and their parents and vice versa. This should be a clearly stated part of our mission with goals and objectives and assessments. The culture of the last days runs directly against this. Paul says that this anti-Christian culture would be . . .

1 Timothy 4:2-3 . . . speaking lies in hypocrisy, having their own conscience seared with a hot iron, [3] forbidding to marry, *and commanding* to abstain from foods which God created to be received with thanksgiving by those who believe and know the truth.

That God identifies Himself as Our Heavenly Father is not a metaphor but rather a fact of creation. Reconsider the example of Jesus and His Heavenly Father Whom He call Abba, Daddy as a grown man! According to Malachi, turning the hearts of the fathers to the children and the children to their fathers is a last-days' work! If Christian schools will not do it, who will? May God stir up our convictions, forgive our misgivings, and deliver us in His mercy and grace from evil to His honor and glory.

Chapter 13: The Battleground: Defining Love for the Next Generation of Christian School Students

1 John 4:16   And so we know and rely on the **love God** has for us. **God is love**. Whoever lives in **love** lives in **God**, and **God** in him.

Romans 5:5   Now hope does not disappoint, because the **love of God** has been poured out in our hearts by the Holy Spirit who was given to us.

Love or Respect

Why do Caesar's, tax funded schools use *respect* as the key ingredient to their discipline and rule systems, but not love? Walk into any public school classroom and look on the walls. It is highly probable you will see a set of classroom rules. The key idea expressed in them will be respect: respect for rules, respect for others, respect for yourself, respect for property, respect for the teacher, etc. Have you ever wondered why they choose *respect*?

Did Jesus teach at length on respect? Actually your concordance will show that He did not teach much on respect, except regarding wives and husbands and children and fathers! Oddly enough, however, when one walks into Christian school classrooms, the same respect rules are often on the walls or in the handbook or on the folders. Now respect for God is found in the word.

Psalm 40:4   Blessed is that man who makes the LORD his trust, and does not **respect** the proud, nor such as turn aside to lies.

Isaiah 17:7   In that day a man will look to his Maker, and his eyes will have **respect** for the Holy One of Israel.

Yet what did Jesus say when He was asked what the **greatest** commandment is? Of what kind of rule did He speak? Did He speak of respect? Did He even list the Ten Commandments? No, He spoke of love. Love God. Love your neighbor. And later He added for us to love as He has loved us and to love the brethren. You do not need to worry about keeping all the other rules or respect if you keep these three!

<u>**Romans 13:10**</u> **Love** does no harm to a neighbor; therefore **love is** the fulfillment of the law.

If your Christian school has these three rules on the wall, God bless you; and, I believe, He will. If it does not, why does it not? Could it be that respect carries that subtle message of pride under the surface; whereas to "rely on the **love God has for us**" speaks so clearly of humility?

Why are we embarrassed to speak about love in the classroom, faculty room, administrative offices, parent meetings, and board room? "**God is love**." Are we embarrassed of Him or of speaking of Him? The Bible is the greatest love story ever told! Can anyone match the love of Jesus? Are we embarrassed because we have let the world define love for us and for our students? Are we embarrassed because we have settled for much less than what God wants for us?

So what should the rules be for Christian school classrooms, offices, and boardrooms? Why not what Jesus said about the greatest commandments and the new commandment: love God, love your neighbor, and love as Jesus loves you!? Why do Christian schools use Caesar's respect rules instead? Should we not aim more highly and differently than that? Why not change the conversation from respect to love?

Who Defines Love?

If we do not define love for our students as God's agape, sacrificial love, how will Hollywood, Madison Avenue, Nashville, Wall Street, Washington DC, the NEA, Planned Parenthood, American Idol, and the ACLU define it for them? Agape is unconditional and sacrificial love, love by choice and by an act of undefeatable and unchangeable good will. It is pure and unselfish and holy and wholesome; it is God's love.

We need to be making agape the central issue in Christian schools: what, how, and why do we love? What, how, and why does Jesus love? We need to unpack and expound upon these questions continually. If we fail here, defining true love by our words and deeds, can we succeed anywhere else that matters? Is this a top priority of our mission statements, our curricular goals, our methods of teaching and learning, our discipline, and our school wide goals and outcomes and assessments?

What would happen in a classroom where the stated, focused, taught, modeled, practiced, enforced, discussed, explained, and followed rules were: 1) Love God, 2) Love your neighbor, and 3) Love one another as Jesus loves us? Why aim lower than this if we are preparing students as citizens of the Kingdom of God?

Colossians 3:14   But **above all** these things put on **love**, which is the bond of perfection.

There is nothing wrong with Godly respect per se, but is it the fullness of what Jesus has in mind and in heart for us under His anointing? What message do we send if we settle for less than love? If "God is love," and if our classroom, office, and boardroom rules are all about love, then our schools are all about God! That is simple logic! God's love rules!

Hebrews 12:2 . . . looking unto Jesus, the author and finisher of our faith, who for the joy that was set before Him endured the cross, despising the shame, and has sat down at the right hand of the throne of God.

1 John 4:10   In this **is love**, not that we **love**d God, but that He **love**d us and sent His Son to be the propitiation for our sins.

Luke 20:13   "Then the owner of the vineyard said, 'What shall I do? I will send my beloved son. Probably they will **respect** him when they see him.'

John 3:16   For God so **loved** the world that He gave His only begotten Son, that whoever believes in Him should not perish but have everlasting life.

It is not wise to count on respect where there is no love. God is the initiator of love; it is He who so loved first. He gives us His love when we do not deserve it but need it so desperately. The love of God should be at the heart of who we are, what we say, and what we do. This glorifies God! Our words and our deeds should be all about God's love!

As a liar and a murderer, Satan tries to command respect out of fear; but Jesus says that, if we love Him [Jesus], we will keep His commandments. Jesus wants our love, not just our respect. Jesus wants us to keep His commandments out of love, not just our respect. Jesus did not say that if respect Him, we will keep His commandments. He sets the highest standard! And so should we in His name in a truly Christian education! Jesus wants our love! God also wants our respect, but even more importantly He wants our love, our devotion, that which moves us from deep within.

Deuteronomy 6:4-7   Hear, O Israel: The LORD our God, the LORD *is* one! [5] You shall love the LORD your God with all your heart, with all your soul, and with all your strength.

[6] "And these words which I command you today shall be in your heart. [7] You shall teach them diligently to your children, and shall talk of them when you sit in your house, when you walk by the way, when you lie down, and when you rise up.

John 14:15   "If you **love Me**, keep My commandments."

John 14:24   He who does not **love Me** does not keep My words; and the word which you hear is not Mine but the Father's who sent Me.

John 15:9   As the Father **love**d **Me**, I also have **love**d you; abide in My **love**.

Why should we focus our students on respect instead of love; it is not the example Jesus has shown us. Caesar's path and Jesus' path are not the same!

Love and the Arts

Now one might ask, furthermore, what does all this have to do with the arts and Christian education? A culture's picture of love is often substantially defined and, as well, mirrored by the arts, either in unity with or in the absence of or in opposition to true theology, knowledge of God, Who is love. For centuries Western culture had a profoundly Christian influence in its literary, visual, and musical arts which helped greatly to bolster an approximation of a larger Christian society and culture. Sadly, with very few yet precious exceptions, this is no longer remotely the case. The love of God is no longer a major theme of the arts in our present day culture. The ugly fruit of this is obvious all around us and within us. And the arts especially influence the youth.

This cultural disparity all the more should urge us to create arts programs that do honor and glorify and please God by showing forth His true love. The beauty of holiness and of wholesomeness in the arts ought to be another chief aim of Christian schools in the preeminence of God's love that makes Christian schools obviously unique within this culture. Do our arts programs love God, do they proclaim the love of God for us and therefore furthermore our Godly love for one another? I can remember people weeping in a shopping mall listening to our Phoenix Christian High School choir singing real Christmas carols from the heart and Spirit of Jesus!

The Battle

Matthew 24:12   And because **lawlessness** will abound, the love of many will grow cold.

We must focus our students on the love of God especially in the times we live in. Repentance and zeal for God keep the heart warm; they are the antidote to the lawless and cold hearted, sin saturated culture of self worship within which the youth are growing up. What our students believe about true love, the models they have concerning Godly love, the opportunities they have to be trained in and to walk in real and faithful love, their personal understanding of God's love for them, their calling to be creative in the expression of true and Godly love through the various curricula, through service programs, through evangelism and true witness, through discipline and discipleship, and through Christian arts and sciences and letters, these are not side issues but rather the heart of the anointed education which Jesus wants for us! Consider that His first miracle was turning water into wine at a wedding feast! Jesus is loving and faithful; we should follow Him.

Who will define love for the next generation of Christian youth? If we do not boldly do this, others gladly will, with certain, terrible consequences! And what a person, young or old, believes about love connects directly to what they believe about God, because "God is love!" If we are made in His image, we are made to love. The question is what, how, and why do we love in such a way that our love blesses God instead of false idols? Should this not be at the very center of our mission statements and curriculum? Why is it not if it is not?

This is another great divide between anointed and supposedly secular education, the question of who defines love, what we should love and how we should love and why we should love. Are our students learning to "know and rely on the **love God** has for us?" Do we make this a central issue in what we are teaching and learning, in education? Does not Jesus? "Whoever lives in **love** lives in **God**, and **God** in him." Do our various curricula lead our students to think about what they love, how they love, and why they love and whether or not these manifestations of their love glorify God or some deadly idol? This is getting to where our students and our selves really live! Jesus talks a good deal about love and then completely demonstrates it! He never even addressed respect. We must not be afraid to address this issue head on, because perfect love casts out fear!

Let us, therefore, train our students to love God, to love our neighbor, and to love as Jesus loves, all in response to the love God has for us! What other curricula could be more important? Should not all curricula of any subject area start, travel through, and end here?! Do they? How do our curricula love God? May God stir up our convictions, forgive our misgivings, and deliver us in His mercy and grace from evil to His honor and glory. Caesar wants our respect, but Jesus wants our love which is much, much, much more important!

<u>1 Timothy 1:5</u> Now the purpose of the commandment is love from a pure heart, *from* a good conscience, and *from* sincere faith . . .

<u>1 Corinthians 13:4-8a</u> Love suffers long *and* is kind; love does not envy; love does not parade itself, is not puffed up; [5] does not behave rudely, does not seek its own, is not provoked, thinks no evil; [6] does not rejoice in iniquity, but rejoices in the truth; [7] bears all things, believes all things, hopes all things, endures all things. [8] Love never fails.

Chapter 14: Postmodern Relativism/Tolerance/Multiculturalism and Christian Education

How is Jesus both the most tolerant and the least tolerant person to ever walk the earth? Misunderstandings about tolerance are rife within our present, macro culture and especially within supposedly secular, educational culture. These misunderstandings even twist the way many see Jesus and the Gospel. Misguided tolerance is one of the chief values of postmodern relativism and one of the most deadly and blinding idols of our time, especially for the youth. Avalanches of sin hide behind false tolerance. Again, let us look unto Jesus for truth and clarity on this issue and how it should apply to truly Christian education.

The Most Tolerant

How is Jesus more tolerant than anyone who has ever walked this earth, even of the most ardent of post-moderns who are, by the way, virulently intolerant of Christians and Christianity? Jesus is supremely tolerant in that He is absolutely no respecter of persons!

Acts 10:34 Then Peter opened his mouth, and said, "Of a truth I perceive that God is **no respecter of persons."**

Our earthly status means nothing to Jesus, zero. He will help **anyone** who is willing and humble, rich or poor, blind or lame, leprous or paralyzed, broken by sin or slaves of Satan's demons, young or old, male or female, Jew or Gentile, powerful or weak, and from any nation, tribe, or tongue, anyone who is willing and will humbly repent and exercise faith in Him. He accepted people of whom we would scorn and from whom we would hide.

Consider a naked, demon possessed, out of his mind Greek chained in a cemetery by the terrified townspeople, an occupying centurion of a foreign, Roman army, an adulteress caught in the act, a prostitute crying on His feet, a thief justly dying on a cross, a traitorous, robbing, corrupt, sinful, tax collector, an adulterous and fornicating, Samaritan half-breed, members of the corrupt, power hungry, God mocking Sanhedrin, a synagogue ruler's dead child, a banished, infectious, and wandering leper begging alongside the highway, and even a murderous and self righteous zealot, named Saul of Tarsus.

Jesus is the most tolerant person in the universe when it comes to helping lost but willing people, people who humbly seek and/or willingly accept and appreciate His mercy and grace to them and to others in faith and obedience and repentance. He turned down no one simply because of race, gender, age, tribe, nation, language, social status, economic status, religious status, success, failure, brokenness, illness, sin, or even demon possession. No one is more tolerant of lost and broken and humbled people than Jesus! None of us get this kind of forgiving tolerance ourselves because none of us as yet love as deeply as He loves. Jesus is the most tolerant of all because He is the most loving of all.

The Most Intolerant

Of course Jesus is the most **in**tolerant person who ever walked this earth as well. This point is lost on God-evading modernism and God-hating postmodernism. His amazing tolerance for lost, God rejecting and even God hating, and undeserving people like all of us is matched by his stalwart, to the point of death, **in**tolerance for sin and lies. All of us try to make light of our sins, our selfishness, our pridefulness . Jesus, however, never tolerated sin or lies on His own part, not even once. Nor does He ever condone sin or lies in us, not even once. He never calls sin, righteous and never calls righteousness, sinful. He alone faced sin in truth and righteousness and in total perseverance and victory.

John 8:46 Which of you **convinceth me** of sin? And if I say the truth, why do ye not believe **me**? KJV

The words *convince, conviction,* and *convicts* all come from the Latin root which literally means *to defeat with, to win over with, to go along with.* Jesus could not be convicted of sin because He was never convinced of it! He never once was defeated by it, won over by it, or went along with it! And He never will! He does not tolerate it absolutely!

We generally act out of our deepest and truest convictions, what we really believe, no matter what we say or even think we believe. We sin because we are not convinced that doing the right thing is always in our best interest or, in transposition, that doing what is wrong is not sometimes in our best interest. We believe lies; we are won over by them. We listen to Satan and our flesh and the world and let them convince us, defeat us.

Jesus does not! He will not tolerate sin, ever. He always calls sin, sin and righteousness, righteousness. And He only always walks in righteousness and truth. Truth is His deepest conviction because He is the Truth and vice versa!

So Jesus always tolerates and accepts all sinners willing to repent and believe, but never tolerates or accepts sin or lies: supremely tolerant of sinners and supremely intolerant of sin!

The postmodernism of our present, sinful culture partially embraces the first truth of Jesus minus the repentance and belief, but not at all the second truth. In fact supposedly secular post-modernists believe if the first truth is true, tolerance for sinners, the second one, intolerance for sin, cannot be true; or conversely, if the second truth is true, intolerance for sin, the first one, tolerance for humbled sinners, cannot be true. They cannot understand how Jesus can hate sin but love sinners nor love sinners but hate sin. They think that if you hate my sin or my lies, you must hate me; and, if you love me, you must accept and love my sin and my lies. They are lost! But Jesus seeks and finds!

Unfortunately, if we look closely, are not some of these falsehoods, these false connections, these false logics, and these lies alive and active in Christian schools also? Has not the macro culture blinded us? Do we consistently expose these falsehoods for what they are when students try to walk in them in their words and deeds? What does Jesus think about these: winking at sin and lies as if that makes us righteously tolerant or hating reachable sinners or liars as if that makes us righteously intolerant?

He never does either of these, and nor should we. These distinctions and discernments about tolerance and intolerance are extremely important to truly Christian education and giving our students a truly Christian worldview regarding the falsehoods of our present, supposedly secular culture and the truth of the scriptures and Godly culture to which we are called to be an example to a lost and dying world and a pleasing praise to our God. Love sinners, hate sin! This is the radical example of Jesus!

This whole discussion leads to another question. What does this seeming paradox say about Christian schools and the willing, or, for that matter, the unwilling? To whom did Jesus minister or not minister? This is an enormous and vital question. We will take it up again in a later chapter, but for now consider the willing. He did not and does not heal and deliver everyone; what does this have to do with the willing?

Judge Not

Moreover, in postmodern culture, blanket tolerance of everything but Jesus is also linked to another twisted misunderstanding of scripture: judge not. This is taken to mean that a real Christian would never judge another's actions or thoughts or teachings or religion because we are not supposed to be judgmental. Like misguided tolerance there is a fatal misunderstanding of scripture here also, which misunderstanding is prevalent in many of our students' minds and hearts.

1 Corinthians 2:15 But he who is spiritual **judge**s all things, yet he himself is rightly **judge**d by no one.

Romans 14:13 Therefore let us not **judge** one another anymore, but rather resolve this, not to put a stumbling block or a cause to fall in our brother's way.

Luke 6:37 "**Judge** not, and you shall not be **judge**d. Condemn not, and you shall not be condemned. Forgive, and you will be forgiven."

These three scriptures are not contradictions, for they come from the same Holy Spirit; the distinction, again as in tolerance, is between people and sin. It is our God-given responsibility to judge "things:" actions, sin, decisions, deeds, teachings, and false doctrines. It is God's place to judge people who are made in His image. We dare not judge people but rather forgive them and not stumble them with our condemnation of them, but we also dare not refuse to judge evil. We are required to leave judging others, even ourselves, to Jesus; but we are also required to judge evil actions, attitudes, thinking, decisions, deeds, or teachings, our own or anyone else's.

Supposedly secular, postmodern tolerance has purposefully confused these truths in too many people's minds, especially the youth. In the name of tolerance we are too quick to pass on judging our own or other's evil deeds and evil teaching and also too quick to call people evil. Judge deeds, not people. It is not that there are not evil people, people given over to evil; rather that it is not our place, given that we too sin, to be their judge. God is willing and able to take that responsibility for us!

We desperately need **good judgment** in these times! Do we teach good judgment in our schools, judging evil and not judging people? Again, this does not mean there are not people given over to evil, just that it is not our place to judge them as opposed to their deeds and thinking and teachings. There but for grace go you or I!

Do our administrators, staff, and students understand and practice what **"Judge not"** really means and does not mean? What are the implications of this truth in school policy and practice and curricula? Compassion for people, judgment for sin!

Multiculturalism

Another postmodern value related to misguided tolerance and falsely not judging, which is running roughshod over education in our times is multiculturalism. As with tolerance and judging, there is a purposeful sleight of hand here that causes much confusion and evil. The confusion comes from the purposeful, inverse linking of racism and multiculturalism. So where does Jesus stand on racism? Is heaven multi-racial?

Revelation 5:9 And they sang a new song: "You are worthy to take the scroll and to open its seals, because you were slain, and with your blood you purchased men for God from **every tribe and language and people and nation**."

Is racism a sin?

1 Samuel 16:7 But the LORD said to Samuel, "Do not look at his appearance or at his physical stature, because I have refused him. For the LORD does not see as man sees; for man looks at the **outward appearance**, but the LORD looks at the heart."

Acts 10:34 Then Peter opened his mouth, and said, "Of a truth I perceive that God is **no respecter of persons** . . .

Peter's revelation of God's heart is in the context of the Holy Spirit falling upon a Roman, a Gentile, Cornelius, and his household, someone who was not of Peter's Jewish race, someone outside of Peter's covenant. How clear can this be?

Not only is God not a racist, but He actually seems to have some kind of quota system in heaven! *Every* means *every*, and it seems very purposeful! If we are racists, eternity could be very uncomfortable! Of course one might not be there, if they really are a racist. Racism is a sin, judging by appearance and not the heart! In fact God probably sees us as one race! And, of course, all races practice racism, not just Caucasians. There is an obvious implication to this. Should Christian schools be multi-racial? I think the answer is abundantly clear, if we are truly preparing our students for heaven!

But now comes the confusion; is, then, heaven multi-cultural?

Ephesians 4:3-6 . . . endeavoring to keep the **unity** of the Spirit in the bond of peace. *There is* **one** body and **one** Spirit, just as you were called in **one** hope of your calling; **one** Lord, **one** faith, **one** baptism; **one** God and Father of all, who *is* above all, and through all, and in you all.

Deuteronomy 6:4 "Hear, O Israel: The LORD our God, the LORD *is* **one**!

The evil sleight of hand referred to earlier now comes into play; it is the postmodern, twisted insistence that one is a racist if one is not a multi-culturalist.

This is preached so often and so heavy handedly in our present, lost culture that you may have to read that last sentence several times before it starts to sink in! It equates preferring a given culture to racism. This lie is very deeply embedded in our tax funded, supposedly secular universities and K-12 schools, not to mention the entertainment and information media. To speak against this lie is, for them, akin to blasphemy; for it strikes at the core of their secular humanist religion, Mystery Babylon.

It sounds so innocent, but it is not. Look again at any of the educational psychology, text books used to educate all most all American teachers. They will begin to define culture as language, dress, customs, foods, etc which makes it sound so racist and trivial to judge them one way or another. Then, once they have your fairness sympathies, they will also add values and beliefs and ways of life as their core definitions of culture.

Finally then they top it off with implications and clear statements that link not being a racist with accepting that all cultures are of equal value (e.g. *Educational Psychology*, Woolfolk, 2005). Sounds great and so fair to our postmodern ears; no one wants to be accused of being prejudiced or biased, because that would be intolerant and judgmental, that would be racist.

But think about this idea; if all cultures are of equal value, does that include Nazi culture or heroin or crack culture or Satanist animal and human sacrifice culture or murderous gang culture or child rape and pornography culture or promiscuous, narcissist, homosexual culture or head hunter, revenge culture or slavery culture or Stalinist, Gulag, totalitarian, state-ist culture or Hirohito, emperor and racist state worship culture or Islamist, terrorist, suicide bomber, we will conquer the earth through deceit and murder culture?

Surely all cultures with their values and beliefs are not of equal value. The post-modernist is stuck here because it is intolerant to see differences in values and beliefs and what they lead to in terms of human actions unless, of course, one is maligning Christians. So this leads to the even greater evil and postmodern idol of moral equivalence: either both sides must be right or both sides must be wrong, but it cannot be true that one side is right and the other wrong, unless, of course again, it is postmodernism versus Judeo/Christian culture!

But we stand for the Gospel, good news as opposed to evil news. Caesar's schools, however, under the guise of multiculturalism teach that all cultures and faiths and values are of equal value and must therefore have an equal voice and an equal respect. The ACLU and the NEA stand for this and will sue you with your own tax dollars if you do not agree.

Should Christian schools do the same? What should Christian schools teach about tolerance and culture? What does it mean that our goal is to become more like Jesus? Are there many Jesuses? What about false Jesuses?

Racism or Culturalism

The key here is that true Christian culture is not tied to any earthly race or to any earthly nation or to any earthly culture because it comes from God's heavenly culture. Jesus taught at length regarding the values and beliefs of the Kingdom of God. This Kingdom is not Western nor Eastern, Northern nor Southern; no language group, tribe, race, gender, political party, nation, or continent can claim it as their own creation; it comes from above and belongs to the Creator of us all, God.

Philippians 3:20   For our citizenship is in heaven, from which we also eagerly wait for the Savior, the Lord Jesus Christ.

1 Corinthians 9:19-22   For though I am free from all men, I have made myself a servant to all, that I might win the more; *20* and to the Jews I became as a Jew, that I might win Jews; to those who are under the law, as under the law, that I might win those who are under the law; *21* to those who are without law, as without law (not being without law toward God, but under law toward Christ), that I might win those who are without law; *22* to the weak I became as weak, that I might win the weak. I have become all things to all men, that I might by all means save some.

There is a sense, however, in which Kingdom culture is very earthly cultures sensitive. Paul clearly expresses this above, but this sensitivity is **not** for the purpose of proclaiming all earthly cultures good or of equal value, but rather to show compassion, mercy, and understanding in order to win some from any earthly culture **to the one true, heavenly culture of God**!

Matthew 6:10   **Your kingdom** come. **Your will** be done on earth **as it is in heaven**.

Earthly cultures are to be judged in relation to the Kingdom culture of our Heavenly Father to the extent to which they align with it or oppose it. We have the yardstick; we should not be ashamed to use it even on our own civil or ethnic or national culture. **And we are not racists because we deem Christian culture that is truly God's heavenly Kingdom culture to be better than all other man made cultures!** This has nothing to do with race, because Kingdom culture is a multi-racial culture by God's design! And it has nothing to do with gender, because Kingdom culture is gender-worth equal by God's design! Postmodern relativism, misguided tolerance for sin, multi-cultural amoralism, and deceitful, moral equivalence doctrines, all as evil, supposedly secular idols of a fallen and spiritually lukewarm age, have no place in a truly Christian education. If our schools bow to them, they lose their power from God.

Romans 1:16   For I am not ashamed of the gospel of Christ, for it is the power of God to salvation for everyone who believes, for the Jew first and also for the Greek.

All of our earthly cultures are deficient including much of American culture. A Christian view of unity, diversity, independence, and dependence is based upon the fact that we are all seeking God's culture which is *echad*, one, unified in God and His Holiness; we are all striving to become more like Jesus, having His beliefs and values, His faith and faithfulness.

Heaven is multi-racial, and heaven is uni-cultural. (Read this last sentence several times!) We all leave our earthly culture behind. God's culture is the best culture, the only redeemed culture, and soon the only fulfilled culture! All Christians are called to leave their earthly culture behind and adopt the culture of the Kingdom of God which is not multi but one.

E Pluribus Unum, **from many, one**, is true of heaven's culture and is what our Christian, American forefathers had in mind when they made it our national motto. Check out the money in your pocket; it still has two proclamations: *In God We Trust* and *E Pluribus Unum*. This is why the universe is called the uni-verse; it is the *singular word* of God. Uni-versities also used to proclaim the unity of God's word. Multi-versities are the product of supposedly secular humanism not Christianity and they worship spiritually and morally compromised diversity.

We depend on God for our new culture in Christ as well as for our new self in Christ, both of which are from above and are above all others! Both of which can only be seen in the Sprit! We accept all brothers and sisters in the Lord regardless of race and their former earthly culture; but this does mean we accept the sinfulness of anyone's earthly person or culture including our own; and this does not make us racists!

All of what has been said above about tolerance, judgment, and multiculturalism as applies equally as well to their sister, postmodern idol, diversity worship. Christianity does not focus on what divides us but rather what unifies us in Jesus! This is another great divide between God's true values and postmodern, man's culture only, hypocritical values which greatly affect the dominant, post-modern, educational philosophies taught to teachers in our universities. This generation desperately needs to hear clearly from us about these matters in words and deeds. We are multi-racial, being of one God created race, and we are uni-cultural, God's Kingdom culture to come!

Hebrews 11:13-16   These all died in faith, not having received the promises, but having seen them afar off were assured of them, embraced them and confessed that they were strangers and pilgrims on the earth. *14* For those who say such things declare plainly that they seek a homeland. *15* And truly if they had called to mind that country from which they had come out, they would have had opportunity to return. *16* But now they desire a better, that is, a heavenly country. Therefore God is not ashamed to be called their God, for He has prepared a city for them.

May God stir up our convictions, forgive our misgivings, and deliver us in His mercy and grace from evil to His honor and glory. Do these truths permeate our policies, practices, and curricula?

Chapter 15: Why Does Educational Psychology Worship the Self and Should Christian Education Follow?

Think about this list: **self-actualization, self-concept, self-determination, self-efficacy, self-esteem, self-fulfilling prophecy, self-instruction, self-management, self-regulated learner, self-regulation, self-reinforcement, self-schemas, self-talk,** and **self-worth** (from the topic index of *Educational Psychology*, Woolfolk, 2005). Now think about this quote: "Interest in the self in psychology has grown steadily. In 1970, about 1 in every 20 publications in psychology was related to the self. By 2000, the ratio was 1 in every 7 (Tesser, Stapel, & Wood, 2002)" (as quoted in Woolfolk, *Educational Psychology*, 2005).

Made to Worship versus Self Esteem

We are made to worship; in the absence of Jesus we will worship something else. Should Christians follow Caesar's schools in the worship of, reliance upon, and preoccupation with self, with the school psychologist as the priest of selfness and self esteem? What does the scripture say? Let us begin with an Old Testament prophecy about Jesus, then the Lord's own words, and last, New Testament teachings.

Isaiah 53:3 He is despised and rejected by men, A Man of sorrows and acquainted with grief. And we hid, as it were, our faces from Him; He was despised, and we did not **esteem** Him.

Luke 16:15 And He said to them, "You are those who justify **yourselves** before men, but God knows your hearts. For what is highly **esteemed** among men is an abomination in the sight of God."

Philippians 2:3 Let nothing be done through **selfish** ambition or conceit, but in **lowliness** of mind let each **esteem** others better than himself.
Hebrews 11:26 . . . **esteeming** the reproach of Christ greater riches than the treasures in Egypt; for he [Moses] looked to the reward.

Romans 12:3 For I say, through the grace given to me, to **everyone** who is among you, not to think *of himself* more highly than he ought to think, but to think soberly, as God has dealt to each one a measure of **faith**.

Are psychologists the new, Godless priesthood; and should we as Christians follow them? Will having pride and esteem in ourselves save us, heal us, deliver us, make us better people, and lead us to success, happiness, and world peace as the supposedly secularists teach? Has esteem for God and others diminished as esteem for self has increased in our culture? Has sin exploded as esteem for self has increased? What is celebrity-ism? What have we sacrificed on the altar of students feeling good about themselves instead of feeling good about God? Do we worship the creation or the Creator? Is our measure of faith in God more important than our self esteem, our conceit in ourselves? Whom do we celebrate? These are hard questions in our times, but ones Jesus is asking us. If we are honest with ourselves, the right answers are obvious even though our flesh fights them fiercely.

Jesus or Socrates; where is our educational focus? The supposedly secular universities worship worldly Greek philosophy and especially Socrates whose famous dictum was to *know thy-self*. Jesus, on the other hand, calls us to *know God* and through God to find our new self in Him, dependently born again in Him, in His Spirit, and in His likeness, a self of no reputation, of humility, and of obedience. Are we teaching our students to always be looking unto Jesus or to always be looking unto themselves or their social group? The fruits of the two are vastly different. How does this manifest itself in our ESLERs and daily lessons?

Along this vain, why is Caesar pushing homosexuality in our tax-funded schools? According to Romans 1, homosexuality is the end result of narcissistic, self love which denies the love of God and the true, sacrificial love of others. Can we dare to try to be neutral here? Caesar will be teaching the children that anyone who stands against homosexuality is a criminal homophobe, someone committing a hate crime. Loving yourself more than God or others is the narcissistic religion of our times, and its proponents are deadly serious. Homosexuality is the epitome of this evil principality.

John 17:4 'I have glorified You on the earth.'

Jesus' focus was on glorifying God the Father, not Himself. This is an example for us. Upon whom do we focus our students? For Whose glory do we call them to work and to live and to worship and to be and to learn and to produce?

This is no trivial matter. The more people worship themselves, the less willing and able are they to worship God. Is not this Satan's goal? He wants them to worship the king of self-worshipers and self esteem-ers, himself!

Self-determination

Furthermore, consider self-determination, a key humanist value. Should we be teaching it in Christian schools? Again, to our postmodern ears it sounds great. Yet, was Jesus self-determined? Like many of these twisted concepts, there is a half truth here which can be very deadly. Jesus was in truth very determined. Consider how He steadfastly set His face to go up to Jerusalem knowing what lay ahead there (Luke 9:51). Yet the Garden of Gethsemane shows us that this was not self-determination but rather His determined obedience to His Father's will, not His own. We need to teach our students to be determined followers of God, not themselves! Determination is a good character quality; it is just a question of the source and the object of this determination! Determination is determined by what we rest or trust in to set and accomplish a task, ourselves or God. If we know what God has called us to do, we should with determination put our hand to the plow and not look back, being moved in the Spirit. But self-determination is a deadly sin, not a Biblical value! Satan again is very self-determined! Jesus is not!

Isaiah 50:7 "For the Lord GOD will help Me; Therefore I will not be disgraced; Therefore I have set My face like a flint, And I know that I will not be ashamed."

A Biblical Developmental Paradigm

If we want to discuss human development as in educational psychology in a Godly manner, we need to turn to scripture and theology and Jesus, not to Freud or Skinner or Piaget or Maslow or Vygotsky or Erickson or Bronfenbrenner or Dewey, all extremely popular in educational psychology text books and none of whom gave God anything that is due Him.

It is not that some of their ideas might not be helpful *if* they align with God's thoughts. There is common grace. But why start with them? Who are they anyway? We can only know if any of their ideas align with God if we first know what God thinks. We should start there!

What follows is a simple syllogism. If we are made in and thus are intended to mirror God's image, and if He reveals His image to us in His word, then we should be able to see a blue print in God into which we should humbly and dependently and obediently grow by His Spirit and grace and mercy. As Christians, our human growth and development is to become more like Him by humbling ourselves to the gracious work of His Holy Spirit upon and within us through our new birth and baptism in His Spirit by our Savior, Jesus, leaving our old man on the cross in Him. Our original *Imagio Deo* was ruined by our sins, but in Christ we can put off our old, ruined self and put on our new self, renewed and reborn by faith in Christ by His Spirit, our anointed Savior; Christ living in us, the hope of glory!

What then are the implications for Christian schools and Biblical, human development of these ideas? We can look to the character of God the Father, the Son, and the Holy Spirit to see what we are humbly to develop into by His mercy and grace and through His Spirit! We cannot do this by our own efforts in our flesh but only by humbling ourselves and dependently surrendering to God's work in us by faith!

Let us look again at Genesis 1:1-5. This is certainly not exhaustive, but it is God introducing Himself to us. What can we see about His image into which we are to develop as by-faith-reborn mirrors of Him?

Genesis 1: 1-5 In the **beginning** God **created** the heavens and the earth. 2 The earth was without form, and void; and darkness *was* on the face of the deep. And the **Spirit** of God was hovering over the face of the waters. 3 Then God **said**, "Let there be light"; and **there was** light. 4 And God **saw** the light, that *it was* **good**; and God **divided** the light from the darkness. 5 God **called** the light Day, and the darkness He called Night.

First of all God is a *beginner*; that is he shows initiative. Should not Christian school teachers, as Christian, human development specialists, then model and encourage Godly initiative for and in our students? Of course, we also know, from Jesus' pronouncement on the cross, that God is a finisher as well; He is the author and the finisher of our faith! He will finish the good work that He has begun in us if we let Him.

We should model and encourage Godly initiative and the Godly perseverance of finishing well in everything we and our students say and do. Christian initiative, however, is not rebelliousness but rather faithful obedience; spiritual character!

Next we see that God is *creative*. Christian, human development encourages Godly creativity. Although human, fleshly psychology associates creativity with rebellion, this need not be the case. God is very creative, but He is not rebellious. True creativity is respectful, loving, submissive, courageous, and worshipful. Satan is not really creative but a twisted and degrading, copy cat and deceiver and thief. We must model and foster Godly creativity that glorifies God in our students. This kind of creativity is wholesome and redeeming and fulfilling.

Next we see that God is *spiritual*; He works through His Spirit. He is Spirit! How deep are the implications here about Christian, human development and Christian education?!

Galatians 5:22-23 But the fruit of the Spirit is love, joy, peace, longsuffering, gentleness, goodness, faith, meekness, temperance: against such there is no law.

Should not these be high on our list of teacher and student outcomes and assessments? They are obviously on God's list! How does our curriculum foster spiritual development across our students' entire experiences and in all their activities and studies? Can we measure and encourage the activity of the Holy Spirit in our lessons, in our assignments, in our school community, and in our students' lives? Is this more important to God than SAT scores, not that SAT scores do not also measure important learning? Are we developing our students' spirits as well as their souls and bodies?

Next we see that God *speaks,* and He speaks *being*; He is a linguist; He uses language; He communicates; He teaches! And His communication causes being. Perhaps the three R's are not such a bad idea after all especially if we think of mathematics as a language used to communicate quantitatively. The arts are also languages as are the sciences. Albert Einstein said that God's thoughts could be seen in the formulas of physics. Albert Greene (1998) says the whole creation is God speaking to us and also a medium through which we speak back to Him and to each other. Christian, human development has to do with communication, all kinds of languages, including other languages of the Spirit such as worship and prayer! Are we teaching our students to communicate in many diverse languages in a Godly manner and for God's glory and for the good news of God's love for us? Are we making them aware of the power and being of these languages for good or evil, that their words create being as do their songs or paintings?

God also *produces*, makes things be. Helping students become productive in a Godly manner is a huge part of Christian, human development. Producing what is good and wholesome and faithful and beautiful and God honoring and beneficial and useful to others and redeeming and fulfilling is Christian stewardship and service. We should model and foster the development of productive stewardship and service.

God also *sees*; He is perceptive. And His perceptions are *evaluative*; He discerns the difference between right and wrong, good and evil. Christian, human development develops the senses and especially so in conjunction with the moral and spiritual sense. Again, as Greene says (1998), perceived facts for the Christian are never neutral but rather loaded with spiritual and moral meaning. We see and evaluate through our worldview and our cosmology and our theology and our anthropology. Can we find a Godly worldview, an anointed worldview, in everything being taught and learned through our students' developing their senses, their sensibilities, and their discernment in our schools, including their moral and spiritual senses? Do we help students see in a Godly manner?

And God *divides*; He makes clear distinctions; He is logical. We should develop Godly logic in children. C.S. Lewis' wise professor in the Narnia series wondered wonderfully and aloud as to why children were not taught logic in their schools anymore (Lewis, 1955). Clear thinking in these dark and confusing times is a great gift from the Holy Spirit for our students! Clear thinking has both form (logic) and content (Truth). Finally, God *names*. His names are true and they are accurate and they are meaningful. Christian, human development trains students to call it like it is, to name reality truthfully and meaningfully and discerningly, to take their words and their word seriously, as trusts from and to God.

Each of these human developmental characteristics must function under the guidance of the Holy Spirit: initiative, finishing well, creativity, spirituality, communication, productivity, perception, moral sense, evaluation, distinction, and naming. When these Godly characteristics are developed in a way that brings glory to God and not to self, we have a partial basis for truly Christian, human development, God's intended and redeemed and fulfilled image in us. And they all take the faith, hope, and love of God to be done as God would have us do them.

2 Corinthians 10:5 . . . casting down arguments and every high thing that exalts itself against the knowledge of God, bringing every thought into captivity to the obedience of Christ,

Independent Learners

Finally a word about independent learners is in order in the context of this chapter. Look at the aims and goals of most supposedly secular schools or universities or curriculum guides or state standards or educational psychology courses, and you will find independent learners or independent thinkers high on the list. This is another subtle twist of the truth. Again in the context of our postmodern culture this sounds very reasonable. Do we not want our students to think for themselves? Of course, this makes sense, but only if you live in a Godless universe. But we do not.

Therefore a logical distinction must be made. It is good to think *independently* of other people, especially unredeemed, fallen people who do not have the mind of Christ; this entire book is based upon this premise; but it is also good to think completely *dependently* upon the Holy Spirit of God and not just upon ourselves, another premise of this book!

Conversely it is wrong to think too dependently on other people but also to think too dependently just on ourselves, and furthermore it is disastrously wrong to ever think independently of God; witness the Garden of Eden. Godless Darwinism, where the randomly-by-chance fittest supposedly survive, hails independent and mutant and chance thinking. But what does scripture say?

Proverbs 3:5-6 Trust in the LORD with all your heart, And lean not on your own understanding; 6 In all your ways acknowledge Him, And He shall direct your paths.

Proverbs 28:26 He who trusts in himself is a fool, but he who walks in wisdom is kept safe. NIV

It is a prideful and arrogant sin to think we can outgrow our need to be taught of the Holy Spirit. Yet a stated goal of supposedly secular education is to produce independent thinkers who no longer need teachers. Listen carefully and you can hear Satan speaking! This is the lie that ends up in murder, as is witnessed in Cain and Abel. Independence from fallen, twisted, and merely human ideas is a good thing; but this independence is itself dependent upon dependence on the living teaching and discernment of the Holy Spirit if it is to lead to truth!

Jesus will be our Teacher and Lord as well as our King, Priest, and Prophet for eternity, even when we are His humble friends and His faithful bride as well as His servants ruling and reigning **with** Him! So we must not be fooled by the independent thinking idol and its God denying half truths and lies. We need to be helping our students transfer their dependence from us and from themselves unto the Holy Spirit. Independent thinking in and of itself is not a Christian goal! Discerning by the Spirit thinking is! Do we need to check and change our stated goals in regard to this issue? May God stir up our convictions, forgive our misgivings, and deliver us in His mercy and grace from evil to His honor and glory.

Chapter 16: Why is Christian Education Personal?

John 14:6   Jesus said to him, "I am the way, the truth, and the life. No one comes to the Father except through Me.

The incarnation is a personal God choosing to become personal with each one of us, His creations. The doors of heaven open or close based upon our own personal relationship with Jesus, God the Son. No one can make that relationship for us; we must do it individually and personally. God the Father is just that, our Father in heaven. This is not just an interesting metaphor or even powerful symbolism. Fatherhood does not exist independent of God, nor did He find it somewhere else and then decided to use it as a symbolic communication tool or a technique. Rather, it is Who He is; it comes from Him! As C. S. Lewis says, God begets as well as creates (Lewis, 1944). He is our Father!

He could be our heavenly boss or president or next door neighbor or uncle or dictator or cosmic consciousness or higher power or whatever; but the fact is that God **is** our heavenly Father; He created us; He begat us in Jesus; He is personal! Jesus called and calls Him *Abba*, Daddy. And God the Father chose to send His Son, His only begotten Son, very personal again! He did not send His lieutenant or lawyer or salesman or detective or heavenly software or technician or politician, or whatever; He sent His Son. These are not abstractions, nor literary symbolisms; they are realities. The Holy Spirit is also identified as the third **Person** of the Trinity and is not an *it*. Therefore Christian education is not an abstract concept or set of principles; it is a personal reality; it is God to person, and person to God, and person to person, just as it is in the Trinity!

Jeremiah 9:23-24   Thus says the LORD:
"Let not the wise *man* glory in his wisdom, Let not the mighty *man* glory in his might, Nor let the rich *man* glory in his riches; 24 But let him who glories glory in this, **That he understands and knows Me**, That I *am* the LORD, exercising lovingkindness, judgment, and righteousness in the earth. For in these I delight," says the LORD.

Christian Teachers

Frank Gaebelein (1954) said over a half century ago: no Christian education without Christian teachers! This is a direct byproduct of the personal nature of God and thus of Christianity and thus of truly Christian education. This leads to the obvious question: What is a Christian teacher?

As many have commented upon, if you are a Christian and a teacher, are you automatically a Christian teacher? In one sense, the obvious answer is logically yes. Yet in many other senses a person who is a Christian can teach very secularly; in fact, given the pervasive nature and influence of our supposedly secular, civil, educational and entertainment and political cultures and the supposedly secular, formal training most teachers receive, most Christian teachers do not teach very Christianly (Gaebelein, 1954; Greene, 1998; Graham 2003). One of the main purposes of this book is to point out the philosophical and practical discrepancies between supposedly secular and truly Christian education in order to stir up Christian thinking about Christian teaching and Christian learning and Christian school practices. It should be a very personal matter for each of us because it is to God!

Consider this. Why did Jesus stay up all night praying (McAlpine, 1982)? This is the only recorded time He did so; therefore we can assume it was very important.

Luke 6:12-13   Now it came to pass in those days that He went out to the mountain to pray, and continued all night in prayer to God. *13* And when it was day, He called His disciples to Himself; and from them He chose twelve whom He also named apostles:

It would appear that choosing who would teach His Gospel once He took His intercessory seat at the right hand of God was extremely important to Jesus. He had a personal relationship with each of His apostles, even Judas, whom He called friend. This was no bureaucracy He was building; it was family; it was community; it is a Kingdom of people. He was not interested in a Christian environment or a Christian atmosphere or climate; He wants Christian disciples who are in relationship with Him and with each other. It is personal. It is a community, a Kingdom that He seeks. It is a bride that He wants; can you get more personal than that?!

What Can be Christian in a Christian School?

According to scripture then, what can be Christian anyway? Where does scripture speak about a Christian environment or a Christian atmosphere or climate or even a Christian place? It does talk about Christian people, Christian teaching, Christian fellowship, the fragrance of the Holy Spirit in Christ and in us, His body, a Christian anointing, and Christian suffering, all of which are very personal! Did Jesus invest in Christian institutions or Christian people? It is always people first with Him!

John 15:5 "I am the vine, you *are* the branches. He who abides in Me, and I in him, bears much fruit; for without Me you can do nothing."

Mark 8:34 When He had called the people **to Himself**, with His disciples also, He said to them, "Whoever desires to come after Me, let him deny himself, and take up his cross, and **follow Me**."

Salvation is personal; to again quote the late Derek Prince, an exceptional Bible teacher, "Salvation is everything provided by the death of Jesus on the cross" (2007, p. 56). Following Isaiah 53, Prince went on to lay out nine **personal** exchanges provided for us **personally** by Jesus on the cross (pgs. 39-40):

1. Jesus was punished that we might be forgiven.

2. Jesus was wounded that we might be healed.

3. Jesus was made sin with our sinfulness that we might be made righteous with His righteousness.

4. Jesus died our death that we might share His life.

5. Jesus was made a curse that we might receive the blessing.

6. Jesus endured our poverty that we might share His abundance.

7. Jesus bore our shame that we might share His glory.

8. Jesus endured our rejection that we might enjoy His acceptance.

9. Our old man died in Jesus that the new man might live in us.

Since none of this wondrous grace can be earned, our only righteous response is humility, thankfulness, repentance, zeal, and a willingness to respond in kind. It is a personal response. Do we make the personal exchanges on the cross, made possible by Jesus' personal sacrifice, personal to our students? It was and is and always will be personal for Jesus! Is the once and forever, personal sacrifice of Jesus, of the cross, for each of us personally central to our curriculum? How deeply does it penetrate what we teach and learn? If it is the most important event in history and reality, how does it have preeminence in all our teaching and learning in every subject? Or do we just settle for a "Christian" environment or atmosphere!

Galatians 4:4-5   But when the fullness of the time had come, God sent forth His Son, born of a woman, born under the law, [5] to redeem those who were under the law, that we might receive the adoption as sons.

Adoption is very personal. Paul made his curriculum clear.

1 Corinthians 11:1   **Imitate me**, just as I also **imitate** Christ.

This is again very personal. Although there is definitely an emphasis on growing the Kingdom throughout the Bible, it is never impersonal. Size is never as important as quality. Although Jesus at times spoke to crowds, He never passed over personal encounters and ministry just to get to bigger crowds. Whether we are a school of 50 or 1,500, Christian education, anointed education is by definition personal. Does size matter? One person at a time! This is family; it is the King and His bride and His kingdom!

Chapter 17: How Should Training and Discipline Be Different in Christian Schools?

This is not a question of whether or not we should train (we train whether we intend to or not), but rather how well we train and toward what ends.

Luke 6:40   A **disciple** is not above his **teacher**, but everyone who is perfectly **trained** will be like his **teacher**.

Here Jesus clearly links discipleship (discipline), teaching, and training. Although training often scares supposed secularists most likely because of their guilt over their own nefarious motives, it should not Christians. Jesus thinks it is very important!

Proverbs 22:6   **Train** up a child in the way he should go, And when he is old he will not depart from it.

Psalm 144:1   Blessed be the LORD my Rock, Who **train**s my hands for war, And my fingers for battle.

1 Corinthians 9:25   Everyone who competes in the games goes into strict **training**. They do it to get a crown that will not last; but we do it to get a crown that will last forever. NIV

2 Timothy 3:16   All Scripture is God-breathed and is useful for teaching, rebuking, correcting and **training** in righteousness.

Distinctive Discipline

Whether by Gaebelein or Greene, Lowrie or Kienel, or even Moses or Jesus Himself, those of us involved in Christian education have always been urged to be spiritually distinctive and scripturally based in all phases of our school programs.

Why should discipline be any different? In fact, when one considers the root meaning of the word as being to disciple, this, then, ought to be a hallmark of our Biblical distinctiveness. Not that we are just tougher or sweeter, but that we also should be substantially different.

Yet in daily practice it is often difficult to see much of a difference, especially where distinctiveness of methods is concerned – pulling of tags, timeouts, positive reinforcements, detentions, suspensions, etc. However, if discipline is really discipleship, every facet of our discipline program should be very distinctive from humanist-based, supposedly secular education. Gaebelein went so far as to say that this is where the tire meets the road in true Christian education (1954).

Isaiah 55:8 "'For my thoughts are not your thoughts, neither are your ways my ways,' declares the Lord".

This distinctiveness begins with as fundamental a question as why we discipline in the first place. While we are also very interested in external, behavior modification and personal, habit formation in the here and now, our real goal should be a regeneration of our internal and personal relationships with God and with our fellow man, a communion that brings God glory for eternity and is based on the redeeming and restorative love and grace of Jesus. Thus Jesus told us, and especially with our hypocritical, legalistic tendencies, to clean the inside of the cup and then the outside will also be clean.

Matthew 23:26 Blind Pharisee, first cleanse the inside of the cup and dish, that the outside of them may be clean also.

Habakkuk 2:4 "For the just shall live by his faith".

In this light, right action is not primarily a matter of only moral reasoning, behavior modification, habit formation, or even character modeling, all of which have their good place; but one also, and primarily, of faith in a loving God. **Moral formation and spiritual formation are codependent because justice and righteousness rest on faith.** Or, put another way, there is no true moral education without spiritual education, something a modern, pioneer, Christian school educator, Mark Fakema (1954), said over half a century ago.

Redemption and sanctification, then, are what our discipline should be all about, to be partakers of God's holiness.

Hebrews 12:10b ". . . but God disciplines us for our good, that we may share in His holiness".

Our discipline should restore relationships with both God and man while it cleans the inside of the heart and thus also the outside behaviors of those disciplined, of those discipled. It is an expression of God's love for His children, even though it may not at the time seem pleasant but often grievous.

Hebrews 12:6-11a For whom the LORD loves He chastens, And scourges every son whom He receives."7 If you endure chastening, God deals with you as with sons; for what son is there whom a father does not chasten? 8 But if you are without chastening, of which all have become partakers, then you are illegitimate and not sons. 9 Furthermore, we have had human fathers who corrected us, and we paid them respect. Shall we not much more readily be in subjection to the Father of spirits and live? 10 For they indeed for a few days chastened us as seemed best to them, but He for our profit, that we may be partakers of His holiness. 11 Now no chastening seems to be joyful for the present, but painful . . .

Remember that God's discipline,

Hebrews 12:11b ". . . yields the peaceable fruit of righteousness to those who have been trained by it".

This fruit is made up of the fruits of the Spirit that come from a Holy Spirit controlled life and against which there is no law, that is,

Galatians 5:22b ". . . love, joy, peace, longsuffering, kindness, goodness, faithfulness, gentleness, self control".

These are the evidences of Christian discipline. This is how we can measure if our discipline is working or not.

Distinctive Methods

But how is it done? How is Christian discipline distinctive in method? For one, there should be no quibbling about what is right and what is wrong. Thank God, we should not be caught in the postmodern, relativists' quagmire.

The Ten Commandments, the greatest commandment of love for God and neighbor, the new commandment to love others sacrificially as Jesus loves us, and Jesus' other commandments are just that, commandments. We have objective yardsticks for sin and righteousness in God's word.

Micah 6:8   He has shown you, O man, what *is* good; And what does the LORD require of you; But to do justly, To love mercy, And to walk humbly with your God?

This clarity regarding both for what and toward what we should discipline should not be lightly taken for granted. Discipline is made much more murky for relativists and supposedly secular humanists, who can't even get to first base in agreeing upon what is right and what is wrong except perhaps hating God, let alone how to proceed from there and what the ultimate goal should be, beyond being a tolerant of evil, non-judgmental, democratic citizen of an earthly civil state. This clarity of standards and goals should be a great blessing to us, which we ought to cherish; but it does not in itself answer the question of how.

How to discipline is where the tire meets the road and is crucial to our integrity (Gaebelein, 1954), and here too we have clear Biblical guidance. It all begins with repentance, and repentance is built upon humility and conviction. This flies in the face of the supposedly secularists' culture and the worldview of tolerance, selfishness, pridefulness, self-esteem, and personal dignity, which underscore their key moral unction of respect. Our discipline should instill an esteem and a love for God and others, not primarily ourselves. This is why the twins of repentance and humility are so important and are necessary first ingredients of Christian discipline.

Philippians 2:5&8b   "Let this mind be in you which was also in Christ Jesus . . . who humbled Himself . . ."

Pride, then, the base rock of the self-esteem movement, is really the enemy of Christian discipline and rather the author of rebellion. And yet supposedly secularists resort to it as a foundational principal; teach children to have pride in themselves and tolerance for evil, and their behavior will improve. This is another watershed understanding. Pride and tolerance do not lead to repentance; humility and conviction do!

James 4:6b   "God resists the proud, but gives grace to the humble."

The Importance of Repentance, Faith, and Humility

So why are repentance, faith, and humility and the freedom to choose them so important? Without them there can be neither redemption, nor regeneration, nor restoration. They are what cleans the inside of the cup.

Repentance and faith change motivations. Only where there is true repentance and faith can there be genuine acceptance of forgiveness and a restoration of trust and fellowship. Repentance and faith lead to a change of heart. And this leads to another key ingredient of Christian discipline, restitution.

Consequences are a big part of discipline. Sometimes Christians think they are showing mercy when they forego consequences or conversely they are upholding crucial standards when they always meet out harsh punishments. These methods are probably brought about by confusion between the Biblical aims of punishment and of restitution. Restitution is good and should be encouraged and required as an outgrowth of individual repentance. Punishment, on the other hand, is the consequence of a failure to repent and is thus quite different from restitution.

The idea of consequences brings up the age-old philosophical and moral dilemma of the one and the many as well as balancing the attributes of God's mercy and justice. How can discipline serve the needs of the individual and the group at the same time? How does one uphold God's mercy and God's justice at once? If one gives the individual no consequence, what signal is being sent to all the others; where is the deterrence, what is the precedent being set? Yet will punishing the one embitter him or her and show a lack of mercy? Into this seeming dilemma many a teacher and/or administrator have fearfully wandered!

Conviction, Repentance, Faith, Restitution, and Punishment

Understanding the Biblical relationships of conviction, repentance, faith, restitution, and punishment, however, should shed some good light here. This is why the common practice of skipping over repentance and faith and going straight to automatic punishment can cause so much trouble and damage, simply dealing with the outside of the cup. We often go straight from infraction to consequence, short circuiting conviction, repentance, faith, forgiveness and restitution, the inside of the cup.

Another quandary with repentance is excuse making, a form of a lack of personal conviction and responsibility, which comes from a lack of humility, faith, and truthfulness. Postmodern culture says we are all victims of others, and sin is therefore always someone else's fault, and therefore not real for us; we have no accountability; we are only victims. There is no need for humility, conviction, faith, or truth, because we are never the problem; it is always someone else's responsibility, the proverbial *they*. This culture of victimization and lack of personal responsibility is at the heart of supposedly secular humanism, and it is a form of Satanic denial and rebellion.

But in truth why should I allow myself to be convicted of my sin or then repent of it? Because without true repentance and faith there can be no redemption, no real acceptance of forgiveness, no change of heart, no restitution, and no restoration, just a papering over of problems. Perhaps the outside of the cup is hosed off by punishment, but nothing happens on the inside.

All that is left is denial, which usually then leads again to punishment in the hope that it leads back to repentance and faith. Listening to excuses in this process of Christian discipline may show compassion, but it does not solve the problem of conviction and repentance and faith. We must therefore be avid, if not gentle and private and humble, excuse busters, if we really believe in the power and importance of conviction and repentance and faith. As all temptation is common to man, we can show understanding and humility but not unaccountability.

Correctly distinguishing between restitution and punishment is important. Restitution is a way for *the one* to willingly make up for the loss of *the many* and/or *the other*, a way to assume responsibility, and is best jointly decided upon and made directly relevant to the loss. It also secondarily acts as a true deterrent for others, *the many*. Punishment also satisfies deterrence, but its goal is furthermore to lead the individual back to repentance, and it does not necessarily tie directly in kind to the problem. The difference between the two is a matter of repentance and faith or not and is vital to understanding Christian discipline. Restitution is based upon humility, real conviction, and true repentance and faith. Punishment is for their lack.

James 4:6b "God resists the proud, but gives grace to the humble."

And how do we know if repentance and faith are true? Because they lead to a desire for and an acceptance of forgiveness **and** to a willingness towards restitution, which all together lead to restoration and the production of Holy Spirit controlled fruit in our students' lives. Repentance, faith, and forgiveness uphold God's mercy. Willing restitution upholds His justice. And all four bring Him glory! The needs of *the one* and *the many* are both met, and God's mercy and justice are both satisfied. And there is also deterrence for others, *the many*. It is interesting, as an aside, to note that God made no provision for prisons in the Old Testament community. One was either innocent, repented and made restitution, or was put to death.

Matthew 18 instructs us to do all this as privately as possible, and we should always take the plank out of our own eye first! But if humility, conviction, repentance, and faith cannot be found due to a hardness of heart and a lack of openness to the Holy Spirit and truth, then punishment has its place; however, even here the goal is still eventual conviction, repentance, faith, restitution, and restoration.

This all may seem a complex and a personally time consuming affair, which it is, but it comes from God's own heart. Thank God, He thinks it is worth the time and effort for us, and thus we would do well to take heed to each of these steps, for they work as an integrated whole: humility, conviction, confession, repentance, faith, forgiveness, restitution, and restoration. Their school-wide application would take much effort and prayer and diligence, but these steps would be distinctly Christian, qualitatively different, and very redemptive! They are worth the effort!

So the next time we are tempted to just skip from infraction to punishment or to ignore the situation all together to save time or effort, or to pretend we are showing mercy when we are showing license, or justice when really showing vengeance, let us realize the importance to God of what we are leaving out. The real hallmark of these steps is God's restorative love for His willing children that they may share in His holiness and the fruits of His Spirit. God disciplines those He loves, and so should we. Yet we should do it God's way! It is His love that takes Him and us the needed extra mile.

This takes a great deal of communication and diligence. Yet it also creates unity within a community. Communication, community, communion, and unity all come from the same Latin, root words, *with oneness*, and are deeply connected in meaning; they also support one another. As an interesting aside, has your school staff or faculty ever taken communion together as a local manifestation of the Body of Christ? And, if they have not, why have they not? Could this not help form a community for discipleship and faithfulness and discipline!? Jesus said it would!

A Word about Saying You Are Sorry

Where does Jesus say anything about saying we are sorry? Is this a secular half truth? Remorse can be a genuine byproduct of repentance and faith. And we are certainly all sorry from God's perspective; that is, in a sorry state in our sins! But is being sorry a substitute for true conviction, repentance, and faith? Is it enough? "I'm sorry if I offended you" might actually mean it is your fault for being offended! Is this the same as admitting it is my fault, I am wrong, I have sinned against God and you, and I repent, please forgive me? One may also be sorry and have remorse, but are remorse and repentance the same thing? What if we taught students to repent and ask for forgiveness instead of just saying, sorry?! If we did nothing wrong, why be sorry; if we did something wrong, why not admit it and repent and ask for forgiveness?! One shows true remorse by repenting.

<u>2 Corinthians 7:9-11</u> Now I rejoice, not that you were made sorry, but that your sorrow led to repentance. For you were made sorry in a godly manner, that you might suffer loss from us in nothing. [10] For godly sorrow produces repentance *leading* to salvation, not to be regretted; but the sorrow of the world produces death. [11] For observe this very thing, that you sorrowed in a godly manner: What diligence it produced in you, *what* clearing *of yourselves, what* indignation, *what* fear, *what* vehement desire, *what* zeal, *what* vindication! In all *things* you proved yourselves to be clear in this matter.

Mutual Blame

Here is one last thought on discipline. What do you do when one says X and the other one says Y, and they both blame each other, and they cannot work it out on their own? Try this. Ask for humility, conviction, repentance, and faith first, instead of blame. Do not let anyone speak unless they are admitting what they did wrong and then apologize for it, repent for it and offer restitution, and then ask for forgiveness. Then do not let anything else be discussed until restitution is agreed upon and forgiveness is given.

Work this both ways to full completion, never allowing accusation or blaming into the conversation. No *yes-buts* allowed. Keep each person listening to the Spirit about their own fault instead of focusing on the fault of the other. Be sure that this moves both ways. Ask what Jesus would ask each person if He were present about his or her own sin. This way Jesus becomes the healer, the reconciler!

Matthew 7:5 Hypocrite! First remove the plank from **your own eye**, and then you will see clearly to remove the speck from **your** brother's **eye**.

Only when this two-way process is exhausted, should we ask if anyone still has an offense. How we see ourselves as kings, priests, and prophets in Him and in our own hearts and convictions and spirits concerning discipline and training makes a huge difference in how we go about the ministries in which He has placed us. May God stir up our convictions, forgive our misgivings, and deliver us in His mercy and grace from evil to His honor and glory.

Proverbs 29:19 A servant will not be corrected by mere words; For though he understands, he will not respond.

Chapter 18: Why Do the Supposed Secularists Prefer Piaget or Kohlberg Over Moses and Jesus for Moral Development and Character Education?

Dewey and Piaget

Again, most supposedly secular, educational psychology text books from which most educators are trained, even for Christian schools, now contain a section or a chapter on moral development and/or character training. That they might look to God, the Bible, Moses or Jesus on such a topic does not seem to cross their minds, so completely have they assumed the psychological to have replaced the spiritual and theological in all things educational, even morals and character. Instead they regularly turn to two secularists, Piaget and Kohlberg, both of whom develop John Dewey's secular humanist, anti-God, religious perspectives. This approach is distinctly anti-Christian because most of Dewey's life was spent trying to substitute the man-made psychological for the God-made spiritual and theological.

For instance, for Piaget (1997) moral development hinges on an awareness of who makes the rules, but only from amongst humans. Development thus means young children just accept the rules as made by adults but developed children see that they are man-made and can thus be negotiated and with their own input, democratized or socialized. There is no thought here that morality could be anything but a man-made construct and a mutual, temporal contract. We-make-the-rules is the highest, moral development possible! What would the snake in the garden think of this idea?

Kohlberg

Kohlberg (1984) is even more prevalent. He seems to be the agreed upon expert for all things moral development amongst humanists educators. He is Jewish, yet his theory is very secular and truly Jewish only in a Talmudic sort of way. It is based upon moral reasoning and moral discussions brought about by carefully crafted, hypothetical dilemmas. Like Piaget, it is constructivist and relativist with no thought of God or God's perspective, though he does see a hierarchy of moral reasoning and thus moral judgment, but somehow based upon secular values of only human crafted democracy and social justice, a perfect fit for God-denying progressives.

Moral judgment is considered more important than personal righteousness or Godly character and values, and it is solely based around man-made reason and social justice criteria. For Kohlberg moral development is equated with only social justice principles; personal morals or eternal or even temporal values or right standing with God are not his humanist, social constructionist perspective. He thus severely limits moral development to the secular and temporal.

Secular education loves Kohlberg's theory because it is essentially mental and unreal and easily fits within moral relativism; it is based on a mind game. It is not the righteous answer but the complex and progressivist one that counts. His levels of moral development are connected to the sophistication and the humanistic and supposedly secular universality of one's moral reasoning but not the truth of God. Sophists were ancient Greek philosophers who were known for their ability to take either side of an argument and then out reason their opponent regardless of any absolute truth or morality of the matter at hand. Sophistication is not a Christian value or virtue. Though Jesus' thinking is obviously elegant and deep and beautiful in the truest senses of the words, its goal is not sophistication but simple and yet real and deep truth.

It is not that Jesus does not apply moral reasoning; it is that reasoning or even moral judgment is not the goal in itself. What matters to God is what one actually does in reality, one's humble, heart motives for doing so, and how one's faith in God is involved. The goal is our real walk with God and neighbor and brother. Kohlberg's dilemmas, on the other hand, are artificial. They pose relativist situations with supposedly only two choices possible where one has to sin one way or the other and thus reason one's justifications on the most universal, humanist principle one can muster.

There is in reality, however, always another or a third way when God is involved in any supposed dilemma.

1 Corinthians 10:13   No temptation has overtaken you except such as is common to man; but God is faithful, who will not allow you to be tempted beyond what you are able, but with the temptation will also make the **way** of **escape**, that you may be able to bear it.

Artificial reasoning within a Godless, closed system does not show moral development but sophistication of moral reasoning and hypothetical self-justification. It says nothing about what one does in reality. There was no dilemma that caused or causes Jesus to sin one way or the other, ever. Kohlberg's dilemmas force one to rely upon unregenerate human reason as our highest moral faculty without the possibility of faith in Godly intervention! This is not Christian character development! Teachers trained in this kind of relativist thinking need retraining.

The Role of Faith in Action

Matthew 7:20   Therefore by **their fruit**s you will know them.

Romans 1:17   For in it the righteousness of God is revealed from faith to faith; as it is written, "**The just shall live by faith**."

Hebrews 11:6   But **without faith** it **is impossible** to please Him, for he who comes to God must believe that He **is**, and that He **is** a rewarder of those who diligently seek Him.

There is no true moral development without the exercise of faith in real choices, and only by the fruit of one's real choices, motives, and actions can moral development be measured or manifested or grown. Moral development without faith in action is dead in the water, an empty, self-justifying, prideful, mind game. Moral judgment must become moral suasion by faith. There is also, therefore, no true moral development without the work of the Holy Spirit. There are plenty of moral scoundrels with sophisticated, moral justifications and universal reasoning and judgments.

True moral development is in the heart, the spirit, the mind, and in one's real choices in faith and in actions and in motives. It is based on faith in the love of God. It takes faith to be good not just reasoning or even good judgment.

Do we, therefore, focus real opportunities for our students to exercise faith in the doing of good for God's glory and in the holding dearly of Godly virtues by faith? Here is true, moral development; it is a spiritual matter not a psychological one. This is where the content of our character is built as referred to by Martin Luther King (1963), not outer appearance. Where does this fit into our curriculum?

Words and Deeds

Luke 24:19   And He said to them, "What things?" So they said to Him, "The things concerning Jesus of Nazareth, who was a Prophet mighty in **deed** and **word** before God and all the people,

Words and deeds must match, and deeds and words must match; hypothetical, constructivist, moral development measures just words and therefore is not enough. This sword cuts both ways, and faith is what connects them.

There are Christian school educators who have the right words but not the deeds to match them. There are also Christians in secular schools who claim their right actions are enough while what they teach is void of God's Word and truth. Neither of these is the example Jesus left for us. He constantly spoke God's truth in both word **and** deed, as well as in deed **and** word! This is a true measure of moral development! Do we use this yardstick with ourselves and our students? Walking in the truth means not being afraid to both speak it **and** do it, and do it **and** speak it! Jesus is our example.

Colossians 3:17   And whatever you do in **word** or **deed**, do all in the name of the Lord Jesus, giving thanks to God the Father through Him.

The giving of thanks is because we can only truly do either and both together by faith, which is God's gift to us! This is another divide, is moral education a full life and faith walk based upon God's love for us and including personal righteous and social justice and right standing with God by faith or just an intellectual exercise solely based upon manmade, universal and democratic, justice principles, as proposed and hypothetical, moral judgments? Is it about truth or sophistry; must it be about both words and deeds or only words or only deeds? Jesus' moral teaching has universal principles within it, but they are deeply rooted in God's virtue and eternal values and character and faithfulness, not just man's, self-serving and relativistic reasoning and ideas of social justice.

However we answer these questions, we are setting a moral example. Let us follow the example of Jesus, faith manifested in deeds and in words, personally and universally and eternally! We bear good fruit by personally abiding in Jesus, surrendering by faith to His life, His Spirit and His truth in us, not by our own intellectual and moral reasoning sophistication! This is why our daughter, Shoshanah, who has Downs Syndrome, is capable of great thoughts and great acts of goodness! Her reasoning is often simple but pure because of the faith motives of her heart!

Truly Christian teachers, who mirror our one true Teacher, cannot teach the truth in words and act like heathens in deeds, nor can they act like Christians in deeds and teach in words like heathens. It takes both to teach as Jesus teaches! Always tell the truth and walk in it no matter the cost! Are these part of our student outcomes in our daily lessons? May God stir up our convictions, forgive our misgivings, and deliver us in His mercy and grace from evil to His honor and glory.

Chapter 19: What Can We Learn from Jesus' Parable of the Talents in Matthew 25 Regarding Christian Education?

One of my earliest experiences as an educator was listening to a dear, Jewish Christian lady, Helen Cooper, give a talk to the students on this parable at the opening of a summer school session at Ojai Valley School, a non sectarian, boarding school in 1971.

Matthew 25:14-30   "For *the kingdom of heaven is* like a man traveling to a far country, *who* called his own servants and delivered his goods to them. 15 And to one he gave five talents, to another two, and to another one, to each according to his own ability; and immediately he went on a journey. 16 Then he who had received the five talents went and traded with them, and made another five talents. 17 And likewise he who *had received* two gained two more also. 18 But he who had received one went and dug in the ground, and hid his lord's money. 19 After a long time the lord of those servants came and settled accounts with them. 20 "So he who had received five talents came and brought five other talents, saying, 'Lord, you delivered to me five talents; look, I have gained five more talents besides them.' 21 His lord said to him, 'Well *done,* good and faithful servant; you were faithful over a few things, I will make you ruler over many things. Enter into the joy of your lord.' 22 He also who had received two talents came and said, 'Lord, you delivered to me two talents; look, I have gained two more talents besides them.' 23 His lord said to him, 'Well *done,* good and faithful servant; you have been faithful over a few things, I will make you ruler over many things. Enter into the joy of your lord.'
24 "Then he who had received the one talent came and said, 'Lord, I knew you to be a hard man, reaping where you have not sown, and gathering where you have not scattered seed. 25 And I was afraid, and went and hid your talent in the ground. Look, *there* you have *what is* yours.'
26 "But his lord answered and said to him, 'You wicked and lazy servant, you knew that I reap where I have not sown, and gather where I have not scattered seed. 27 So you ought to have deposited my money with the bankers, and at my coming I would have received back my own with interest. 28 So take the talent from him, and give *it* to him who has ten talents.

29 'For to everyone who has, more will be given, and he will have abundance; but from him who does not have, even what he has will be taken away. 30 And cast the unprofitable servant into the outer darkness. There will be weeping and gnashing of teeth.'

This is obviously a parable about Jesus leaving His servants here to continue working on His behalf with His goods until He returns to take account; but what can it also say to us about education, about teaching and learning? Furthermore, it is also a parable about the fruit of our chosen conception of God and about faithfulness or laziness and about talents and expectations and accountability and about good or evil and finally about rewards or punishments. All of these concepts have their place in education.

For instance, should rewards be tied to abilities or to what one differentially does with their given abilities? The parable shows that there is an expectation that one use faith to responsibly multiply whatever talent or ability one has been given; but it also reveals that the five talent and the two talent servants did not have to both return ten talents to be rewarded. Moreover, "to each according to his own ability," clearly implies that we each have differing amounts of ability. Although this is obvious to teachers and learners, politically correct, humanist, educational theory and its universal, equity outcomes religion tries to deny it. Christian education should not.

One wonders what the third servant would have had to do to receive the same reward as the other two servants received. If he had brought back the one talent along with just one other, would he not have had the same reward? What the Lord was after was faithful use or multiplication, in this case doubling, regardless of where one began or ended. Do we teach students to mix faith with whatever level of ability or talent they have to use and to double their service, and do we reward them for growth without comparison to others' totals? Note that the one who ended up with ten and the one with four got the same reward as good and faithful servants who did well. The faithful use and growth of talent for service is the key point.

Luke 12:48 For everyone to whom **much** is **given**, from him **much** will be required; and to whom **much** has **been** committed, of him they will ask the more.

To whom much is given, much is expected. The one with five talents could have complained about having to make ten when the other one only had to make four. But the faithful use of whatever the level of talent given is what is responsibly expected of all! Conversely "outer darkness" and "weeping and gnashing of teeth" are Biblical code for Hell. Burying our God given talents of any level in laziness and fear and refusing to mix them with faith is not a good idea!

Our Conception of God, Faithfulness, and Good Will

Furthermore according to the Lord's parable what do our chosen understanding and picture of God, our obedient faithfulness to use and grow what has been given to us, and our good will have to do with achievement and success? Conversely what do a chosen negative picture of God, a rebellious fear, and a neglectful laziness have to do with failure? Does this have anything to do with teachers and learners, with education?

How does this compare with the supposedly secular, self esteem movement with pride or its lack as the reason for success or failure of students? The question is whether real success is a matter of self esteem or of faith in and humble responsibility toward God? So, who is right, Jesus or the prideful humanists, and how would this manifest itself in our schools? Clearly the one, who lost even what he had, considered God a hard and unjust man to be feared and not to be honored or loved or served. He used his picture, that he had created, of God as an excuse to be fearful and lazy. He pridefully and resentfully buried his talent instead of faithfully using it for God's glory. He had ill will toward God and did not serve Him. Jesus called him wicked, and he lost everything! God did not agree with his assessment of Him that He was a hard and unjust man, but simply verified that that was how the servant had chosen to see Him. Just how important, then, is our chosen picture of who God is, what we really believe about God? And what is the blessing of faithfully obeying a loving and expectant God?

Whose talents and goods are they, anyway? Are humility and pride at play here again, and what of thankfulness? What does God require of us regarding the talents and goods He gives us regardless of our ability level in any given area of our lives? And will we not have to give an account for them? What lessons can be drawn from this parable for the Christian school? Just how important is it to mix faith and good will and a true conception of God with our given gifts, abilities, talents, and goods for His glory and service?

For example, all schools group students somehow; but why do most do it sacrosanctly by age? Did Jesus group His followers and learners by age? Did Paul with Timothy and others? Why did the Lord create people with differing abilities? Why did the Lord give to some one, to some two, or to some five talents in some area of their lives? Why are the challenges different but the rewards potentially the same for all of us? Do we appropriately challenge and help our one, two, and five ability students regardless of age to reach their maximum potential? Do we let the one talent students slide and the five talent students only make six or seven because they are already ahead? Does it matter what you start with or where you end up compared to others if you do your best?

Did Jesus ability or readiness or willingness group? Who were James, Peter, and John? Who were the 12 or the 72? Do we all develop in the same way at the same pace by age? And what do humility, hope, love, and faith have to do with learning as opposed to pride and self esteem or even age?

Hebrews 11:1 Now **faith is** the substance of things hoped for, the evidence of things not seen.

Hebrews 11:3 By **faith** we **understand** that the worlds were framed by the word of God, so that the things which are seen were not made of things which are visible.

A Possible Application

Here is a possible application of these thoughts and questions: what if parents made the decisions in an ability and readiness and willingness, flexible grouping system for learning? God gave me the grace and chance to help lead the birthing and growth of Monte Vista Christian School's middle school from 10, 7th graders and 10, 8th graders in one room with me in 1977 to 325 students in 1990 in Watsonville, CA, at which point He called me to do other things for Him. By God's grace and the guidance of His Spirit, we actually created a program of classes based on truths from the parable of the talents.

We created a flexible system where parents chose between five levels per grade of pairs of classes, math/science, reading/social studies, and Bible/grammar from remedial to low grade level to high grade level to advanced to high advanced.

It was flexible in two ways. First these pairs of courses could be on different levels depending on student readiness, gifting, interest, and willingness. Second placement was changeable at any time, and the parents were in the driver's seat. You read that correctly, we eventually grew into giving them the final say. Of course they often asked us for advice; test scores, rankings, grades, teacher recommendations, and the principal's advice were always available; but they came to have the final word. This unique system evolved by trial and error over 14 years. The results were excellent for all three groups of students: high, middle, and low. Yearly gain scores were excellent for all students as well as mean group percentiles compared to other Christian schools and national averages; and we accepted students across a broad range.

At the time, two colliding perspectives guided the creation of this unique system. One was the parable of the talents and the urging of the Spirit and another was Jeannie Oaks, then from the Rand Corporation and now the holder of UCLA's Multicultural and Diversity Education Chair, and a point person for secular, anti-tracking or readiness grouping ideology, completely contrary to what we were doing. Her criticisms, however, were taken to heart, not to junk the idea as she propounded but rather to improve it, but so was the Lord's parable taken to heart. What came out of that crucible was a list of compound ideas about readiness grouping across middle school classrooms within grade levels done well and done poorly.

Done Well	Done Poorly
1. Assignment to classes by parent choice via readiness meeting with principal	1. Assignment to classes by the school by group IQ or achievement test
2. Assignment changeable	2. Assignment set in stone
3. Assignment variable by subject pairs according to parents & readiness	3. Assignment across all classes regardless of varying readiness
4. Smaller lower level classes with equally qualified teachers	4. Lower classes receive low-quality instruction & worst teachers
5. Objectives & procedures creatively done for lower level readiness	5. Lower-level objectives & procedures routine and boring

6. Smaller classes in readiness zone engages lower students	6. Lower level more behavior problems and disengagement
7. Hi and Mid level readiness students challenged to their full capacity	7. Bored and unchallenged hi and mid level students
8. Competent & ethical administrators & compassionate teachers	8. Decreased teacher enthusiasm for lower levels
9. All improve with real & unembarrassed learning	9. Low attendance and self esteem for lower levels
10. High expectations for LL	10. Low expectations for LL
11. Parents' choice	11. School fiat racial or SES inequity
12. Student/parent choice	12. Friendships limited
13. Elective courses, PE & sports, co-curricular activities & variable course levels by parent choice	13. Somehow segregated socially

The key here is parent, student, and school collaboration with the parents with the final word. This is Biblical. It puts fathers in control, and it makes the school a servant of the Lord and the family. You can see why Caesar and the NEA might not like this! Much of Oaks' criticisms were based on bias regarding race, gender, and low achievers getting inferior educational opportunities, reflecting a rather dim view of educators. Parental choice effectively negated the first two criticisms. There was no evil *they* using bias to hurt students because of race or gender or ability or SES; there was *we* with parental final word.

Did all the parents always make wise choices? Not really, but they learned from their mistakes and made better choices as they went, and they were empowered, honored, and involved. Usually they took our advice. Sometimes they chose differently. Sometimes this worked, and sometimes it did not, but we remained flexible, and lessons were always learned.

We also took to heart Oaks' criticism regarding low learners that they often got the worst teachers and curriculum. In this particular school a single teacher often taught all five levels of a particular grade level's subject plus a Bible class. The Bible class idea came from Gaebelein (1954) as a way of increasing Bible integration across subject areas. Therefore the high, middle, and low students all had the same quality of teacher and different levels of similar quality curriculum! At other times people of special compassion took a larger share of the remedial classes.

Of course, there is also a fairness issue with the five talent students which is so often overlooked with the emphasis on slow learners. Should they be held back for the sakes' of the one and two talent students? Grouping within classrooms instead of across different classrooms often means the high ability students are either left on their own and thus not stretched to their fullest or are used as forced tutors again not stretching them to their fullest. We found, however, that all three groups benefited from freely chosen, readiness and willingness grouping.

Here are some of the benefits of well done grouping among leveled classes within a grade level versus grouping within each class and/or purposeful heterogeneous grouping in classes for politically correct, social reconstructivist reasons:

1. All students get a **full** period, not just a fraction, of expert teacher instruction and teacher help and teacher feedback in their readiness zone.

2. Whether high, mid, or low readiness, all students are less embarrassed to ask meaningful questions regarding their needs because the other students in their classes are much more likely to be in the same boat.

3. Whether high, mid, or low readiness, all students are less likely to be bored or frustrated with direct instruction or group work and thus create less discipline problems.

4. Whether high, mid, or low readiness, all students are more likely to benefit from class discussions and individual teacher feedback to other students.

5. Whether high, mid, or low readiness, teacher preparation is more focused and in depth and efficient and effective and targeted.

6. Whether high, mid, or low readiness, students can be fairly and justly held accountable to complete assignments and to engage in appropriate classroom behavior and participation.

7. A school has less frazzled teachers not trying to run a constant, three ring circus and thus happier, more attended to and more productive students.

8. More teaching and more learning; less time fillers while the teacher is helping others with work that is not germane to various groups of other students.

9. Less practicing of mistakes in unsupervised groups before the teacher knows it.

10. Less blind leading the blind as a primary source of learning, where the students try to teach each other while the teacher is helping another group.

11. Less unsupervised busywork while the teacher is teaching other groups.

12. Better use of the teacher's and students' talents and time.

13. More meaningful and expert feedback for all students at their readiness and willingness levels.

All this came from the parable of the talents. Parents making choices; students able to move ahead as they were willing and ready; and the school serving, not lording it over! This is not theory, it happened!

Of further note is how the middle level students thrived under this system with their new found confidence, responsibility, and leadership opportunities. And the high students, being appropriately challenged took off. And those low students who really wanted to learn progressed rapidly in an unembarrassed learning group. Not that this should always be copied, but it is an example of looking to the word for inspiration for educational methods.

A High School Application

Something similar was also done later at Phoenix Christian High School, where I was superintendent, but on a high school level where a seven diploma, parent/student choice program was put together in the early 1990s with these parent/student driven, diploma program choices: general education, community college prep, NAU prep, ASU prep, U of A prep, math/science honors, language/social science honors, and double honors. Academic requirements went from three solids a year (general diploma) all the way up to seven with AP courses (double honors). Again parents and students chose. Again parents and students could change plans as they progressed. Again many differing groups of readiness and willingness flourished. They set their appropriate goals and worked diligently to reach them with the school serving them. This offered a wide variety of students with differing goals and abilities the possibility of a distinctly Christian education. The point is not that the author thinks these two examples are the only Biblical ways to do these things, but they are examples of creatively using Biblical truths as a foundation and as a way to develop school philosophies and practices instead of just blindly imitating Caesar's schools and philosophies.

Competition and Cooperation

Christian schools should be different based on Biblical truth. These are just two schools that broke the mold, but there are many ways of flourishing in the Lord.

Competition among un-equals is unfair and often debilitating, but what about competition among equals, is it a good thing if done in an honorable and Godly way? God applauds when anyone grows in their faith and talent by being appropriately and fairly challenged. We found that high and middle and low readiness groups flourished competing and cooperating among themselves.

Proverbs 27:17   As **iron sharpens iron**, so a man **sharpens** the countenance of his friend.

1 Corinthians 9:24   Do you not know that those who run in a race all run, but one receives the prize? Run in such a way that you may obtain *it*.

2 Timothy 4:7 I have fought the good fight, I have finished the **race**, I have kept the faith.

Hebrews 12:1-2 Therefore we also, since we are surrounded by so great a cloud of witnesses, let us lay aside every weight, and the sin which so easily ensnares us, and let us run with endurance the **race** that is set before us, looking unto Jesus, the author and finisher of *our* faith, who for the joy that was set before Him endured the cross, despising the shame, and has sat down at the right hand of the throne of God.

Cooperative learning can be Godly, though the secularists have made a god and an idol of it as secular, progressivist socialism; but fair competition can also be Godly, though the secularists hate it. Thank God Jesus chose to compete with Satan for our souls! And Paul certainly was competitive for good. Cooperative or competitive learning are not automatically Godly or un-Godly; it depends upon the manner and spirit and the fairness in which and righteous goals towards which they are done. We should teach our students to cooperate and to compete in ways that glorify God, and all should be appropriately challenged to reach in faith their fullest potential, to run so as to obtain the prize set before them. May God stir up our convictions, forgive our misgivings, and deliver us in His mercy and grace from evil to His honor and glory.

Chapter 20: School Wide, Practical Problem Solving and Conflict Resolution According to Jesus in Matthew 18; How Does it Work?

Why is this important? Are there ever conflicts that need to be resolved or problems among people that need solving in Christian schools? In fact, because of the spiritual warfare involved, there are probably more! This true, silver bullet has been recognized for a long time, but let us unwrap it to see what we can find that will help us both as individuals and as truth learning communities. I first heard Dr. Paul Kienel speak of this in a forerunner of ACSI workshop in the 1970s, but it took time and experience to start to see a fraction of what is potentially here.

Matthew 18:15-20 "Moreover if your brother sins against you, go and tell him his fault between you and him alone. If he hears you, you have gained your brother. 16 But if he will not hear, take with you one or two more, that *'by the mouth of two or three witnesses every word may be established.'* 17 And if he refuses to hear them, tell *it* to the church. But if he refuses even to hear the church, let him be to you like a heathen and a tax collector. 18 "Assuredly, I say to you, whatever you bind on earth will be bound in heaven, and whatever you loose on earth will be loosed in heaven.

Gaining Our Brother

How is gaining your brother the focus of these procedures straight from the lips of Jesus? It really is not so much about offenses or procedures as it is about maximizing our chances of gaining our brother, building the unity of the Spirit within the Body of Christ. Because humans are involved and in a fallen world, these procedures are not fool proof; they simply promise the greatest possible success and the least possible collateral damage for those who are willing to embrace their wisdom.

Why does Jesus use concentric circles of privacy? How is this the opposite of our fleshly inclinations? Why is it the most effective way to win our brother? To follow this prescription to offenses, we must exercise humility instead of pride and restraint instead of revenge; we must seek in love to gain our brother. Pride and revenge would lead us to run to others with our self righteous complaint and create a mountain out of a mole hill and also spoil any chance of gaining our brother but rather of defeating him. This is always the real temptation, to nurture the offense.

Humility and restraint and love for our brother, on the other hand, lead us to bite our tongue and go in private to him or her alone and first. While this may maximize our discomfort, it minimizes our offender's. We give our brother or sister the best chance to repent without everyone else knowing; it is actually a gift given. Our brother only has to deal with us and God and not everyone else. As well, Jesus asks us to focus on the "fault" and not the person. We have the responsibility to judge the sin and not the sinner.

But there is a potential place to stumble here. What do repentance and forgiveness have to do with why we try to avoid this righteous path of conflict resolution? What if our brother does repent when we show the fault to him or her? Now the ball is in our court; for we should forgive and have no excuse not to. If we run to everyone else first, we do not have to worry about forgiving, instead we get revenge. Or even more what if in going to our brother we find out we also have something for which to repent? Now it is we who must ask for forgiveness. What do we actually want, to gain our brother and solve the problem or to further grieve our brother and the Holy Spirit and gain the sympathy of others?

Further Steps and Practical Applications

Beyond this Jesus does add further steps. Of note is that, as the circle widens, it also stays within the church of believers, and it is still aimed at restoring trust. The design is to encourage private conviction, repentance, forgiveness, restitution, and restoration. This works in any personal situation; but it also works as a community practice.

What would happen if a whole school (students, teachers, administrators, office staff, parents, and board members) followed this path as a truth-learning community? What does this path do to malicious gossip for example? As a community this works best when it is a two way street by mutual pact.

For instance, the administrators promise the teachers to do two things. First, if they take offense at a teacher's action, they will speak to no one else about their offense before they first go directly to the offending teacher to try to gain back their fellowship through repentance and forgiveness.

Second and in parallel, they promise not to hear a complaint from anyone, including other teachers, parents, or students, unless that person has proven to them that they have first gone to the teacher themselves in private to attempt to gain them back through repentance and forgiveness. If someone comes and starts, they promise to stop them and turn them to the teacher first and let them know that will not listen until they have done so. This is very reassuring to the teachers, and it shows them love in action, but there is a second side to this street. In return the teachers pledge to do the same for the administrators.

If an administrator offends them, before they say a word to anyone else, they go directly to the offending administrator in private to try to gain back their fellowship through repentance and forgiveness. Second, they also promise not to hear a complaint from anyone, including other teachers, parents, or students, unless that person has first gone to the administrator themselves to attempt to gain them back through repentance and forgiveness. If someone comes and starts, they promise to stop them and turn them to the administrator first and let them know that will not listen until they have done so. This is also very reassuring to the administrators, and it shows them love in action as well!

But why stop here, why not make the same pact between teachers and students, and students and teachers. Then there are pacts between staff and parents, and parents and staff, board members and constituents and constituents and board members, coaches and players, and the lists can go on. And what then happens to the scourge of gossip and concomitantly the loosing of our brothers and sisters when this is done as a whole, truth-learning community?

1 Timothy 5:13 And besides they learn to be idle, wandering about from house to house, and not only idle but also **gossip**s and busybodies, saying things which they ought not.

Proverbs 16:28 A perverse man stirs up dissension, and a **gossip** separates close friends. NIV

Proverbs 26:20 Without wood a fire goes out; without **gossip** a quarrel dies down. NIV

Again, this is not just theory. I have made these pacts with board members, staff, teachers, parents, and students, and they work. I also had to go and ask forgiveness when I slipped and broke the very pact I asked for, but this is itself part of the process. It takes great effort to break a gossip/revenge/victim culture within a community, but it is well worth the efforts of all. This is a win, win. Gaining our brothers and sisters in the unity of the Spirit as often as possible is the result. Jesus knows what He is talking about!

So here is another divide, humbly and graciously winning your brother in private through humility, conviction, repentance and forgiveness or pridefully losing your brother through gossip and self-righteousness vindication. A whole community can learn either side of this divide with the God ordained consequences of each! It is our choice. May God stir up our convictions, forgive our misgivings, and deliver us in His mercy and grace from evil to His honor and glory.

Chapter 21: What Should Christian Schools Teach about History, Israel, And the Jewish People?

Why is this, an important question? The short answer is because it is important to God as He makes very clear in His word. I personally can recall the late Jerry Falwell at an ACSI convention in the 1980s in Northern California. He was the keynote, convention speaker. He spoke on a list of tough, moral issues upon which Christian schools could not compromise. The crowd was with him, salty point by salty point. When he came to standing up for Israel and the issue of anti-Semitism, the tensions and, yes, even uncomfortable spiritual opposition in the room noticeably rose, but to his great credit it did not deter him. As a Jewish believer in the audience, I was very humbled, predictably saddened at the spiritual opposition, and also very blessed by his courage.

When we speak of spiritual warfare, there are few issues where demons more bare their teeth than the God ordained, prophetic place of the Jewish people; yet, as we will see, this is because this topic is very close to God's heart and to His integrity, as well as to His purposeful plan for history. Trying to terminate the Jewish people or to bring down Israel and stop God's prophetic clock is Satan's last stand. So expect some especially difficult, spiritual testing as you read this chapter.

Genesis 12:1-3 Now the LORD had said to Abram: "Get out of your country, from your family and from your father's house, to a land that I will show you. **2** I will make you a great nation; I will bless you and make your name great; And you shall be a blessing. **3** I will bless those who bless you, and I will curse him who curses you; And in you all the families of the earth shall be blessed."

Genesis 17:7-8 And I will establish My covenant between Me and you and your descendants after you in their generations, for an everlasting covenant, to be God to you and your descendants after you. 8 Also I give to you and your descendants after you the land in which you are a stranger, all the land of Canaan, as an everlasting possession; and I will be their God."

Genesis 17:19 Then God said: "No, Sarah your wife shall bear you a son, and you shall call his name Isaac; I will establish My covenant with him for an everlasting covenant, *and* with his descendants after him.

It is clear that God made a covenant with Abraham through Isaac and the land of Israel that is "everlasting." This was the beginning of the Jewish people. It is God Who makes this everlasting covenant special, not the Jewish people. It is God's choice and anointing, not their flesh. The everlasting covenant holds because of Him, not them; but it holds nonetheless! His integrity is involved; His integrity is on the line here.

Romans 11 *I say then, has God cast away His people? Certainly not! For I also am an Israelite, of the seed of Abraham, of* the tribe of Benjamin. 2 God has not cast away His people whom He foreknew. Or do you not know what the Scripture says of Elijah, how he pleads with God against Israel, saying, 3 *"LORD, they have killed Your prophets and torn down Your altars, and I alone am left, and they seek my life"*? 4 But what does the divine response say to him? *"I have reserved for Myself seven thousand men who have not bowed the knee to Baal."* 5 Even so then, at this present time there is a remnant according to the election of grace. 6 And if by grace, then *it is* no longer of works; otherwise grace is no longer grace. But if *it is* of works, it is no longer grace; otherwise work is no longer work.
7 What then? Israel has not obtained what it seeks; but the elect have obtained it, and the rest were blinded. 8 Just as it is written:
"God has given them a spirit of stupor, Eyes that they should not see And ears that they should not hear, To this very day."
9 And David says: *"Let their table become a snare and a trap, A stumbling block and a recompense to them. 10 Let their eyes be darkened, so that they do not see, And bow down their back always."* 11 I say then, have they stumbled that they should fall? Certainly not! But through their fall, to provoke them to jealousy, salvation *has come* to the Gentiles. 12 Now if their fall *is* riches for the world, and their failure riches for the Gentiles, how much more their fullness!
13 For I speak to you Gentiles; inasmuch as I am an apostle to the Gentiles, I magnify my ministry, 14 if by any means I may provoke to jealousy *those who are* my flesh and save some of them. 15 For if their being cast away *is* the reconciling of the world, what *will* their acceptance *be* but life from the dead?
16 For if the firstfruit *is* holy, the lump *is* also *holy;* and if the root *is* holy, so *are* the branches. 17 And if some of the branches were broken off, and you, being a wild olive tree, were grafted in among them, and with them became a partaker of the root and fatness of the olive tree, 18 do not boast against the branches. But if

you do boast, *remember that* you do not support the root, but the root *supports* you.

19 You will say then, "Branches were broken off that I might be grafted in." 20 Well *said.* Because of unbelief they were broken off, and you stand by faith. Do not be haughty, but fear. 21 For if God did not spare the natural branches, He may not spare you either.

22 Therefore consider the goodness and severity of God: on those who fell, severity; but toward you, goodness, if you continue in *His* goodness. Otherwise you also will be cut off. 23 And they also, if they do not continue in unbelief, will be grafted in, for God is able
to graft them in again. 24 For if you were cut out of the olive tree which is wild by nature, and were grafted contrary to nature into a cultivated olive tree, how much more will these, who *are* natural *branches,* be grafted into their own olive tree?

25 For I do not desire, brethren, that you should be ignorant of this mystery, lest you should be wise in your own opinion, that blindness in part has happened to Israel until the fullness of the Gentiles has come in. 26 And so all Israel will be saved, as it is written:
" *The Deliverer will come out of Zion, And He will turn away ungodliness from Jacob; 27 For this is My covenant with them, When I take away their sins."*

28 Concerning the gospel *they are* enemies for your sake, but concerning the election *they are* beloved for the sake of the fathers. 29 For the gifts and the calling of God *are* irrevocable. 30 For as you were once disobedient to God, yet have now obtained mercy through their disobedience, 31 even so these also have now been disobedient, that through the mercy shown you they also may obtain mercy. 32 For God has committed them all to disobedience, that He might have mercy on all.

33 Oh, the depth of the riches both of the wisdom and knowledge of God! How unsearchable *are* His judgments and His ways past finding out!
34 *"For who has known the mind of the LORD? Or who has become His counselor?"* 35 *"Or who has first given to Him, And it shall be repaid to him?"*
36 For of Him and through Him and to Him *are* all things, to whom *be* glory forever. Amen.

Romans is a very popular book amongst contemporary preachers, yet this section is most often overlooked. It is the Holy Spirit using a Jewish apostle to the Gentiles to explain God's dealings with the Jewish people to the Roman believers, Gentiles par excellence! His explanation is humbling for both Jews and Gentiles and is full of warnings about pride and conceit and also full of praise for the mercy and grace of God's goodness. God is not done yet!

Replacement Theology

Unfortunately there is presently a popular teaching among some Christians called replacement theology. It is most likely popular because it appeals to spiritual pride, which is not only perilous, but should also be an automatic red flag to the true, Christian believer. Basically its teaching is that dumb Israel failed, so God has now chosen a new chosen people, smart us! God has thrown Israel under the bus and has chosen you instead. Our church has replaced Israel. A scripture often quoted by these misguided folks is:

Acts 13:46 Then Paul and Barnabas grew bold and said, "It was necessary that the word of God should be spoken to you first; but since you reject it, and judge yourselves unworthy of everlasting life, behold, we turn to the Gentiles.

This scripture, however, is about some specific Jews in a specific place and time, and yet it is falsely, pridefully, and perversely universalized to say that God is permanently through with all the Jewish people for all time. But Paul was speaking about a specific group of Jewish people in a specific place! This is made obvious by the first verse of the next chapter in the chronologically written Book of Acts.

Acts 14:1 Now it happened in Iconium that they went together to the synagogue of the Jews, and so spoke that a great multitude both of the Jews and of the Greeks believed.

If Acts 13:46 is meant to be universal and permanent, why Acts 14:1 which follows it? So, how could something so obvious be ignored? Being wise in our own eyes is a great temptation! I have sadly heard so many sermons in many different denominations that exhibit this attitude. It portrays the Jews as failures and the replacing us, as the church, as great successes! How could the Jews have been and now be so blind, it goes?

This is very sad. It is not that the Jews did not fail often trying to hypocritically live out the law in their prideful flesh as the Bible makes abundantly clear, but they also humbly succeeded often in the Spirit!

Derek Prince again makes this clear in his booklet, *Our Debt to Israel* (1984). Consider this, without the Jews, we would not have the Old Testament, nor the New Testament, nor the Ten Commandments, nor the patriarchs, nor King David and his throne for Jesus to return to, nor the prophets, nor the apostles, nor the apostle to the Gentiles, Paul, nor the original spread of the Gospel, nor John the Baptist, nor Mary, nor even Jesus!

"But if you do boast, *remember that* you do not support the root, but the root *supports* you." So just how badly have the Jews failed? How much of our faith would exist without the Jews?

While it is clear that, with a few exceptions like Nicodemus and Joseph of Arimathea and a contingent of the wives of some of the high officials, the Jewish religious and political leadership of His time spurned Jesus as a threat to their earthly power; this is not so, however, of the common Jewish people.

Mark 12:37b And the common people heard Him gladly.

It is also true that large numbers of Jews became believers after the resurrection and thus helped to found the church and to spread the Gospel.

Acts 21:20a And when they heard it, they glorified the Lord, and said unto him, Thou seest, brother, how many thousands of Jews there are which believe; (KJV)

I do not know what "how many thousands" means, but it seems quite illogical that it would be 6 or 7 thousand or even 60 or 70 thousand, but more likely it would refer to something for instance like 600 or 700 thousand which would be a huge number in that day's demographic context! For this is not a few thousand, nor several thousand, but "many thousands!" The point is that the Jewish leaders rejected Jesus, but the Jewish people did not! You do not hear this idea much in the Gentile churches of our day and certainly not from the sad and self righteous, replacement theologians!

Now let us consider in comparison how successful the New Testament church has been: a billion and a quarter Muslims going to hell, another billion atheistic communists and humanists in China, another billion Hindus in India, an apostate Europe, North America, and South America, all fading fast, and a totally un-unified, lukewarm church with hundreds of warring denominations and factions and continual cultural retreats in the face of rabid, supposed secularism and other progressivist, humanist, false religions!

How about all the wars in Europe fought between Christian nations? How about the church's horrifying retreat from and/or treatment of the Jewish people in inquisitions, crusades, pogroms, and concentration/death camps over the centuries? Has the church always behaved Christianly? Were Hitler, Chamberlain, Mussolini, and Stalin products of Christian nations? The point is there is plenty of failure as well as success to go around for both Israel and the Church.

"For God has committed them all to disobedience, that He might have mercy on all." The temporary, partial blindness of the Jews is actually a gift of opportunity from God to the Gentiles, not something with which to ridicule the Jews or with which to minimize their contributions to us all. "I say then, have they stumbled that they should fall? Certainly not! But through their fall, to provoke them to jealousy, salvation *has come* to the Gentiles. 12 Now if their fall *is* riches for the world, and their failure riches for the Gentiles, how much more their fullness!" God is not through with Israel nor the Jews; in fact they are His prophetic, time clock for us all. Their prophetic "fullness" will be a blessing to all who believe!

I am painfully aware that regarding the Gospel, for our sakes, the secular Jews are often our enemies, as are, by the way, the secular Gentiles for that matter. Some secular Jews have done great damage to our culture. Freud, Marx, and Madeline O'Hara come to mind, and the ACLU and Hollywood are full of others and the list is long; "but concerning the election *they are* beloved for the sake of the fathers. 29 For the gifts and the calling of God *are* irrevocable." Consider, moreover, just how good would God's promises to us, His church, be, if His "everlasting" covenant to the Jews and Israel means nothing? Thank God, God is not done yet with Israel or the church!

"For I do not desire, brethren, that you should be ignorant of this mystery, lest you should be wise in your own opinion, that blindness in part has happened to Israel until the fullness of the Gentiles has come in. 26 And so all Israel will be saved."

How many times have I reread this scripture?! Clearly the blindness will come off, the failure ends, and this is connected to a full number of saved Gentiles coming in, which number only God knows. Also only God knows what "and so all Israel will be saved" means. It is obviously clear, however, that He is not yet done. When I got saved 40 years ago, there were a handful of Jewish Christians hidden here and there in Europe and America and around the world, and there were basically none in Israel.

The explosion of Jewish believers over this past generation is a little discussed phenomenon; secular and religious Jews either pretend it is not happening or treat it as a scourge, and Gentile Christians often more or less ignore it as well. Now, however, estimates in America and Europe are as high as a 250,000 Christians with Jewish backgrounds (Jews for Jesus), and Israeli TV (Mabat- Israel, Channel 1 TV) estimates that there are 20,000 Messianic believers of Jewish descent in Israel, Israeli Jewish Christians!

This is prophecy being fulfilled right before our eyes! "For if their being cast away *is* the reconciling of the world, what *will* their acceptance *be* but life from the dead?" After personally visiting Israel in 2009, I can attest to the fact that God is moving among the Israelis including the founding of fledgling Christian schools for the children of Jewish believers and their Gentile brethren! We should take heart in this!

The Mystery of Anti-Semitism

Have you ever wondered at the mystery of anti-Semitism? Israel is the size of Rhode Island and has only 5 million Jews in its population. Driving from top to bottom is like driving from Santa Barbara to San Diego in Southern California. What happens in Rhode Island regularly that continually keeps the world's leaders' attentions as well as the U.N.? Finland, Turkmenistan, and Kyrgyzstan also have a population of roughly 5 million, how many U.N. resolutions are there concerning them? There are 250 times as many Muslims, 1.25 billion, in the world than Israelis. There are also 13.2 million Jews total in the whole world out of a population of 6.6 billion people. That is roughly 1 Jew for every 500 non Jews, 1/500th of the people on the planet. "I will make you a great nation" from Genesis is obviously not meant solely numerically.

But consider the world influence of say Abraham, Moses, David, Jesus, Mary, and John, Peter, and Paul. Add to this Albert Einstein, Sigmund Freud, or Karl Marx, or the fame of Spinoza, Mahler, Maimonides, Bohr, Mendelssohn, Disraeli, Kafka, Rothschild, Gompers, Mayer, Durkheim, Gershwin, Bernstein, Brandeis, Bernhardt, Strauss (as in Levis), Buber, Salk, Kissinger, Miller, Pasternak, Spielberg, Chagall, or even Dylan (Zimmerman!). Of course Jesus alone is more than enough. Why so much from such a small people? How many influential and famous people from Finland, Turkmenistan, and Kyrgyzstan do you know?

Then there is the history to consider. Egypt, Babylon, Medes, Persians, Assyrians, Philistines, Canaanites, Crusaders, Spanish Inquisitors, Russian pogroms, Nazi death camps, and now the Iranians with nuclear bombs, and Saudi Arabian Wahabi-ism with its oil riches and blackmail, who can explain such constant attempts at annihilation of so small a people in so small a country over so many millennia of history in simple human history terms? It is neither logical nor natural.

Revelation 12 Now a great sign appeared in heaven: a woman clothed with the sun, with the moon under her feet, and on her head a garland of twelve stars. 2 Then being with child, she cried out in labor and in pain to give birth. 3 And another sign appeared in heaven: behold, a great, fiery red dragon having seven heads and ten horns, and seven diadems on his heads. 4 His tail drew a third of the stars of heaven and threw them to the earth. And the dragon stood before the woman who was ready to give birth, to devour her Child as soon as it was born. 5 She bore a male Child who was to rule all nations with a rod of iron. And her Child was caught up to God and His throne. 6 Then the woman fled into the wilderness, where she has a place prepared by God, that they should feed her there one thousand two hundred and sixty days.
7 And war broke out in heaven: Michael and his angels fought with the dragon; and the dragon and his angels fought, 8 but they did not prevail, nor was a place found for them in heaven any longer. 9 So the great dragon was cast out, that serpent of old, called the Devil and Satan, who deceives the whole world; he was cast to the earth, and his angels were cast out with him.
10 Then I heard a loud voice saying in heaven, "Now salvation, and strength, and the kingdom of our God, and the power of His Christ have come, for the accuser of our brethren, who accused them before our God day and night, has been cast down. 11 And they overcame him by the blood of the Lamb and by the word of their testimony, and they did not love their lives to the death. 12 Therefore rejoice, O heavens, and you who dwell in them! Woe to the inhabitants of the earth and the sea! For the devil has come down to you, having great wrath, because he knows that he has a short time." 13 Now when the dragon saw that he had been cast to the earth, he persecuted the woman who gave birth to the male *Child.* 14 But the woman was given two wings of a great eagle, that she might fly into the wilderness to her place, where she is nourished for a time and times and half a time, from the presence of the serpent. 15 So the serpent spewed water out of his mouth like a flood after the woman, that he might cause her to be carried away by the flood. 16 But the earth helped the woman, and the earth opened its mouth and swallowed up the flood which the dragon had spewed out

of his mouth. 17 And the dragon was enraged with the woman, and he went to make war with the rest of her offspring, who keep the commandments of God and have the testimony of Jesus Christ.

The woman with the sun and the moon and the twelve stars is from Genesis 37:9 and is clearly symbolic of the twelve patriarchs and tribes of Israel, the fountain of the Jewish people.

Genesis 37:9   Then he dreamed still another dream and told it to his brothers, and said, "Look, I have dreamed another dream. And this time, the sun, the moon, and the eleven stars bowed down to me."

The child caught up to God's throne who will rule all nations with an iron rod can only be Jesus. The woman who gave birth to the child can only be Israel, the Jewish people, through whom Jesus incarnated.

John 4:22   You worship what you do not know; we know what we worship, for **salvation is** of the **Jews**.

And this is why the dragon is enraged with the women and her offspring, the followers of Moses and of Jesus. Satan knows that Jesus is his demise, and he hates the women because she brought Him forth in obedience to God. Satan also keeps trying to thwart God's plan of salvation, and he especially hates the peoples through whom God has fulfilled and is still fulfilling this plan.

This is the source of the irrational persecutions of anti-Semitism that have scared human history and made otherwise seemingly rational people totally insane. It cannot be explained in natural terms because it is supernatural. Its source is the father of all liars and murderers. The war is in heaven as well as on earth. Through all this suffering, however, the resurrection and the fulfillment are the victory. I speak of course of the resurrection of Jesus, our Savior, His victory over Satan and Death at the cross and the empty tomb and His triumphal soon return.

Yet there is another resurrection that has prophetically taken place right before our eyes that defies all the laws of merely human history; and that is the modern nation of Israel. No other people in the history of mankind have mainly lost their land, lost their spoken language, and been scatter throughout the world for nearly two thousand years without losing their identity. But that is only half of it; no other people have then returned to their land (and against such amazing odds and opposition) and resurrected their dead language and their lost sovereignty.

Moses and Elijah (Revelations 11) will understand the Hebrew spoken on the streets of Israel today. It would be akin to the Italians deciding to start speaking Latin again after it has not been used for centuries as a daily spoken language! Israel is a prophetic resurrection, which is another reason why Satan so hates it; she constantly reminds him of Jesus and his own defeat at the cross and the empty tomb and also of the Lord's soon return to reclaim what is His, the Earth, and David's throne!

King of the Jews

Consider the question asked by the Magi (Matthew 2:2), the title on the sign which Pilot put on the cross (Matthew 27:37), and the identity of the resurrected Lion of Judah eternally in heaven (Revelation 5:5).

Luke 23:3 Then Pilate asked Him, saying, "Are You the **King** of the **Jews**?" He answered him and said, "It is as you say."

Jesus was born, crucified, and resurrected, "**King of the Jews**." He is forever identified with them. He is the most Jewish Jew to ever live, the King of the Jews! Therefore one cannot be an anti-Semite and be a Christian; it is impossible.

There are many ways of seeing or levels of understanding just who *the sheep* and *the goat* nations and *the least of these My brethren* are in Matthew 25:31-46 where Jesus brings each nation under judgment upon His return; but one inescapable one, from what we have seen above, is how people treat the nation Israel and the Jewish people, Jesus' brethren. "I will bless those who bless you, and I will curse him who curses you." It is clear Satan is on one side of this line and Jesus on the other. Whose side are we on? Whose side are we teaching our students to be on and how and why?

Psalm 122:6 Pray for the peace of Jerusalem: "May they prosper who love you."

When we pray for the peace of Jerusalem, for what are we really praying?

Zechariah 12:2-3 "Behold, I will make Jerusalem a cup of drunkenness to all the surrounding peoples, when they lay siege against Judah and Jerusalem. 3 And it shall happen in that day that I will make Jerusalem a very heavy stone for all peoples; all who would heave it away will surely be cut in pieces, though all nations of the earth are gathered against it."

This certainly sounds like current world history; who can solve the Middle East problem, the Jerusalem problem, the one national capital the peoples of the earth will not recognize? The world looks to human politics and eventually will look to the anti-Christ, Satan's puppet disguised as a peace loving, religious secularist, to answer these questions; but the real answer is the return of Jesus!

So, when we pray for the peace of Jerusalem, we are really praying for His return, because there will be no real peace in Jerusalem or Israel or the world until then. Not that this absolves us of standing by His brethren now; but only Jesus solves the Middle East problem!

Acts 1:6-11   Therefore, when they had come together, they asked Him, saying, "Lord, will You at this time restore the kingdom to Israel?" 7 And He said to them, "It is not for you to know times or seasons which the Father has put in His own authority. 8 But you shall receive power when the Holy Spirit has come upon you; and you shall be witnesses to Me in Jerusalem, and in all Judea and Samaria, and to the end of the earth."

9 Now when He had spoken these things, while they watched, He was taken up, and a cloud received Him out of their sight. 10 And while they looked steadfastly toward heaven as He went up, behold, two men stood by them in white apparel, 11 who also said, "Men of Galilee, why do you stand gazing up into heaven? This *same* Jesus, who was taken up from you into heaven, will so come in like manner as you saw Him go into heaven."

The clear reading of this scripture, Jesus' last words before taking His place at the right hand of the Father in heaven, is that the kingdom will be restored to Israel, but in the Father's timing when this same Jesus will return "in like manner" to this same spot in Israel. Jesus will sit on David's throne! In the meanwhile the job of those Jewish believers and us who have been grafted in by extension was and still is to become filled with the Holy Spirit's power and then share the Gospel as a witness to Jesus from Jerusalem to the ends of the earth. This job holds to the end of this harvesting age.

The second coming will be the fulfillment of the second half of Jesus' mission statement. In the meantime, we must keep our eyes and our hearts on Israel as well as the full number of the Gentiles to come in; Jesus is. This is not either/or; it is both/and. If Jesus keeps His word to Abraham, Isaac, Jacob, Moses, and David, He will also keep it to you and me as well! Of course the inverse of this would also be true. If God would break His promises to the Jews, why would we believe He would keep them to us? Moreover, the land of Israel has miraculously had the continuous and faithful presence of the Jewish people for thousands of years even if only as a remnant at various times (Grobman, 2010), yet the world would try to convince us that the land belongs to Palestinian Muslims who despised it until the Jews returned and not to the ones to whom God has given it. But God keeps His promises!

Christian Education and Israel

Why is all this important to a truly Christian education? There are at least six reasons. First, God will bless those that bless Israel and curse those who curse her, including our schools! Second, this is a key issue in our times; we cannot walk in the prophetic ministry of Jesus by ignoring it or getting it wrong in order to be politically correct or spiritually proud.

Third, it makes the Bible alive and relevant to our students in their times, not just a book of ancient history! Fourth, we must prepare our students to fight the lies of the spirit of the anti-Christ while we are still here. Fifth, remember the importance to this generation of the second half of Jesus' mission statement. Sixth, we must teach our students to look forward to His return, the hope of glory, the helmet that protects our sanity in a world dominated by Mystery Babylon.

2 Peter 3:1-4 Beloved, I now write to you this second epistle (in *both of* which I stir up your pure minds by way of reminder), 2 that you may be mindful of the words which were spoken before by the holy prophets, and of the commandment of us, the apostles of the Lord and Savior, 3 **knowing this first**: that scoffers will come in the last days, walking according to their own lusts, 4 and saying, "Where is the promise of His coming? For since the fathers fell asleep, all things continue as *they were* from the beginning of creation."

It is another great divide between supposedly secular education and truly Christian education; is God in control of history or man or a meaningless, evolving or devolving, material universe? Who is running the show? Are we purposefully designed in the image of God or a chance accident of Mother Nature? How we answer this question for ourselves and our students is crucial to their faith. King, Priest, and Prophet, they are inseparable, the whole Jesus for the whole student, spirit, soul, and body! May God stir up our convictions, forgive our misgivings, and deliver us in His mercy and grace from evil to His honor and glory.

Chapter 22: How is Meditative Learning a Christian Pedagogy?

Psalm 1:1-3   Blessed *is* the man who walks not in the counsel of the ungodly, nor stands in the path of sinners, nor sits in the seat of the scornful; But his delight *is* in the law of the LORD, And in His law he **meditates** day and night. He shall be like a tree planted by the rivers of water, That brings forth its fruit in its season, Whose leaf also shall not wither; And whatever he does shall prosper.

The counsel of the *ungodly* can be thought of in two ways; first is a person who in rebellion purposely counsels against the Godly way, but another is counsel that simply leaves God out, that is God-less, that does not give God His rightful place perhaps out ignorance or cowardliness. Standing in the path of sinners and sitting in the seat of the scornful also does not bring a blessing. These are apt descriptions of postmodern, supposedly secular education, opposing, mocking, and ignoring God. The contrast is delighting and meditating in God's word and Spirit, a God-filled education, drinking deeply, producing fruit, and prospering in Godliness!

Deuteronomy 18:9   When you enter the land the Lord your God is giving you, do not learn to imitate the detestable ways of the nations there.

Eastern or Biblical

So what is meditating? The root word is connected to median and medicine. It connotes the center, the middle, the core and thus medicine that reaches the heart of the matter. Interestingly the Biblical understanding of meditation has been replaced by the false, Eastern religious understanding in our apostate culture. These understandings are diametric opposites. To Eastern mysticism, meditating means emptying one's mind and spirit in order to experience nothingness. Biblical meditation, however, is filling your mind and spirit with the truth of God's word, chewing on it, digesting it, letting it sink into your core as medicine, planting and watering its seed, letting it grow within you. Emptying yourself or filling yourself with God so He can transform you; these are completely different visions of reality!

Genesis 24:63   And Isaac went out to **meditate** in the field in the evening; and he lifted his eyes and looked, and there, the camels were coming.

What does meditating on God, His Word, and His works in a quiet place have to do with receiving His best for us, in this case, Rebecca!?

Joshua 1:8   This Book of the Law shall not depart from your mouth, but you shall **meditate** in it day and night, that you may observe to do according to all that is written in it. For then you will make your way prosperous, and then you will have good success.

What does meditating on God, His Word, and His works have to do with our obedience, prosperity, and good success?

Psalm 1:2   But his delight is in the law of the LORD, and in His law he **meditate**s day and night.

What does meditating on God, His Word, and His works have to do with our delight in His laws?

Psalm 4:4   Be angry, and do not sin. **Meditate** within your heart on your bed, and be still. Selah

What does meditating on God, His Word, and His works have to do with our ability to overcome angry temptation and find peace?

Psalm 63:6   When I remember You on my bed, I **meditate** on You in the night watches.

What does meditating on God, His Word, and His works have to do with our remembering God in quiet rest?

Psalm 77:6   I call to remembrance my song in the night; I **meditate** within my heart, and my spirit makes diligent search.

What does meditating on God, His Word, and His works have to do with our heartfelt private worship and our diligent spiritual search?

Psalm 77:12   I will also **meditate** on all Your work, and talk of Your deeds.

What does meditating on God, His Word, and His works have to do with our speaking of God's deeds to others?

Psalm 119:15   I will **meditate** on Your precepts, and contemplate Your ways.

What does meditating on God, His Word, and His works have to do with our Godly contemplations of His ways?

Psalm 119:27   Make me understand the way of your precepts; so shall I **meditate** on Your wonderful works.

What does meditating on God, His Word, and His works have to do with our understanding God's ways and wonderful works?

Psalm 119:48   My hands also I will lift up to Your commandments, which I love, and I will **meditate** on Your statutes.

What does meditating on God, His Word, and His works have to do with our loving and honoring God's commandments?

Psalm 119:78   Let the proud be ashamed, for they treated me wrongfully with falsehood; but I will **meditate** on Your precepts.

What does meditating on God, His Word, and His works have to do with our being able to deal rightly with those who are proud and treat us wrongly or falsely?

Psalm 119:148   My eyes are awake through the night watches, that I may **meditate** on Your word.

What does meditating on God, His Word, and His works have to do with seeing God even in the darkness?

Psalm 143:5   I remember the days of old; I **meditate** on all Your works; I muse on the work of Your hands.

What does meditating on God, His Word, and His works have to do with our being able to muse upon His work rightly and remember the days of old.

Psalm 145:5   I will **meditate** on the glorious splendor of Your majesty, and on Your wondrous works.

What does meditating on God, His Word, and His works have to do with our seeing His glory and splendor and majesty?

Malachi 3:16   Then those who feared the LORD spoke to one another, and the LORD listened and heard them; So a book of remembrance was written before Him For those who fear the LORD and who **meditate** on His name.

What does meditating on God, His Word, and His works have to do with our being in God's book of remembrance?

Philippians 4:8   Finally, brethren, whatever things are true, whatever things are noble, whatever things are just, whatever things are pure, whatever things are lovely, whatever things are of good report, if there is any virtue and if there is anything praiseworthy — **meditate** on these things.

1 Timothy 4:15   **Meditate** on these things; give yourself entirely to them, that your progress may be evident to all.

As Christian school educators: What do we put in the *medi*, the middle, of our thinking? What do we put in the middle of our hearts? What do we put in the middle of our spirits? What do we put in the middle of our curricula? What do we put in the middle of our teaching and learning? This is not just the beginning and the end, but also the middle, the core, the heart!

How is meditating different; rather than just hearing, reading, memorizing, or recollecting? Is this just a prayer at the beginning and/or a dessert at the end, or the whole meal of a lesson? Moreover how does this relate to Bloom's cognitive taxonomy (Bloom, 1956) looking at the what, the how, and the why of our learning? What would a meditative pedagogy look like? Certainly a meditative pedagogy would be deep learning, much more than just surface knowing. It would include knowledge, understanding, application, analysis, synthesis, and evaluation.   I think Benjamin Bloom, as a Jew, saw this; he had apparently simply lost the content, God's living word.

Christian education ought to shine when it comes to the why questions and our curricula and lessons. Theology is at the heart of why. It is what fills the empty void of supposedly secular education.

Matthew 12:44-46   "When an unclean spirit goes out of a man, he goes through dry places, seeking rest, and finds none. [44] Then he says, 'I will return to my house from which I came.' And when he comes, he finds *it* empty, swept, and put in order. [45] Then he goes and takes with him seven other spirits more wicked than himself, and they enter and dwell there; and the last *state* of that man is worse than the first. So shall it also be with this wicked generation."

Emptying ourselves is not enough; we must also then fill ourselves with what is of the Holy Spirit, with what is Godly. Again, this is why Biblical meditation is so different from eastern or mystical meditation.

Hebrews 4:12 For the word of God *is* living and powerful, and sharper than any two-edged sword, piercing even to the division of soul and spirit, and of joints and marrow, and is a discerner of the thoughts and intents of the heart.

A meditative pedagogy has the Word alive and powerful and as a discerner and filler of the thoughts and intents of the heart, medicine for the middle of our being. This must be personally deep learning, heart learning, personally applied learning. Learning that is meditative works in deepening circles of truth, not just surface knowledge; it is loaded with value and values, the very character of God. It is also loaded with conviction and repentance and forgiveness and restitution and restoration. It also focuses on bringing glory to God by faith and obedience and love.

A meditative pedagogy is poetic and beautiful and wholesome and full of joy and even Godly sorrow. It goes deeper and deeper until it gets it right, until it gets to the truth of it, the core value of it! It is anointed methodology, Christian methodology. Do we see this in our lessons? May God stir up our convictions, forgive our misgivings, and deliver us in His mercy and grace from evil to His honor and glory.

Chapter 23: Can Technology Help the Future of Christian Education?

This is an intriguing question. The confluence of financial realities within the contemporary economy, the growth of Christian home schooling, and the possibilities of regionally linked and shared high schools may give birth to new frontiers in Christian education. For instance, if four, 100-200 student high schools link up technologically, one French teacher could simultaneously teach, live and interactive over the internet, the students from all four schools, from perhaps a 600 student population, when none of the individual schools could afford French because of too small class sizes. Then each school would pay a quarter of the French teacher's salary or swap it with the availability of another subject area teacher. Physics, AP Chemistry, Calculus, even specialty Bible or history or literature classes could all be handled in similar fashion. So, as a student, another student against whom one competes on the basketball court might also be in his or her AP Spanish class! The technology for this is present and also constantly coming down in price. Of course humility and cooperation among schools of common vision would be a necessary prerequisite!

Even within a single school technology can greatly improve communication, a vital key to community building. The two words have a common root. Technology can have a large role in putting fathers back in charge and increasing their ability to parent responsibly. Emails, direct information access, and asynchronous responses can bring busy fathers back into the loop, closing the loopholes between parents, teachers, students, curricula, and Godly learning. As internet access becomes as ubiquitous as telephones, there is no excuse for not knowing and not being involved on a very up-to-date basis with proactive initiative from both sides. These communication and information access devises work in all directions between teachers, parents, students, and administrators. They can easily help grow Godly community.

Another possibility of new technology is breaking the grip of Caesar's schools and universities and their publishers over curriculum. Is the time coming when individually well done and spiritually integrated curriculum guides that go well beyond text books can be electronically traded, swapped, or bought and sold between quality Christian schools and thus by-passing ungodly, anti-Christian, agenda-pushing publishers altogether. Could this be a supplemental source of income for creative, Spirit lead, energetic Christian educators?

Paying Christian educators justly and also affording quality Christian education for economically distressed families are important issues. Can technology help Christian schools and home schools form more effective hybrids? Finances are the number one stumbling block to many families who would prefer a Christian education. The Gallup Poll has shown for decades that many more families would choose a faith-based education if they did not have to unjustly pay double for it, taxes and tuition. Could technological collaboration among Christian schools and between these schools and home schoolers open new doors to help with these problems?

Jesus and Technology

Is Jesus pro or con technology? Can you picture Jesus asking his disciples to take Him just off shore in their boat in a half moon cove on the northwest end of the Sea of Galilee so the acoustics over the calm water would help Him reach the large crowd seated in the natural amphitheatre in the round on the shore hillside? You can actually see this kind of spot in Israel. Although we do not know of any books that Jesus may have written while here, the Holy Spirit clearly instructed His disciples to write the New Testament. Why?

Use of tools in a Godly manner for Godly content and Godly purposes is something Jesus does and blesses! We cannot afford the luxury of passing on these possibilities just because they are new; new wineskins for new wine! Furthermore the cooperation and unity among Christian ministries, true to the truth and the faith, that these efforts could bring about is another thing Jesus wants to and would bless. We are one body in Christ! Perhaps we should act like it! There is only one school in heaven, Jesus'.

Which Christian leaders will have the faith, courage, wisdom, and humility to take these vital steps? Our modern technology is no surprise to Jesus; He revealed it! May God stir up our convictions, forgive our misgivings, and deliver us in His mercy and grace from evil to His honor and glory.

Finally consider the Millennials generation we are now educating. Information technology is not a new toy to them; it is simply a ubiquitous part of their world. It is not going away; if we want to speak to them, we had best learn their language. It is the world they live in for better or worse. We must educate them how to live in it Christianly! We cannot stick our heads in the sand here; they need to learn truth and wisdom and understanding in the context of their times.

Chapter 24: Are Our Assessment Instruments for Students, Teachers, and Administrators Aligned with Our Mission Statements, Job Descriptions, and the Will of the Lord?

Assessment is where the proof is in the pudding for education; it shows both the inside and outside of the cup if done well. A key truth here is that what we assess is what our employees and teachers and students and parents will take seriously. Conversely what we do not assess is what our employees and teachers and students and parents will not take seriously. Assessment tells what we really think is important. Good assessment tools also guide us as to how to get where we are trying to go. They are both formative and summative in function; that is they both shape direction and goals as well as test whether or not they are being or have been reached. The Spirit speaking through Peter seems to suggest that there are certain virtues of spiritual development that can be measured.

II Peter 1:5-9   For this very reason, make every effort to add to your faith, goodness; and to goodness, knowledge; and to knowledge, self-control; and to self-control, perseverance; and to perseverance, godliness; and to godliness, brotherly kindness; and to brotherly kindness, love. For, **if you possess these qualities in increasing measure**, they will keep you from being ineffective and unproductive in your knowledge of our Lord Jesus Christ. But if anyone does not have them, he is nearsighted and blind, and has forgotten that he has been cleansed from his past sins.

So we must ask ourselves, do our assessment instruments and practices look like those of Jesus or like those of Caesar? Helping our teachers become the best Christian teachers they can become is one of the best gifts we can give our students and our families and our Lord! What kind of assessments we use is directly connected to these truths, for blessing or ill.

Do our assessment policies and instruments and practices call our teachers to become more like Jesus or more like Caesar? Are we serving a Caesar salad with a little Christian dressing on the side as an add-on or the bread and the wine of our communion with Jesus? Note that knowledge is only one eighth of Peter's measurable recipe!

1 Thessalonians 5:21 Test all things; hold fast what is good.

My experience at California Baptist University in my professorship with the leadership for faith-based schools, master's students and their representation of their respective schools from many differing denominations comes into play here. With over 60 Christian schools across Northern and Southern California, Nevada, Arizona, Utah, New Mexico, Texas, Missouri, Illinois, Alabama and Malawi and Sierra Leon, Africa represented thus far, I must humbly confess that it does not look like we take the alignment of our statements of faith, our mission statements, our job descriptions, and our assessment instruments and practices nor the full spiritual integration and foundation thereof as seriously as we ought to take them. Some Christian schools actually just use secular assessment instruments, or sometimes those very instruments with a couple of spiritual add-ons. These may be verbatim from a Godless and Spiritless, tax funded, school district or from state legislature standards or the tax funded university down the road where Jesus is an outlaw! Teaching is teaching, right? We must seriously ask ourselves how Jesus would answer that question! The implication from the above scripture is that "all things" can and should be tested and held, not just supposedly secular knowledge! The goal of testing is the goodness of God!

Romans 12:1-8 I beseech you therefore, brethren, by the mercies of God, that you present your bodies a living sacrifice, holy, acceptable to God, *which is* your reasonable service. **2** And do not be conformed to this world, but be transformed by the renewing of your mind, that you may prove what *is* that good and acceptable and perfect will of God. **3** For I say, through the grace given to me, to everyone who is among you, not to think *of himself* more highly than he ought to think, but to think soberly, as God has dealt to each one a measure of faith. **4** For as we have many members in one body, but all the members do not have the same function, **5** so we, *being* many, are one body in Christ, and individually members of one another. **6** Having then gifts differing according to the grace that is given to us, *let us use them:* if prophecy, *let us prophesy* in proportion to our faith; **7** or ministry, *let us use it* in *our* ministering; he who teaches, in teaching; **8** he who exhorts, in exhortation; he who gives, with liberality; he who leads, with diligence; he who shows mercy, with cheerfulness.

Mark 1:22   And they were astonished at His **teaching**, for He taught them as one having authority, and not as the scribes.

Matthew 15:9   And in vain they worship Me, **Teaching** as doctrines the commandments of men.

Teaching is a gift of grace from God, Who is Spirit; it is therefore a spiritual gift to be faithfully, spiritually, humbly, and yet authoritatively grown and used to bless the Body of Christ, including our Christian youth! The gift is not for vainly teaching the commandments of men as doctrine, as though they were truth and all that is needed for the successful, good life. Nor is the gift to be used in conformity to this world!

Christian teaching comes from a renewed and transformed mind that is focused on God's truth in the Spirit. Some have this spiritual gift of teaching, and some do not. Not everyone can be a teacher, especially a Christian or anointed teacher; it is a very complex calling and not an easy task or walk. But all who have the gift can be helped to open it up and to grow in it regardless of whether or not they possess worldly university degrees or state certificates. These might help or hinder, but they are not the heart of the matter.

James 3:1-2a   My brethren, let not many of you become teachers, knowing that you shall receive a stricter judgment. 2 For we all stumble in many things. If anyone does not stumble in word, he is a perfect man . . .

What teachers say and do not say, building up or stumbling themselves and their learners in and through their words, leads to the stricter judgment. What we teach matters! How and why we teach matters also! Jesus as our one Teacher never said what He should not have said and also never omitted to say what He should have said. He always spoke the truth, the whole truth, and nothing but the truth and did it in love! He was never politically correct! Helping teachers grow in their Christian teaching is a sacred calling and a humbling privilege. Two sins can be prevalent here: the commission of teachings lies and the omission of teaching truth! And the reason for these is sadly most often the desire to appease worldly Caesars and avoid the suffering that is necessary to bring the youth to Jesus in all their learning.

Two Problems

Two problems can also arise here. The first is simply a lack of commitment to partnership with the Holy Spirit in growing truly Christian teachers. Do we make it a priority? The older term *headmaster* literally meant *head master*, meaning the teacher of teachers, the leading teacher, or the head teacher. Principal can also be seen this way as in the principal teacher. Large, bureaucratic, tax funded, supposedly secularized schools have changed this to principals as administrators or institutional, bureaucratic managers. So much is lost here! This supposedly secularized version is not the role Jesus chose for Himself in His school! Jesus focuses on people, not institutions.

A key truth here is that the school leader does have a class of students; the leader's students are the teachers or the sub leaders of teachers in bigger schools. A corollary to this truth is that how the principal does or does not educate and assess the teachers in accordance with the school's mission sets an example for how the teachers will or will not educate and assess the students in accordance with the school's mission! The principal is to the teachers as the teachers are to the students; it is simple logic, which is also unfortunately not taught much anymore either!

Do principals look at the teachers as their class? Does the principal only help the teachers he or she likes? What is the example of this for a teacher and his or her students? Does the principal preoccupy themselves with other duties and neglect assessing and helping the teachers grow? What is the example of this for a teacher and his or her students? Does the principal only assess classroom management and lesson polish and technique through yearly visits and only student, knowledge attainment through supposedly secular, standardized testing? What is the example of this for a teacher and his or her students? Are bureaucracies, and unions, and the entrapment of tax dollars what Jesus died and rose again for? Was this His focus? And what is it now?

1 Peter 5:1-5   The elders who are among you I exhort, I who am a fellow elder and a witness of the sufferings of Christ, and also a partaker of the glory that will be revealed: 2 Shepherd the flock of God which is among you, serving as overseers, not by compulsion but willingly, not for dishonest gain but eagerly; 3 nor as being lords over those entrusted to you, but being examples to the flock; 4 and when the Chief Shepherd appears, you will receive the crown of glory that does not fade away.

The second problem is using assessment practices and tools that are badly mismatched to the stated mission and goals of the school. Regarding assessment, after noticing this missing- and mis- alignment, our CBU graduate course, EDL 535 Analysis of Teaching and Learning, has grown to focus on creating new lesson and teacher assessment instruments, policies, and practices. They focus on Christian outcomes and the aligning of statements of faith, mission statements, job descriptions and assessment instruments and practices to guide in the improvement of what we really should be all about in our schools, distinctly Christian teaching and learning. Again, if we only assess classroom management, lesson polish and secular technique, and even student, knowledge attainment, what message does this send our teachers and students and parents about what we consider to be important?

This is, however, not an either/or question.

Matthew 5:41   And whoever compels you to go one mile, go with him two.

Going beyond does not mean ignoring or simply replacing; you have to walk the first mile before you can walk the second one. But if we only walk the first mile, even if we do it better, we are saying the second one is irrelevant!

We can ask the related question, what happens when assessment practices, job descriptions, mission statements, and God's Word are or are not aligned? There is either integration of intents and outcomes or disintegration of intents and outcomes. Godly intents and goals mismatched to supposedly secular assessments will not get us where we want to go. Any program for teacher development, help, and improvement must have various forms of lesson, student products, and teacher methods evaluation to be personally meaningful to individual teacher's practice, where the tire meets the road (Good & Brophy, 2008).

This also requires a context of concepts and vocabulary and practiced practices shared by all involved; in our case a theologically and philosophically and Biblically sound, educational context of concepts and vocabulary and practices, founded upon and saturated in Biblical truth and all the virtues it breeds, as well as upon knowledge of teaching skills put into practice and student responses. And as stated above, these concepts and vocabulary and practices need to flow from our statements of faith through our mission statements and Godly goals through our job descriptions right down to our assessment and teacher development instruments and practices.

They need to be founded upon and full of truth and wisdom and a philosophy according to Christ as well as knowledge and technical skills. If not we will end up unwittingly instilling worldly values and practices in our teacher improvement programs which will undoubtedly filter into our students!

Matthew 7:13-14 & 18-20   "Enter by the narrow gate; for wide *is* the gate and broad *is* the way that leads to destruction, and there are many who go in by it. 14 Because narrow *is* the gate and difficult *is* the way which leads to life, and there are few who find it . . . 18 A good tree cannot bear bad fruit, nor *can* a bad tree bear good fruit. 19 Every tree that does not bear good fruit is cut down and thrown into the fire. 20 Therefore by their fruits you will know them.

Luke 13:6-9   He also spoke this parable: "A certain *man* had a fig tree planted in his vineyard, and he came seeking fruit on it and found none. 7 Then he said to the keeper of his vineyard, 'Look, for three years I have come seeking fruit on this fig tree and find none. Cut it down; why does it use up the ground?' 8 But he answered and said to him, 'Sir, let it alone this year also, until I dig around it and fertilize *it*. 9 And if it bears fruit, *well*. But if not, after that you can cut it down.'"

The broad way will not do here. It is Jesus who has the words of life. Growing truly Christian teachers and truly Christian teaching in a faculty and truly Christian curricula in a school, so as to grow truly Christian learning in the students, is a narrow gate and a difficult way. It is the way of Jesus, our Master Teacher. Assessment is by their fruits; in what ways did their students grow or not grow under their servant leadership? Can we see the mission of the school being fulfilled in his or her students? Do the students have the robustness, sweetness, productivity, and nourishment of Jesus in them?

Roots, Trees, Leaves, and Fruit

Interestingly enough this requires inspection of both the fruit and the tree, not just the leaves. Is the tree just taking up valuable ground purchased by the blood of Jesus? Does it have lots of outward leaves but no inward fruit? But before we go to cut it down, we must ask ourselves if we have gotten our hands dirty trying to help it produce?! Digging around the roots and fertilizing it (the Old King James says *dung it*) is hard and unpopular work, not to mention difficult for the tree itself to endure! It means breaking up hardened ground and exposing roots and adding sources of nourishment.

Many *administrators* would rather shuffle papers or even attend meetings! It also requires years of perseverance, diligence, and patient, loving involvement. You cannot dig around someone's roots while ignoring them! Digging around roots without breaking them off probably means getting down on our knees and prayerfully, carefully, and patiently loosening the hardened soil so the rain and nutrients just do not run off but rather sink in time after time. Then the fruit as well as the leaves will flourish! Interestingly, from the parable it takes the keeper to do this; it is hard for the tree to do it for itself! As teachers of teachers, like Jesus, are we not to do this as leaders in Christian education?

Psalm 1:2-3 But his delight *is* in the law of the LORD, and in His law he meditates day and night. 3 He shall be like a tree planted by the rivers of water that brings forth its fruit in its season, whose leaf also shall not wither; and whatever he does shall prosper.

And meditating together in God's word can change everything! His created word, His written word, His living Word, and His ever-present Word make the difference. They are medicine for the tree and thus for its fruit! But the word must be lovingly and diligently unwrapped and applied.

John 13:12 So when He had washed their feet, taken His garments, and sat down again, He said to them, "Do you know what I have done to you?

Washing disciples' feet, those who will carry on the daily teaching to the students, this is the example Jesus, our Lord and **Teacher**, left for us. Watch out, those feet can be very tired and sore and dirty, but Jesus knows that! Bring the word, break up the hardened ground, add nourishment, be patient yet firm, and tend to the roots not the leaves!

The leaves are helpful, but the roots bring forth the fruit. They are like the inside of the cup, the spirit and heart of the matter. This is what Jesus calls the teacher of teachers to do. If we do not want to be the teacher of teachers, perhaps we are the one taking up ground ourselves where someone else who is willing should be planted?!

1 Thessalonians 5:21   Test all things; hold fast what is good.

This summarizes the Godly purpose of assessment: find what is good and hold dearly to it and by implication discard what is evil. Is the goodness of God our assessment goal?

Ministering to the roots of the trees in His vineyard has interesting parallels to the washing of the disciples' feet, the example as our teacher of teachers that Jesus left for us! They both require humility, love, compassion, and personal gentleness. They also paint a picture of us on our knees.

Examples

Some professor edited examples of mission-aligned, assessment instruments from some previous CBU master's students are included in Appendix A by permission. They are shared here not as perfected examples, but as first attempts in the right direction. They have also been used in real schools by real administrators!

Ephesians 4:13   . . . till we all come to the unity of the **faith** and of the knowledge of the Son of God, to a perfect man, to the **measure** of the stature of the fullness of Christ

Chapter 25: For Whom Does Christian Education Exist?

This is an enormous and crucial and culminating question. It is also one that is not easily answered by us; or, to put it in the converse, it is one we can on our own most easily distort. Every Christian school has wrestled with it. Of course, the key again is: what is Jesus' answer to this question, not yours or mine or someone else's? Let us never forget that it is He who bought Christian education with His own blood! A Christian education should be for whom ever Jesus wants it to be! The flip side of this truth is that the selfish or prideful answer is always the wrong answer.

What, therefore, glorifies God in Christian school admissions? Is a Christian school supposed to be a seminary for only the redeemed and sanctified, a hospital for the sick and wounded, a country club for the safe and rich, a partner for only Christian families, a fortress for the saved and harassed, a boot camp for the willing, strong, and adventurous, a reclamation center for the lost and bewildered, a factory for the successful and the skilled, a hopeful junkyard for the dispossessed and politically incorrect like David's cave, a gracious surprise for the willing and yet unwanted and wandering wayfarers when the expected guests decline, a helping hand to the poor and meek, or some variable combination of all or some thereof? You might see a part of any of these in any given school! How a school defines itself hugely impacts for whom it exists and vice versa.

There are all kinds of arguments coming from many differing perspectives on this issue. But what does Jesus say? To whom did and does Jesus minister? Who does He want to see in His Christian schools? You may recall this scripture from way back in Chapter 1.

Psalm 25:8-9 Good and upright is the Lord; therefore He teaches sinners in the way. The humble He guides in justice, and the humble He teaches his way.

Of course there are also these:

Matthew 7:6 "Do not give what is holy to the dogs; nor cast your pearls before swine, lest they trample them under their feet, and turn and tear you in pieces.

2 Peter 2:22 But it has happened to them according to the true proverb: "A dog returns to his own vomit," and, "a sow, having washed, to her wallowing in the mire."

Mark 2:17 When Jesus heard it, He said to them, "Those who are well have no need of a physician, but those who are sick. I did not come to call the righteous, but sinners, to repentance."

And furthermore:

Galatians 5:9 A little leaven leavens the whole lump.

1 Corinthians 15:33 Do not be deceived: "Evil company corrupts good habits."

Luke 19:10 ". . . for the Son of Man has come to **seek** and to **save** that which was lost."

And what about Jesus and the willing and the unwilling, the humble and the proud, what do these have to do with the question of for whom Christian education should and does exist in Him?

Truths from Scripture

Several truths could be distilled and made clearer from the above scriptures and others. First, swine, dogs, leaven, and evil company exist and are to be avoided. Anyone who has suffered to bring the youth to and/or to strengthen the youth in Jesus through Christian education has witnessed trampling and rending of this precious gift and even of themselves as ministers thereof. That is why Jesus says to not do that! It is a command, not a suggestion. Similarly we have all seen the effects of leaven on the rest of a group's bread. So, by the Lord's own testimony, swine, dogs, evil company, and/or leaven do exist and are to be avoided; but the question must be asked, how?

How do you know a swine? What was Jesus getting at with this imagery that He purposefully chooses? Why did He say this? It certainly seems clear that it must be possible to attempt to give what is so precious to the wrong people. Not anyone will do. We also know that Jesus is no respecter of persons; so this has nothing to do with race, class, money, or gender.

Perhaps it is that swine are symbolic of indiscriminant and selfish eaters or by analogy perhaps learners; truth and lies, spiritual health or disease, righteousness or sin are all the same to them as long as it temporarily fills their belly! From the Old Testament dietary and Jesus' Jewish cultural context, swine do not chew their cud, they do not meditate on what they take in or learn from it, and they just swallow anything whole. They believe anything without discernment as long as it pleases them. But, in doing so, it does not seem to change their heart or spirit or behavior; after being washed on the outside, they return to the mire.

Much as supposed secularists would refuse to admit, this is possible regarding people; Jesus says it is true for some! He is not talking about pigs but rather people. Avoid them because they will not only waste your treasure but will also turn on you.

And why dogs, those who run with the pack and give their affection to whoever will feed them or dominate them, good or evil, and then return to their own vomit when they hunger from eating what is rotten? Jesus also thought this was real and warned us against them, the pack dominated scavengers who take the broad road and will bite the hand that feeds them. And as far as leaven goes, one clear characteristic is certainly that it puffs up, as well as spreads quickly! It therefore can easily point to the proud, and not the humble, and their effects on others. Conceit is to be avoided. Again Jesus warns us against this also.

Of course imagery is in the eye of the beholder. Yet the Spirit has something in mind in using these images. So, would these scriptures speak to the idea that the all roads indiscriminant, the unwilling to learn truth and repent and change; the peer pressured, undiscerningly bribed or dominated, and former sins controlled; and the spreaders of selfish pride but not God glorifying humility; all of which types seem to be on His possible *no list*!? Evil company has no place in a Christian school, and it does exist! But do we define it the way Jesus does? Jesus surrounded Himself with formerly evil doing people who were humbled and repentant! Look who he let into His, all important school! Are His ideas of false doctrines our ideas as well?

But then Jesus' obvious concern for and focus upon sinners, the humble, the sick, and the lost, even the demon possessed can make this all confusing to us in our smallness of heart and mind! Did Jesus just go and gather the already righteous for His school?

Think of Levi, the turncoat and thieving, tax collector, renamed Matthew or Mary Magdalene of seven demons and first to see Him raised from the dead or Saul, the instigator and accomplice to the murder of believers, renamed Paul! Are they not members of His school, the writer of the first Gospel, the first one to see Jesus raised from the dead, and the late born apostle to the Gentiles? There is a reason that Jesus did not come to call the righteous; He would have been very lonely! How do we integrate all these truths?

Polar Temptations

There are often two polar temptations here: 1) selfishly and/or self righteously wanting a school full of only perfect, Christian students from totally supportive and righteous, Christian families in the name of discipleship or 2) selfishly and/or self-righteously wanting to be willing to accept anyone who has a need or who can pay tuition in the name of evangelism or compassion.

I personally do not see how either of these extreme models is what Jesus has in mind and in heart in accordance with the above scriptures and His own example. I also keep coming back to the idea of to whom Jesus ministered and still does minister. He did not and does not ever force Himself on the unwilling or waste time and resources on the pridefully disinterested or permanently hostile; but did or does He ever turn away the willing or the humbled or the faith seeking no matter how horrendous the shape they are in? And would whom He saw or now sees as the unwilling or pridefully disinterested or the willing or humbled and faith seeking match our view of them?

Isaiah 1:19 If you are willing and obedient, you shall eat the good of the land;

Perhaps questions like these could help clarify the situation. "Are you willing to humbly accept Jesus' help and thankfully let Him change you into His own image as the author and the finisher of your faith?" "Are you willing to humbly consider and listen to and learn of Him Who is the Truth?" "Are you willing to learn to honor and accept Jesus as the King, Priest, and Prophet of this school, this truth seeking and truth learning and truth honoring and truth walking community that still has a long way to go to reach its hope?" "Are you willing to repent and let Jesus make you whole?" "Are you interested and open to letting Jesus birth and/or grow your faith in Him and change your spirit?"

Or: "Do you want the Holy Spirit to grow your God given gifts to the service and glory of God and your neighbor and your brothers and sisters in Christ?" "Are you willing to put your faith in Jesus and see what happens?"

2 Corinthians 8:12   For if there is first a willing mind, *it is* accepted according to what one has, *and* not according to what he does not have.

While this last scripture is about financial gifts to God and the ministry, the principle could easily apply to admissions in Christian schools.

Willingness and humility and obedience and faith, regardless of present attainment, seem to be His key criteria for His school as well as perseverance thereof! So how do we measure degrees of willingness and humility and obedience and faith, and does He allow different people of differing circumstances to start in different places as long as they keep moving forward in faith and mercy and grace?

Clearly a set of rules may help or perhaps may even cloud these complex matters; reliance on the Holy Spirit is, therefore, really the only truly safe haven, because it is His work! Another truth that is clear from His own example is that a Godly and challenging curriculum often solves this problem of willingness and humility and obedience and faith on its own. Truly pressing forward in God calls some and removes others by self-choice and self-selection. He invites many, but only some will actually follow. His curriculum did not change to accommodate the unwilling and the proud and the habitually disobedient. All of this is an issue of preparation for His Kingdom, not ours or theirs.

God Glorifying Admissions

Let us go back now to our earlier question. What therefore glorifies and pleases and serves God in Christian school admissions? If we are to glorify, please, and serve God in all that we do, this includes how we conduct our admissions. Our admissions practices are a witness of something to the community within and to the community without and to the community all around us! In fact these practices may be the only witness some families, both as parents and as children, experience regarding Christian education as a local manifestation of the Body of Christ (Gangel, 1997). What kind of a witness in His name is it?

And then there is retention policy. Admissions and retention are not the same, but they are very closely linked and often define who we become as a community of truth seekers and truth walkers attempting to glorify God in our education. In fact their philosophies should be considered together with the same set of truths guiding them, and then both should be clearly put forward together for all to see. Jesus had and has no hidden agendas.

So how do we mix Godly compassion and outreach with Godly righteousness and purity? Do we emphasize evangelism, or discipleship, or evangelism and discipleship? Who needs to be willing and humble and obedient and faith seeking, the parents, the student, or both the parents and the student? And what kind of willingness and humility and obedience and faith seeking do we require: an openness, an intention, or some degree of an accomplished fact, and how do we judge them, by words or by deeds or by both words and deeds and which ones?

Some schools differentiate student willingness and humility and obedience and faith between above or below twelve years old, the Old Testament age of accountability. Under this approach those below twelve are admitted on their parents' faith and willingness and humility and obedience, but after twelve on the student's own manifestations of these.

But what do we do about the defiant, nine year old from a believing family and the open, fourteen year old from an ungodly home? And is it a parent, a biological parent, a step parent, a legal parent, a foster parent, a grandparent, a residing parent, a parent in one of two sharing, divorced families or both parents and of what kinds of both parents? In our shattered culture this is obviously not an easy assessment to make with neat and clear formulas. And how deep must a parent's and/or a student's faith, willingness, humility, and obedience go at what points in time? And what about those who would profess a different faith?

Finally what truth about God does all of this show to the parents and to the children who come to our doors? We will accept, and we will turn down; we will retain, and we will let go. How and why we do it in a way that always glorifies, pleases, and serves God and gives a true witness of His love and truth and grace and righteousness and judgment, and blesses the families and children around us in God's Spirit is the question? Accepting or denying anyone Jesus would not is truly a mistake and/or a tragedy and a poor witness. There can be eternal implications for one or many!

Revelation 3:20 Behold, I stand at the door and knock. If anyone hears My voice and opens the door, I will come in to him and dine with him, and he with Me.

Admissions and Retention More Broadly

Of course the concepts of admissions and retention are broader than students and parents. We admit, reject, retain, and remove board members, leaders, administrators, staff, teachers, donors, and volunteers as well. These decisions and criteria and judgments are certainly as important if not more so in creating and maintaining our identity and our blessing and favor in Jesus. Remember Gaebelein's dictum, no Christian education without Christian teachers (1954); this needs to be broadened.

Or for instance, if boards are our stewards of leadership and vision under Jesus, how crucial is the recruitment, selection, retention, and removal of their members? All too often worldly criteria are used. Business and/or financial success can be an asset, but they are not enough and can easily lead to a spirit of Mammon as a master.   Again many Christian school boards have present or past, secular-school teachers or administrators who are Christians as members to supposedly show us how education should be done more professionally. Should we really be asking Caesar's employees how to do Jesus' work even if they are Christians? Did Jesus ask the Romans or the Greeks or the Pharisees or those who worked for them how to run His school? Why would we want to emulate a Godless education where Jesus is an outlaw and where it is illegal to openly base anything upon His truth?

Or conversely why are there not more pastors or believing, Christian university professionals or leaders of para church, organization personnel or youth ministers or missionaries or Christian artists or authors or even church elders with a heart for Christian education? And what about board members who do or did not send their own children to Christian schools? The keepers of the vision must actually have the vision! And of course what has been said above obviously applies to all the other stakeholders and servants of the mission. Each one either gathers with Jesus or scatters against Him.

A Three Legged Stool

Of course all of this must also be done realistically. Christian schools can be viewed through the metaphor of a three legged stool: a ministry, a school, and a business. The unique thing about a three legged stool is that, if any one leg is broken, the stool falls. All three functions must be sound and Biblical; they support and depend on one another. We are not just a school or just a ministry or just a business if we are truly a Christian school as a local manifestation of the universal Body of Christ. All three functions must be strong and thoroughly Biblical and anointed for the whole to be what Jesus wants us to be. This is true whether we are overseen by a church, a denomination, an independent board, or an owning individual or group. We therefore must seek His blessing and His anointing in all three functions.

Without Biblical, faithful, honest, and realistic business practices and planning, the ministry and the school fail. Without fulfilling our anointed and Biblically unique and spiritually integrated educational ministry, the ministry and the business fail; there are free (mandatorily tax funded), supposedly secular schools down the road. And without fulfilling our Godly ministry as a local manifestation of the universal Body of Christ, the school and the business become irrelevant to His Kingdom and thus lose their power and anointing and His favor.

The Present American Culture

Of course, the *whom* of Christian schools would drastically change if there was education, tax justice in America via something like vouchers or tax credits to parents without Caesar's encroachment. We can wonder if Caesar, the NEA, and the ACLU will ever play fairly or if the American people will ever again awake from our moral and spiritual stupor and demand so.

Tax funded, supposedly secular, pre-K to graduate school education to the tune of a trillion dollars a year is not free public education; we all pay for it and dearly so! That is $1,000,000,000,000 every year!

This is a justice issue. However, this is really not just about money but rather also ideology and truly warring religious faiths. It is a spiritual warfare issue, and the lukewarm church has yet to show herself up to the fight! Yet Godly individuals must still stand up and be counted!

Right now self-worshipping humanism and materialistic scientism have beaten God serving and glorifying Christianity in the American public arena. And this is so because it has also won in the private arena of individual people's lives and faith and consciousness and hearts (Pearcey, 2004).

Therefore, without a move of the Holy Spirit, a great humbling and repenting of a majority of the American people, and thus a great awakening, which have happened before in our history, current historical trends do not make it likely that Christians will get educational, tax justice or relief from Caesar on mass, regardless of the political party in power though there are definite differences! There is not presently the spiritual will for it in the people, regardless of politics and despite the desire of the Lord. When sexual perversion is the cause cerebra rather than Jesus, it is obvious how deeply we are as a nation in trouble! Look at who President Obama picked as the federal Education Secretary.

The question then is will individual families and local churches and larger denominations as manifestations of the universal Body of Christ step up in the midst of an anti-child, broken family, God-denying, unwholesome culture? The Supreme Court has actually opened the way for any state legislature courageous and just enough to walk through the voucher door (2002, US Supreme Court, Zelman v. Simmons). The general culture, however, is bogged down in sin with 50,000,000 abortions, 40% of born children being born outside of wedlock and thus clearly and grossly negligent, parental commitment, and half of the remaining 60% whose parents give up on their family through divorce, and huge sections of the population choosing to not have children at all. There is no other way to describe this honestly than an anti-children, anti-family, anti-faithfulness, and anti-God culture that has turned its back on God in order to worship self and selfishness. This is not something democracy or capitalism (or socialism) can fix. Yet there are a few states like Indiana (April, 2011) who have started stepping through the door!

Moreover God knows all of this and foretold it, and His call to the faithful and their children's education has not changed because of it, even to the end of the age. It was not so much different in Jesus' day. Perhaps all of this will force a more collaborative model of Christian education with willing and humble groups of schools and home schools working technologically together more, and less in competition. Choosing between the dream of the Kingdom and the American, often greed driven dream may become more evident; yet God knows this too.

We must remember that Christian education is His idea, that He is the author and the finisher of our faith, and that He blesses the faithful in any generation under any circumstances! Jesus knows whom He wants in His schools even and especially in these times; we need to ask Him! May God stir up our convictions, forgive our misgivings, and deliver us in His mercy and grace from evil to His honor and glory.

Isaiah 1:18-19 "Come now, and let us reason together," Says the LORD, "Though your sins are like scarlet, They shall be as white as snow; Though they are red like crimson, They shall be as wool. [19] If you are willing and obedient, You shall eat the good of the land;"

Chapter 26: So What Then Are the Godly Goals and Godly Purposes of Christian Education?

They are first and foremost the ones Jesus has in mind and heart and Spirit! If Christian education is in fact His idea, His heart, His will, His possession bought with His blood, His providence, then should not its goals and purposes be His also? How wrong would it be for us to try to substitute, instead, our own or even some, modern or postmodern, politically correct goals and purposes in His name as self serving for ourselves? For whose glory and blessing should our goals and purposes really exist? Whose goals and purposes will best prepare our youth for this life and the next, ours or His? Who loves them more? Who knows best? He did not come to help us on our own way but to lead us into His way, for He is the way, the truth, and the life! We end with this all important heart of the matters at end: what is our target? This must be right for anything else to go well in His eyes!

The Parable of the Wise and the Foolish Virgins

<u>Matthew 25:1-13</u>   "Then the kingdom of heaven shall be likened to ten virgins who took their lamps and went out to meet the bridegroom. [2] Now five of them were wise, and five were foolish. [3] Those who were foolish took their lamps and took no oil with them, [4] but the wise took oil in their vessels with their lamps. [5] But while the bridegroom was delayed, they all slumbered and slept.
[6] "And at midnight a cry was heard: 'Behold, the bridegroom is coming; go out to meet him!' [7] Then all those virgins arose and trimmed their lamps. [8] And the foolish said to the wise, 'Give us some of your oil, for our lamps are going out.' [9] But the wise answered, saying, 'No, lest there should not be enough for us and you; but go rather to those who sell, and buy for yourselves.' [10] And while they went to buy, the bridegroom came, and those who were ready went in with him to the wedding; and the door was shut.

[11] "Afterward the other virgins came also, saying, 'Lord, Lord, open to us!' [12] But he answered and said, 'Assuredly, I say to you, I do not know you.'

[13] "Watch therefore, for you know neither the day nor the hour in which the Son of Man is coming.

Let us first look carefully at this parable of Jesus about wisdom, foolishness, and being prepared at His return, *"those who were ready."* God help us if both eternal and timely, faith, wisdom, and truth built up within our students is not a key purpose and goal for our schools! And this is all the more so in our times of utter foolishness and lies in the general culture, despite all our worldly knowledge, and also the more so in the clear, eternal importance of Jesus' soon return. May our students be *"those who were ready"* because of the Godly faith and truth and wisdom in which they have learned to walk regarding all of their studies and in all of their ways.

"Then the Kingdom of heaven shall be . . ." when, then? There is evidently a certain quality about the Kingdom at a certain point in history, at a certain *"then."* Are we at that *"then"* with the wise and the foolish?

This parable is not written about or to the spiritual and/or the physical fornicators or adulterers of that time, that *"then,"* the impure who have no thought of God, but rather it is written about and to ten virgins. It is not written to unbelievers, those who scoff at the Lord's return and live life for themselves and/or live for the Godless idols of our times. As such it is pointed at the universal church and even perhaps particularly at the youth of the church. It does, to be sure, apply more widely, but it also clearly focuses on Christian youth and young people at that time, that *"then,"* our students and graduates.

This parable is about those preparing to go out to meet Jesus, the soon coming and returning, bride groom. It is about His betrothed, those promised to Him. It is about those saving themselves for Him and His Kingdom, looking for His return, watching for His coming. It is for those who have focused their hope on His wedding feast and His Kingdom come, and yet are also busy faithfully multiplying their God given talents for service now and for His eternal return, His pleasure, and His glory in the present and for the future. Are we preparing our students to go out to meet the returning Jesus? Should not this be a major goal of ours? Who else will do this?

Yet, even within this group of ten virgins, there is a split between wise and foolish. The wise, *"those who were ready,"* are more prepared to go out to meet Jesus, the bride groom, than the foolish.

The hidden question is why? Why bother being pure and having a lamp but with no oil in one's vessel? The wise had oil *"in their vessels with their lamps,"* but the foolish did not. Why? What is the symbolism and meaning of the oil? What is Jesus trying to tell us who are helping to prepare this generation of Christian youth? And what does all this have to do with the true purposes of Christian education in our times in His eyes?

Several things are clear from this teaching of Jesus. Those who had oil went into the wedding feast, and those who did not met a shut door, even after scrambling trying to make up for their lack of preparation. These "*foolish*," beside that lack of preparation, were also unknown to the Lord. Late, with someone else's oil, apparently, will not do.

Perhaps key understandings here are that the oil goes on the inside, it makes the lamp work, and it is the fuel that gives off the needed light, and the implication is that it is somehow connected to being known a forehand by Jesus. So we may ask how deeply did the foolish believe, were they really betrothed to Jesus? On the outside the foolish may have looked like they believed in Jesus and even in His return just like the wise. But why, then, were they without oil? Why empty vessels?

When the Lord's arrival was delayed, all slept. Jesus will return to take the faithful to the wedding feast, but it appears it will be past the eleventh hour in the middle of the night at the darkest point. Some see this delay as proof that He is not coming back at all as He said He would. Yet those who had the oil inside had the faith and the light to be prepared to go out to meet Him regardless of everyone else's skepticism and unbelief.

Is this a different depth of belief, not just going through the motions, but truly believing, not just trusting in Christian principles or in the earthly church as a social or religious group or in just ourselves as good people, but trusting in Jesus even from within the earthly church? Could *churchianity* as a personal or social or political or even cultural movement without true faith in our returning King Jesus be at play here? Some have staked their faith on the church victoriously winning the world and then Jesus coming back or just being back spiritually within the church, but will He know them as His betrothed if they have tried to do all this on Christian principles and not in and with and through Him according to His already prophesied plans and will?

Or again, when we look at oil and no oil, are we looking at the difference between omission and commission as well as the inside and outside of the cup. The ones without the oil stayed pure in that they apparently did not commit themselves to other gods or idols at least outwardly, as virgins they omitted that spiritual sin; but did they fully commit themselves to Jesus and His return inwardly as their blessed hope?

There are failings of commission as well as omission in the Christian walk. The Laodicean, lukewarm church is fully committed to neither sin nor Jesus; they are the fence sitters with one foot on both sides, the dualists. Was there outward appearance but no inward preparation or conviction, or repentance and zeal, no dependent relationship with Jesus as His betrothed?

John 14:1-3 "Let not your heart be troubled; you believe in God, believe also in Me. ² In My Father's house are many mansions; if *it were* not *so,* I would have told you. I go to prepare a place for you. ³ And if I go and prepare a place for you, I will come again and receive you to Myself; that where I am, *there* you may be also.

Is it our goal and purpose that our students will be where Jesus is and be received there because they are already known by Him and because they have learned to rely on Him for their very life as well as their cosmology and their worldview as well as the oil of faith and joy in their lamps that lights their way!?

The "*there*" that Jesus speaks of is the wedding feast and His Kingdom to come thereafter, when He comes again to reign on the earth. We have a foretaste and promise of it now within the true church, but the real deal is not yet here; just look around and inside with honest eyes. If the foolish had really believed all this, would they not have been better prepared for His return, to go out to meet Him and to enter in to the wedding feast of the Kingdom? Would they not have had lamps with oil, their own oil from their own betrothed relationship with Him? Would He not have already known them? One could ask are we preparing a place for Him, or is He preparing a place for us?

Proverbs 21:20 There is desirable treasure, and **oil** in the dwelling of the wise, but a foolish man squanders it.

Speaking of Jesus,

Psalm 45:7 and Hebrews You love righteousness and hate wickedness; Therefore God, Your God, has anointed You with the **oil** of gladness more than Your companions.

Psalm 23:5 You prepare a table before me in the presence of my enemies; You anoint my head with **oil**; My cup runs over.

Speaking of our oppression from our enemies,

Isaiah 10:27 It shall come to pass in that day that his burden will be taken away from your shoulder, and his yoke from your neck, and the yoke will be destroyed because of the anointing **oil.**

Isaiah 61:3   To console those who mourn in Zion, To give them beauty for ashes, The **oil** of joy for mourning, The garment of praise for the spirit of heaviness; That they may be called trees of righteousness, The planting of the LORD, that He may be glorified."

Mark 6:13   And they cast out many demons, and anointed with **oil** many who were sick, and healed them.

Regarding the Pharisees in contrast to a repentant sinner,

Luke 7:46   You did not anoint My head with **oil**, but this woman has anointed My feet with fragrant **oil**.

Luke 10:34   So he went to him and bandaged his wounds, pouring on **oil** and wine; and he set him on his own animal, brought him to an inn, and took care of him.
Spoken by the hypocrite and thief, Judas,

John 12:5   "Why was this fragrant **oil** not sold for three hundred denarii and given to the poor?"

And in general,

James 5:14   Is anyone among you sick? Let him call for the elders of the church, and let them pray over him, anointing him with **oil** in the name of the Lord.

Genesis 28:18   Then Jacob rose early in the morning, and took the stone that he had put at his head, set it up as a pillar, and poured **oil** on top of it.

Regarding the eternal lamp in the temple,

Exodus 27:20   And you shall command the children of Israel that they bring you pure **oil** of pressed olives for the light, to cause the lamp to burn continually.

Psalm 119:105   Your **word** is a **lamp** to my feet and a light to my path.

Luke 11:33   No one, when he has lit a lamp, puts it in a secret place or under a basket, but on a **lampstand**, that those who come in may see the light.

Oil is obviously an important reality and symbol in the Bible. There is the oil of God's joy and gladness, the oil of God's anointing (Christos, Mashiach), the oil of light in darkness, the oil of commemoration in meeting God, the oil of healing, the absent oil of hypocritical contention and lack of faith from the Pharisees and Judas who were seeking their own earthly kingdom rather than His prophetic one, the oil that breaks bondage and mourning, and the oil of preparation. All have to do, one way or another, with **faith in God** as well as the wisdom and truth of His anointing and fellowship and followership therein.

This oil of faith ought to be the bedrock of our goals and purposes of Christian education because it is so for Jesus, the Author and the Finisher or Perfecter of our faith, our King, Priest, and Prophet. Are our students half believing or wholly believing in Him and in His promised return; do they have, in faith, both feet in a Christian view of reality or only one foot; are they looking through His eyes or the world's eyes or trying to do both; are they the wise or the foolish; the anointed or the not anointed; getting by on others' faith or deeply rooted in the faith God makes available to each one of us as a gift through repentance and rebirth and sanctification, the opportunity for a personal and eternal relationship with Jesus, first as His betrothed and then as His bride?

Do they have the oil of their own walk with Him with their lamps and vessels full because of the education they have received and walked in and because of the way they see and understand all of reality and because of the way they have been led to walk faithfully and wisely in the truth no matter what they are studying or doing? Are they faithfully looking forward to the Lord's Kingdom or to their own kingdom or to someone else's promised kingdom?

Hebrews 11:6 But **without faith** it is impossible to please Him, for he who comes to God must believe that He is, and that He is a rewarder of those who diligently seek Him.

1 Thessalonians 5:1-4 But concerning the times and the seasons, brethren, you have no need that I should write to you. [2] For you yourselves know perfectly that the day of the Lord so comes as a thief in the night. [3] For when they say, "Peace and safety!" then sudden destruction comes upon them, as labor pains upon a pregnant woman. And they shall not escape. [4] But you, brethren, are not in darkness, so that this Day should overtake you as a thief.

A midnight cry is coming. The whole world will be crying out for a supposedly secular peace and a supposedly secular safety backed by a Godless, worldly religion and government. We will not know by the day or by the hour the Lord's return, but we will by the season, that it will not catch us unaware if we are truly His children of the day. It will be delayed, late, when all are asleep, past due, after the eleventh hour, in the middle of the darkness; but the wise will be watching and will be prepared, exercising their faith, staying busy doing His work as examples of a better city to come and as being loving witnesses and ambassadors to His coming Kingdom, already in promised relationship with Jesus. Is this not Jesus' goal and purpose for Christian education in these times, helping to bring forth good and faithful servants, sons and daughters of His kingdom, His true friends, even to the end of the age, preparing to go out to meet Him, preparing for His wedding feast with us?

Psalm 18:28   For you will light my lamp; The Lord my God will enlighten my darkness.

Luke 12:37-38   Blessed *are* those servants whom the master, when he comes, will find watching. Assuredly, I say to you that he will gird himself and have them sit down *to eat,* and will come and serve them. [38] And if he should come in the second watch, or come in the third watch, and find *them* so, blessed are those servants.

Acknowledgement and Warnings Regarding the Diligent and Thoughtful Reform Thinkers and Writers

Amongst the various streams of Christianity in our times, one should acknowledge the thoughtful and committed work of Calvinist writers on the topic of faith-based, Christian education. They have thought and written deeply and extensively on the subject, much more so than others, perhaps save the Catholics. There is a good deal to be learned from these brothers and sisters. As the citations in this book attest to, I personally have found in particular Albert Greene, Harro Van Brummelen, Donovan Graham, and Nancy Pearcey very helpful, inspiring, and insightful; and I use their works extensively with our graduate students at California Baptist University in our MSE, Educational Leadership for Faith-Based Schools, program.

Within the realm and confines of their theology and eschatology, they are very edifying and thought provoking. There is much Godly and scriptural truth here that should be honored, but I also personally believe there is more, relevant, and scriptural truth beyond the confines of this particular theology. There are even dangers here.

Harro Van Brummelen (2002), for instance, carefully lays out three mandates as the foundations for goals and purposes for Christian education: 1) the creation or culture building mandate from Genesis, 2) the greatest commandment mandate from Jesus' teachings on love, and 3) the great commission mandate from Jesus to His disciples after His resurrection. Each of these mandates has very important truth in it, though one may ponder alternate interpretations of their meaning and import from God's perspective. And one can consider that there are more mandates than these, handpicked three in the scriptures.

Van Brummelen does, for instance, end his book on Christian curriculum with this recurring and concluding idea and principle as an ultimate goal of Christian education, "how we can restore the earth to a safer, more just, and healthier state" (p. 248). Herein, I believe, lays a clear example of the possible danger from this particular theological perspective regarding the purposes of Christian education.

We should therefore, I believe, look further at three areas of truth here: 1) what is good and right about the three scriptural mandates proposed by these Godly, Calvinist, Christian educators, 2) what could be theologically bent from their particular interpretations of these mandates, and 3) what other mandates might scripture suggest beyond these three mandates for goals and purposes of Christian education? Finally it should be noted that prophetic and eschatological differences in these theological perspectives and how they match up with the whole of scripture and Jesus as Prophet of prophets are most possibly at play here.

For instance how do Jesus' last direct words to the church from heaven in the Book of Revelations add to and further explain these mandates? Interestingly enough how one views Jesus as Prophet and His eminent return and the fulfillment of the ages makes a big difference here. He has been in this book our purposeful model, not just as King and Priest, but also as Prophet and Lord. So I humbly offer some additional perspectives here and some possible warnings about particular interpretations. Goals and purposes are so important!

The Three Mandates

All three writers, Greene, Van Brummelen, and Graham, and I am sure many others, make much of God's call to create culture. Though this is not explicitly stated in Genesis, it is not too far a stretch to see it clearly implied. The question is whose culture? For instance, is the present, universal church of true believers or any true local manifestation of the Body of Christ such as a truly Christian school (Gangel, 1997) supposed to save and sanctify American culture or to bear witness in word and deed of the Kingdom of God culture within and to America or any other nation without? And who does the saving and sanctifying and creating; is it the church or the Lord and His Holy Spirit working in and through the believing community? Is a Christian school, as a local manifestation of the universal Body of Christ, called to help create a theocracy in the national culture or to be led forth to be an example of one within the body of believers who are also a witness and salt and light to the national or local community culture as the Holy Spirit leads? Are we preparing the bride for the returning King or trying to take over the world now in His name before He returns? These are very important questions about goals and purposes and help shape who we become.

There is no argument here that any supernatural, local manifestation of the Lord's Body should humbly strive to influence the general culture around it and strive to produce through the Spirit's leading a Godly culture within itself as a true witness. Our graduates are by faith and by spiritual rebirth citizens of the eternal Kingdom of God and by natural birth citizens of earthly societies and civilizations. This is what is good and right in the expressed cultural mandate. It addresses the important question of what kind of community are we allowing God's Spirit to create in our schools?

Yet Van Brummelen's question "how we can restore the earth to a safer, more just, and healthier state" or again "transform the world" (p. 50) may put a burden on the betrothed that only the returning King can bear.

More importantly, as noble as this burden sounds, it may not match what the scriptures say about the last days, thus putting us at odds with God's Word and purposes. In short, is this our agenda or Jesus' agenda in our times? This church victorious emphasis may also lead to a sense of being overwhelmed by a task we cannot do or lead to an abandonment of the cause of Christ as frustratingly unreachable. Our hope is in Him, not ourselves.

This is not a call for retreat or cynicism but for focus and realism based on the whole of the prophetic scriptures. God expects us in the Holy Spirit to have a tremendous burden for and outreach to the lost, to be true witnesses, love letters, ambassadors, intercessors, harvesters for the Kingdom, and salt and light to the world facing God's coming judgment; but Jesus is the conqueror, not us! Every knee shall bow and every tongue shall confess to Him!

Again, along these lines of the creation mandate, that to which God called Adam and Eve, Graham states that **the** present purpose of education is "to help students learn to creatively care for the creation in righteousness" (2003, p. 238). While one might see that this should be **a** purpose of Godly education, would Jesus agree that this is **the** purpose of Christian education in our times? Is this the main focus of His teaching? What about personal repentance, and faith in God, and truth, and spiritual rebirth, and right relationship with God, and evangelism, and preparing for the coming Kingdom? Was, for instance, helping students "learn to creatively care for the creation in righteousness" the focus of Paul's teaching?

There is a theology behind Graham's definition of education. It has at least two foundations regarding the fall and redemption of the image of God in man: 1) "the fall marred the image but did not destroy it" and 2) "that God's call for us to rule with Him and to reflect His character was not rescinded but misdirected" (2003, p, 239). In response to this, one might ask several questions. Did the fall only mar the image of God in us or did it ruin it? As redeemed believers are we only fixing ourselves according to Christian principles or being reborn into a whole new man, a whole new creation, by God's Holy Spirit in Jesus, the Anointed One?

Do we rule [and reign?] with Him now over the earth or when we return with Him from the wedding feast as His bride and eternal companion, one with Him in His kingdom and then rule and reign with Him? Is the fallen creation fixable now before Jesus returns?

Are we just misdirected or fallen beyond our means? Moreover, is man's present rule just misdirected or in need of a whole new Kingdom along with its ruling King present on His earthly throne in Jerusalem? Moreover which of these prophetic visions instills pride [or dignity] in ourselves and which humility and worth in dependence upon God Who loves us even in our brokenness?

While we are certainly called to reflect His character in this present age, are we destined to rule the earth before His return? Are we preparing the bride awaiting the groom's return or walking as the already presumed wife with an absentee husband?

John 18:36 Jesus answered, "My kingdom is **not** of this **world**. If My kingdom were of this **world**, My servants would fight, so that I should **not** be delivered to the Jews; but **now** My kingdom is **not** from here."

Culture is of vital importance. Christian schools need to hold as a key purpose and goal the living of, the modeling of, and the spreading of Kingdom culture to the willing and the humble and the obedient as a foretaste and hope of that which Jesus Himself will soon bring to the whole earth. We should also stand firmly against the fallen cultures all around us and within us that deny the Lord's return and the fulfillment of history and that instead call on us to save ourselves. Trusting in Jesus and His return is what brings true hope.

The two other identified mandates add to this creating of Godly culture through community in the Holy Spirit. Modeling and learning and walking in the love of God, love of neighbor, and love of the brethren are another key set of purposes and goals of Christian education and a witness to a world facing eminent judgment, where the love of most has grown and will grow cold due to lawlessness, a rejecting of God's commandments. These loves should be evident in everything we are and say and do as teachers and learners, as truth seeking communities of teaching and learning, written large from our mission statements to our daily lessons. God, neighbor, and brethren include these three: the Trinity, those outside the Body of Christ, and those within it. Learning to walk in God's agape love is the key. These are the three loves of which Jesus spoke, two from the Old Testament and one He added as a new commandment.

Finally the Great Commission of evangelical outreach, discipleship, and teaching should be cherished goals and purposes of Christian education. As stated in this scripture, all the things He commanded us should be included, written large from our mission to our daily lessons. Revelations, moreover, makes it clear that people from all nations will comprise the Lord's bride but that most of Earth's inhabitants will reject the invitation.

Furthermore Van Brummelen states that, "Christian schools want their aims to reflect a biblical worldview" (2002, p. 14). This is certainly true, though one might add a Christian cosmology, theology, eschatology, and philosophy as well. There are truly many false worldviews that compete for the hearts, minds, and spirits of our students which we must refute and replace in faith with a Biblical worldview. How we view the world is very important. Van Brummelen enumerates the following abbreviated aims of a Biblical worldview for Christian education (p. 15):

1. Christian vision of life

---

2. Learn about God's word

3. Mandate to take care of the earth

4. Contribute positively to God's Kingdom

5. A transformational impact on culture

6. Discern and confront idols

7. Committed to Christ and a Christian way of life

8. Serve God and neighbor

These are generally excellent! They could also be broadened, deepened, elucidated, and added to.

All Things Jesus Commanded

Here is a partial list of further or expanded goals and purposes regarding our truth seeking communities of teaching and learning for God's chosen students that includes world view but perhaps also goes beyond it.

1) to sit at the feet of Jesus, 2) to help bring in the eternal harvest, 3) to help heal and deliver the willing and believing, 4) to help prepare the bride of Christ, washing her in His word for His return, helping her to have her lamp and oil ready, 5) to help rescue the weak and fatherless, 6) to be salt and light for Jesus by being a Godly example of good works before men, 7) to prayerfully follow the Holy Spirit and engage in spiritual warfare against evil principalities and powers which ensnare the lost and oppress the saved, 8) to bring glory to God in word and deed, 9) to exalt truth, 10) to bring down lies, 11) to love God and neighbor and one another sacrificially, 12) to worship God in Spirit and truth, 13) to build up the body of Christ in faith and holiness and obedience, 14) to obey Jesus and the Holy Spirit, 15) to walk in truth and wisdom and understanding and love, 16) to hasten His return by preaching the Gospel in word and deed in the whole world, 17) to bring every thought captive to Christ, 18) to make disciples worldwide, 19) to teach everything Jesus has commanded us,

20) to be a love letter from God to the lost, 21) to be a true witness to Jesus speaking and doing the truth, the whole truth, and nothing but the truth so help us God from Jerusalem to the ends of the earth, 22) to be humbly conformed to the King of kings, the Priest of priests, and the Prophet of prophets, 23) to walk in humility, mercy, and grace, 24) to be crucified with Christ, 25) to show forth God's mercy, grace, and favor, 26) to warn and prepare the world for God's coming judgment both as comfort and vengeance, 27) to be ambassadors for His Kingdom to come, 28) to shepherd His flock, 29) to find favor with God through faith, humility, obedience, stewardship, and service, 30) to live moderate, gentle lives, 31) to esteem others better than ourselves, 32) to restore others and bear their burdens, 33) to know and live the biblical truth of sowing and reaping, 34) to have and display and share the fruits of the Spirit, 35) to be fruitful in every good work, 36) to speak that which is edifying and gives grace, 37) to allow the Spirit to redeem our thinking and feelings - live by truth, 38) to love mercy and justice and walk humbly with God, 39) to bear the reproach of Christ, 40) to protect our hearts from bitterness and walk in forgiveness, 41) to run the race for the prize, 42) to hold fast to the three things that remain: faith, hope, and love, 43) to put on the mind of Christ, 44) to abide in Christ, 45) to be ever watchful in faithfulness for his return, 46) to raise up students who are strong in God's Spirit, 47) to be wise as serpents but gentle as doves, 48) to suffer to bring others to Christ, 49) to preach the Gospel in season and out of season, 50) to study the word to show ourselves approved, 51) to test the spirits, and 52) to fix our eyes on Jesus, the Author and Finisher of our faith.

Of course this list could go on and on. All things Jesus commanded and taught and did are quite large! John said it could fill the whole world with books thereof! And we do have four books of His to read of them: the God sustained, though still in bondage through man's sin, continuous creation as His spoken Word; the Bible as His Spirit revealed and written Word of truth; Jesus Himself as the ever living and redeeming and fulfilling Word; and the Holy Spirit as the ever present and convicting and comforting, teaching Word!

The goals and purposes of truly Christian education, anointed education, must be founded upon the integration of these four, their *echad*, their oneness, written large from our mission to our daily lessons and lives! For their witness is one!

The Seven Churches

Here, in conclusion, is a truncation of some of the direct teachings from heaven of Jesus in the Book of Revelations, the revelation of Jesus to the local manifestations of His body on earth. Should not these too impact the purposes and goals of Christian education? What does Jesus say from heaven to the church? Surely this should be important to us!

Revelation 2 & 3

Ephesus: 1) you cannot bear those who are evil, 2) tested those who say they are apostles and are not, and have found them liars, 3) have persevered and have patience, and have labored for My name's sake and have not become weary, 4) nevertheless I have *this* against you, that you have left your first love, 5) remember therefore from where you have fallen; repent and do the first works, 6) you hate the deeds of the Nicolaitans, which I also hate.

Smyrna: 1) works, tribulation, and poverty (but you are rich), 2) do not fear any of those things which you are about to suffer, 3) you may be tested, and you will have tribulation ten days, 4) be faithful until death, and I will give you the crown of life.

Pergamos: 1) you hold fast to My name, and did not deny My faith even in the days in which Antipas *was* My faithful martyr, who was killed among you, where Satan dwells, 2) but I have a few things against you, because you have there those who hold the doctrine of Balaam, who taught Balak to put a stumbling block before the children of Israel, to eat things sacrificed to idols, and to commit sexual immorality, 3) thus you also have those who hold the doctrine of the Nicolaitans, which thing I hate.

Thyatira: 1) I know your works, love, service, faith, and your patience, 2) nevertheless I have a few things against you, because you allow that woman Jezebel, who calls herself a prophetess, to teach and seduce My servants to commit sexual immorality and eat things sacrificed to idols, 3) I am He who searches the minds and hearts. And I will give to each one of you according to your works, 4) but hold fast what you have till I come.

Sardis: 1) be watchful, and strengthen the things which remain, that are ready to die, 2) remember therefore how you have received and heard; hold fast and repent, 3) if you will not watch, I will come upon you as a thief, and you will not know what hour I will come upon you.

Philadelphia: 1) you have a little strength, have kept My word, and have not denied My name, 2) you have kept My command to persevere, I also will keep you from the hour of trial which shall come upon the whole world, to test those who dwell on the earth, 3) hold fast what you have, that no one may take your crown.

Laodiceans: 1) I know your works, that you are neither cold nor hot. I could wish you were cold or hot. So then, because you are lukewarm, and neither cold nor hot, I will vomit you out of My mouth, 2) because you say, 'I am rich, have become wealthy, and have need of nothing'—and do not know that you are wretched, miserable, poor, blind, and naked— I counsel you to buy from Me gold refined in the fire, that you may be rich; and white garments, that you may be clothed, *that* the shame of your nakedness may not be revealed; and anoint your eyes with eye salve, that you may see, 3) As many as I love, I rebuke and chasten. Therefore be zealous and repent.

These are the abbreviated teachings of Jesus from heaven to the church in the first century, the beginning of our present age. One would think we, as followers of Jesus, would pay great attention to them and their obvious themes, aimed directly from heaven to us and our present era. Jesus is, of course, the best theologian we will ever have! No pope or reformer or contemporary thinker or writer need apply; we have the very words of Jesus Himself from heaven to the church on earth in this age!

So what are His themes? What does He think we need to hear? And what might they have to do with His goals and purposes for a truly Christian education?

There is commentary here on both words-thoughts-teachings-beliefs-doctrines **and** deeds-works. There is recognition of spiritual warfare and exhortation and encouragement in our battle with our temporary and contemporary adversary, Satan. There is understanding and encouragement regarding persecution, tribulation, testing, and suffering from without in this age. There is warning and judgment for apostasy from within, false teaching, lukewarmness, sexual immorality, blindness, and idols which take our eyes off of Jesus. There are exhortations to hold fast, to strengthen what remains, to be faithful in our first love to Him, to persevere, to be watchful of His return, to hate false doctrine and evil deeds, to be faithful witnesses of Him even to death, to magnify instead of deny His name, to love, to good works, to patience, to repentance, and to be zealous for truth and purity and devotion to Jesus.

Are not these worthy goals and purposes for a truly Christian education, an education paid for by His blood? Is not this truth and wisdom for our times and its perils for our youth? Is not this oil for our lamps with which to go out to meet Him? Where do we find these teachings of Jesus in our mission statements, aims, goals, objectives, and daily lessons?

There is no mention, however, here from Jesus of "how we can restore the earth to a safer, more just, and healthier state" by our own efforts before His return. It is not that He would be against this or that we should be against this truly happening; it is just that this is not His focus for us now! In fact, He Himself will do just these things upon His return and much, much more. But for now it is primarily those who have no faith in Him or His promised return or His coming judgment who have taken up the cause of supposedly saving the earth and themselves by their own means and to their own ends despite our and their obvious corruption. Do we need to try to outdo them in this to prove ourselves politically correct in their fallen eyes? And at what price to His teachings and true callings do we do this?

We do need to take our earthly citizenship seriously and do what we can to walk in personal righteousness and social justice in a fallen world, but our focus needs to be on taking our heavenly citizenship even more seriously, letting the Holy Spirit have His way with us as children of the Father, born again in Jesus to His pleasure and glory, as heralds and witnesses of His coming Kingdom.

We need to protect our students from God hating, atheistic, and worldly teachers like Darwin, Marx, Freud, Nietzsche, and Dewey and their progeny in supposedly secular, humanistic, progressivist, modernism and postmodernism and their false teachings, lies, and manifestos that would point us toward the anti-Christ and his false kingdom instead of the true Christ and His true, coming Kingdom at His imminent return. We need to be changing our hearts and our understandings as well as our vocabularies and stated missions, aims, goals, objectives, and daily lessons to match His true calling. The lost in the world point one way, and Jesus calls us to a different way. To whom are we listening? Where does true hope lay?

And above all we must proclaim now personally and in the end historically that Jesus wins! We have read the end of the book, and the present world is headed toward judgment, even the just wrath of God as well as His gracious comfort, and Jesus humbly, gloriously, and righteously wins! May He win in us as leaders in Christian education, spiritual education! May He win in the students and families to whom He has called us to minister in Him.

May we have oil in our lamps to go out to meet Him and be let in to His wedding feast that He has prepared for us where there will be rejoicing for ever more because He already knows us because we are leaning on Him and not ourselves in all things! May the Holy Spirit in God's mercy and grace be our teacher in our truth seeking communities of teaching and learning, reaching our whole persons, sanctifying us in spirit, soul, and body to humbly represent Jesus as King, Priest, and Prophet, walking in faith, hope, and love to God, in faith, hope, and love to the lost world facing judgment, and in faith, hope, and love to one another within His body until He comes.

Ephesians 3:10 . . . to the intent that now the manifold **wisdom** of God might be made known by the church to the principalities and powers in the heavenly places.

In the end it is all about eternal truth and love because it is all about Jesus, Who is the way, the truth, and the life and Who is love. Jesus is the turning point of history and also of eternity in word and in deed. There is a truly anointed education only in Him, and without Him education necessarily becomes meaningless and deceptive and corrupted. He is either at the center or He becomes an outlaw; lukewarmness about Him is not an option that He gives to us as His betrothed no matter what we are studying. May God stir up our humble convictions, forgive our prideful misgivings, and deliver us in His mercy and grace from evil and our worldly fears in the closing of this age to His honor and His glory.

John 18:37 Jesus answered, "You are right in saying I am a king. In fact, for this reason I was born, and for this I came into the world, to testify to the truth. Everyone on the side of truth listens to me."

1 John 4:16 And so we know and rely on the **love God** has for us. **God is love**. Whoever lives in **love** lives in **God**, and **God** in him.

Jude 1:20-21 But you, beloved, building yourselves up on your most holy faith, praying in the Holy Spirit, [21] keep yourselves in the love of God, looking for the mercy of our Lord Jesus Christ unto eternal life.

Matthew 11:6 And blessed is he who is not offended because of Me.

May God bless, encourage, and anoint you as you move forward in humility, faith, hope, obedience, and the love of God in this precious ministry of truly Christian education and leadership so dear to our Lord's heart!

Shalom in Jesus, our King, Priest, and Prophet, Who is sanctifying us in spirit, soul, and body even to the end of the age to the glory of the Father!

Jesus, Jesus, Jesus

There's just something about that name

Master, Savior, Jesus

Like the fragrance after the rain

Jesus, Jesus, Jesus

Let all Heaven and Earth proclaim

Kings and kingdoms

Will all pass away

But there's something about that Name.

Index of Authors, Topics, and Scriptures

Reference List

Bloom, B. S. (1956). *Taxonomy of Educational Objectives.* Boston, MA: Allyn and Bacon.

De Tocqueville, A. (2000). *Democracy in America.* New York: Perennial Classics.

Gaebelein, F.E. (1954). *The Pattern of God's Truth: The Integration of Faith and Learning.* Colorado Springs, CO: Association of Christian Schools International.

Gangel, K.O. (1997). *Team Leadership in Christian Ministry: Using Multiple Gifts to Build a Unified Vision.* Chicago, IL: Moody Press.

Gorbman, A. (2010). *the Palestinian right to Israel.* Noble, OK: Icon Publishing Group, LLC.

God. (Eternity). *The holy Bible NKJV.*

Good, T. & Brophy, J. (2008). *Looking in Classrooms (10th edition).* New York, NY: Longman Inc.

Graham, D.L. (2003). *Teaching Redemptively: Bringing Grace and Truth into Your Classroom.* Colorado Springs, CO: Association of Christian Schools International.

Greene, A.E. (1998). *Reclaiming the Future of Christian Education: A Transforming Vision.* Colorado Springs, CO: Association of Christian Schools International.

Fakema, M. (June 15, 1954). The Case for the Christian Day School. *United Evangelical Action, 13* (June 15, 1954), 220-22.

Hunkins, F.P. & Ornstein, A.C. (2009). *Curriculum Foundations, Principles, and Issues.* Boston, MA: Allyn and Bacon.

Jews for Jesus. (2009). www.jewsforjesus.com

King, M.L. (August 28, 1963). *I Have a Dream - Address at March on Washington.*

    http://www.mlkonline.net/dream.html

Kohlberg, L. (1984). *The Psychology of Moral Development: The Nature and Validity of*

    Moral Stages. London, England: Harper Collins Publishers.

Lewis, C.S. (1944). *Beyond Personality.* NY, NY: Macmillan Pub. Co.

Lewis, C.S. (1950). *The Lion, the Witch, and the Wardrobe.* NY, NY: Harper Collins

    Publishers.

Lewis, C.S. (1955). *The Magician's Nephew.* NY, NY: Harper Collins Publishers.

Mabat – Israel Channel 1 TV. *www.iba.org.il/mabat/*

McAlpine, C. (2001). *The Leadership of Jesus.* Kent, England: Sovereign World
Ltd.

McDermott, E.J. (1985). *Distinctive Qualities of the Catholic School.* Washington
D.C.

    National Catholic Education Association.

McGuffey, W.H. (1879). *McGuffey's Readers.* Hoboken, NJ: John Wiley & Sons.

Nietzsche, F. (1989). *Beyond Good and Evil.* Amherst, NY: Prometheus Books.

Nord, W. & Haynes, C. (1998). *Taking Religion Seriously Across the Curriculum.*

    Alexandria, VA: Association for Supervision and Curriculum

    Development.

Pearcey, N. R. (2004). *Total Truth: Liberating Christianity from its Cultural Captivity.*

    Wheaton, IL: Crossway Books.

Piaget, J. (1997). *The Moral Judgment of the Child.* NY: Free Press Paperbacks.

Prince, D. (1984). *Our Debt to Israel.* Charlotte, NC: Derek Prince Ministries-

    International.

Prince, D. (2003). *War in Heaven: God's Epic Battle with Evil.* Ada, MI: Baker Pub

Group.

Prince, D. (2007). *Bought with Blood: The Divine Exchange at the Cross.* Ada, MI: Baker Pub Group.

Sellars, R.W. (May-June, 1933). Humanist Manifesto I. *The New Humanist* (May-June, 1933): 58-61.

Smith, C. (2006). KWAVE radio address.

U.S. Census Bureau. (Internet release date: April 11, 2000). *Population Estimates Program.*

U.S. Supreme Court. (1993). *Zobrest v. Catalina Foothills School District (92-94).*

Van Brummelen, Harro. (2002). *Steppingstones to Curriculum: A Biblical Path.* Colorado Springs, CO: Association of Christian Schools International.

Wallerstein, J., Lewis, J., & Blakeslee, S. (2000). *The Unexpected Legacy of Divorce: A 25 Year Landmark Study.* New York: Hyperion Books.

Woolfolk, A. (2005). *Educational Psychology (tenth edition).* Upper Saddle River, NJ: Pearson Inc.

About The Author

Dr. James R. Heyman has been Associate Professor of Education and Program Director of the Educational Leadership for Faith-Based Schools specialization for a Masers of Science in Education at California Baptist University, Riverside, CA since 2001.

He holds a bachelors degree in philosophy from the University of California Berkeley, a masters in educational administration and supervision from San Jose State University, and a doctorate in private school administration from the University of San Francisco.

He is former principal of Rancho Capistrano Christian School, San Juan Capistrano, CA; Superintendent of Phoenix Christian Jr./Sr. High School, Phoenix, AZ; Headmaster, Mount Paran Christian School, Marietta, GA; founder and principal of the middle school, Monte Vista Christian School, Watsonville, CA; and Headmaster of the lower campus, Ojai Valley School, Ojai, CA.

Dr. Heyman and his wife, Susan, have raised five children: Justus Heyman, a missionary pastor in France, Dr. Nathanael Heyman, a medical researcher at the University of Nevada Reno, Joshua Heyman MBA, Concordia University, Anna Puffer, Educational Specialist, and Shoshanah Heyman who has Down's syndrome and lives with her parents.

Because his father was Jewish, Dr. Heyman was raised within the Jewish community and came to Christ along with his wife in their mid twenties during the early 1970s Jesus Movement. They now have seven grandchildren and counting! The family has always enjoyed hiking, camping, backpacking, and snow skiing in the Sierra Nevada Mountains.

Dr. and Mrs. Heyman and their daughter Shoshanah, now 29, reside in San Clemente, California. He is reachable at **jheyman@calbaptist.edu**.

Appendix A: Student Examples of Integrated Assessment Forms

CLASSROOM SPIRITUAL AND ACADEMIC

OBSERVATION REPORT

Indicate teacher performance by placing a checkmark in the appropriate box. Use the following rating scale:

NA/NO	**Not Applicable or Observed**
1	**Unsatisfactory**
2	**Needs Improvement**
3	**Meets Expectations**
4	**Exceeds Expectations**

Teacher: _____

Grade: _____

Date(s) of Observation: _____

Time(s) of Day: _____

Evaluator: _____

Type of Observation:　　　( )　Formal　　　( )　Informal

Type(s) of lesson and subject matter:

TEACHER EFFECTIVENESS FACTORS

Level of Performance

The teacher	4	3	2	1	NA/ NO
Creates a classroom community conducive to learning. *James 2:22 You see that his faith and his actions were working together, and his faith was made complete by what he did.*					
Establishes and maintains a positive Christian community in the classroom *1Cor 12:27 Now you are Christ's body, and individually members of it.*					
Looks for the best in each student, acknowledging that students are special and unique, made by the Creator. *Psalm 139:14 I praise you because I am fearfully and wonderfully made.*					
Interacts spontaneously with students. *Romans 8:14 For all who are led by the Spirit of God are children of God.*					
Maintains positive relationships with students. *Psalm 133:1 How good and pleasant it is when brothers live together in unity.*					
Allows opportunities for the students to express ideas, prayer needs, and special interests. *Phil 4:19 And my God will meet all your needs according to his glorious riches in Christ Jesus.*					
Recognizes and responds positively to the students' efforts. *Col 1:29 That's why I work and struggle so hard, depending on Christ's mighty power that works within me.*					
Praises the student and acknowledges God as the source of the student's abilities. *Phil 4:13 I can do everything through Him who gives me strength.*					

The teacher	4	3	2	1	NA/ NO
Creates an environment conducive to developing Christ-like character. *1 Cor 11:1 And you should imitate me, just as I imitate Christ.*					
Teaches students how to have an obedient heart, reflected in words and actions. *Hebrews 13:17 Obey your leaders and submit to their authority. They keep watch over you as men who must give an account. Obey them so that their work will be a joy, not a burden, for that would be of no advantage to you.*					
Cultivates in students a desire to please and honor God. *Acts 17:28 For in Him we live and move and have our being.*					
Encourages students to grow as disciples of Christ. *John 15:8 This is to my Father's glory, that you bear much fruit, showing yourselves to be my disciples.*					
Cultivates a wholesome respect and fear of the Lord. *Psalm 34:11 Come, you children, listen to me; I will teach you the fear of the LORD. Psalm 111:10 The fear of the LORD is the beginning of wisdom; a good understanding have all those who do His commandments.*					

Maintains student attention. *1 Peter 5:8 Be self-controlled and alert. Your enemy the devil prowls around like a roaring lion looking for someone to devour.*					
Creates a community of cooperative learners. *Phil 2:2 Then make me truly happy by agreeing wholeheartedly with each other, loving one another, and working together with one mind and purpose.*					
Teaches students how to be responsible citizens of their classroom and Christ's kingdom. *Matthew 25:23 "The master said, 'Well done, my good and faithful servant. You have been faithful in handling this small amount, so now I will give you many more responsibilities."*					

	4	3	2	1	NA/NO
Models and encourages students to be content. *1 Corinthians 7:24 Brothers, each man, as responsible to God, should remain in the situation God called him to.*					
Promotes service to God. *Deuteronomy 13:4 It is the LORD your God you must follow, and him you must revere. Keep his commands and obey him; serve him and hold fast to him.*					
Promotes service to others. *1 Cor 4:1 So then, men ought to regard us as servants of Christ and as those entrusted with the secret things of God.*					

	4	3	2	1	NA /NO
The classroom evidences the presence of the Holy Spirit. *Luke 10:21 At that time Jesus, full of joy through the Holy Spirit, said, "I praise you, Father, Lord of heaven and earth, because you have hidden these things from the wise and learned, and revealed them to little children.*					
The Holy Spirit is mentioned, welcomed, and is present in the classroom. *Acts 5:32 We are witnesses of these things, and so is the Holy Spirit, whom God has given to those who obey Him.*					
The fruits of the spirit are present in the teacher's actions. *Gal 5:22 But the fruit of the Spirit is love, joy, peace, patience, kindness, goodness, faithfulness, gentleness, and self-control.*					
The fruits of the spirit are present in the students' actions. *Gal 5:22 But the fruit of the Spirit is love, joy, peace, patience, kindness, goodness, faithfulness, gentleness, and self-control.*					

	4	3	2	1	NA/ NO
The teacher manages the classroom to ensure an efficient use of instructional time. *Eccl 8:5 Whoever obeys his command will come to no harm, and the wise heart will know the proper time and procedure.*					
Directions for transitions between activities are clear and concise. *Ephesians 5:15-16 See then that you walk circumspectly, not as fools but as wise, redeeming the time, because the days are evil.*					
Materials for student distribution are organized and available when needed. *1 Cor 14:40 But everything should be done in a fitting and orderly way.*					

	4	3	2	1	NA/NO
Student-to-teacher and teacher-to-student interaction is evident. *Romans 12:10 Be devoted to one another in brotherly love. Honor one another above yourselves.*					
Uses instructional time wisely. *2 Cor 6:2 I tell you, now is the time of God's favor, now is the day of salvation.*					

	4	3	2	1	NA/NO
The teacher demonstrates effective implementation of student behavior management program that promotes redemption in Christ. *Deuteronomy 5:27 Go near and listen to all that the LORD our God says. Then tell us whatever the LORD our God tells you. We will listen and obey.*					
Treats students fairly, listening to them and responding with love. *John 13:35 By this all men will know that you are my disciples, if you love one another."*					
Reinforces/rewards appropriate social and academic behavior in the classroom. *Luke 20:21 "Teacher, we know that you speak and teach what is right, and that you do not show partiality but teach the way of God in accordance with the truth."*					
Students are taught how to solve problems effectively using Matthew 18. *Matthew 18:15 If your brother wrongs you, go and show him his fault, between you and him privately. If he listens to you, you have won back your brother.*					
Manages students in a manner that sustains academic and spiritual focus in the classroom. *2 Cor 13:11 Aim for perfection, listen to my appeal, be of one mind, live in peace. And the God of love and peace will be with you.*					
Students are encouraged to make the right decisions for the right reasons and are led to true repentance when they make a mistake. *Romans 3:23-24 For all have sinned and fall short of the glory of God, and are justified freely by his grace through the redemption that came by Christ Jesus.*					

	4	3	2	1	NA/NO
The teacher demonstrates appropriate instructional planning and procedures, evidencing a Biblical foundation and spiritual integration of learning objectives. *1 John 1:6 If we say that we have fellowship with Him, and walk in darkness, we lie and*					

do not practice the truth.					
Identifies and selects appropriate learning objectives. *Hebrews 11:3 By faith we understand.*					
Acknowledges the Creation is made and sustained by God. *Isaiah 42:5 This is what God the LORD says— he who created the heavens and stretched them out, who spread out the earth and all that comes out of it, who gives breath to its people, and life to those who walk on it. Gen 1:27 So God created man in his own image.*					
Recognizes that teaching and learning involve a response from/to God. *Acts 17:28 For in him we live, and move, and have our being.*					
Instructs students that God's word is truth and helps students develop a Christian worldview. *Col 2:8 See to it that no one takes you captive through hollow and deceptive philosophy, which depends on human tradition and the basic principles of this world rather than on Christ.*					
Worship is a part of the learning experience in the classroom. *Psalm 29:2 Ascribe to the LORD the glory due his name; worship the Lord in the splendor of his holiness.*					
Selects and demonstrates appropriate teaching procedures and techniques that magnify the nature, character, and role of God. *John 4:24 God is spirit, and his worshipers must worship in spirit and in truth."*					
Is well prepared, as evidenced by comprehensive lesson plans and appropriate use of curriculum and textbook materials. *Proverbs 21:5 The plans of the diligent lead surely to plenty, But those of everyone who is hasty, surely to poverty.*					
Communicates to the student(s) the instructional intent or plan at the beginning of each lesson. *Psalm 33:11 The counsel of the LORD stands forever, the plans of His heart to all generations.*					
Demonstrates knowledge of subject area(s) through instructional practices. *2 Timothy 2:15 Study to show thyself approved unto God, a workman that needeth not to be ashamed, rightly dividing the word of truth.*					
Is able to deliver directions, explanations, and instructional content in a manner understood by students. *John 16:29 Then Jesus' disciples said, "Now you are speaking clearly and without figures of speech."*					

Uses a variety of teaching techniques effectively to address various student learning styles and to help students achieve learning objectives. *1 Corinthians 9:19 For though I am free from all men, I have made myself a servant to all, that I might win the more*					
Individualizes instruction for students with varying abilities. *1 Corinthians 9:22 I have become all things to all men, that I might by all means save some.*					
Students are told how much God loves them and love has an important place in the learning process in the classroom. *John 4:16 & 19 And we have come to know and have believed the love which God has for us. God is love, and one who abides in love abides in God, and God abides in him. We love, because he first loved us.*					

Attempts to motivate all students to become involved in instructional activities (e.g., encourages student participation using various teaching/motivational techniques). *Exodus 35:21 And everyone who was willing and whose heart moved him came and brought an offering to the Lord.*					
Voice is used effectively to emphasize key points, monitor student behavior, and draw student attention. *Isaiah 28:23 Listen and hear my voice; pay attention and hear what I say.*					

Evaluator's Comments:

Commendations:

Recommendations:

The signature of the teacher indicates that the report has been read and discussed. It does not necessarily indicate agreement with the evaluation or recommendation.

_____

Teacher's Signature   Date

_____

Evaluator's/Administrator's Signature

Culver City Christian School
Teacher Self-Evaluation of Spiritual Formation in the Classroom

The mission of Culver City Christian School is to glorify God by means of educating children-spirit, soul, mind, and body by:

- *Leading students into a transforming relationship with Jesus Christ*

- *Instilling a Christian worldview*

- *Providing a community of academic excellence*

- *Cultivating a lifetime commitment of doing God's will*

Purpose of this evaluation: This form is to be used by the teacher and the administrator for the <u>development and assessment of spiritual formation</u> that is taking place in the classroom and for the professional development of the teacher.

Teacher's Name: _____

Grade/Subject Taught: _____

Ratings: When using this form for evaluation, please follow this rating scale:

5 = with high consistency	2 = inconsistently
4 = with good consistency	1 = rarely or not at all
3 = with moderate consistency	

Presence of the Spirit

_____ 1. How often is God glorified in my classroom?
"Glorify the Lord with me; let us exalt his name together." Psalm 34:3

_____ 2. Is the leading of the Holy Spirit evident in me as I use teachable moments to instruct

and mold the students entrusted to me?
"This is what we speak, not in words taught us by human wisdom but in words taught by the Spirit, expressing spiritual truths in spiritual words." I Corinthians 2: 13

_____ 3. Do I teach *Truth* and *Wisdom* rather than just mere facts and knowledge?
"Surely you desire truth in the inner parts; you teach me wisdom in the inmost place." Psalm 51:6

_____ 4. Are the Fruits of the Spirit evident in my life and the lives of my students?

"But the fruit of the Spirit is love, joy, peace, patience, kindness, goodness, faithfulness, gentleness and self –control." Galatians 5: 22-23a

_____ 5. Are the Spiritual gifts of my students recognized, encouraged, and appreciated by
myself and others?

"Now to each one the manifestation of the Spirit is given for the common good. To one there is given through the Spirit the message of wisdom, to another the message of knowledge by means of the same Spirit, to another faith by the same Spirit, to another gifts of healing by that one Spirit, to another miraculous powers, to another prophecy, to another distinguishing between spirits, to another speaking in different kinds of tongues, and to still another the interpretation of tongues" I Corinthians 12: 7-10.

"It was he who gave some to be apostles, some to be prophets, some to be evangelists, and some to be pastors and teachers, to prepare God's people for works of service, so that the body of Christ may be built up until we all reach unity in the faith and in the knowledge of the Son of God and become mature, attaining to the whole measure of the fullness of Christ." Ephesians 4: 11-13

"We have different gifts, according to the grace given us. If a man's gift is prophesying, let him use it in proportion to his faith. If it is serving, let him serve; if it is teaching, let him teach; if it is encouraging, let him encourage; if it is contributing to the needs of others, let him give generously; if it is leadership, let him govern diligently; if it is showing mercy, let him do it cheerfully." Romans 12: 6-8

_____ 6. Do I encourage students to use discernment and critical thinking skills regarding life
issues?

"My son, preserve sound judgment and discernment, do not let them out of your sight." Proverbs 3: 21

_____ 7. Are my students encouraged to be dependent on God rather than just be independent
thinkers?

"Trust in the LORD with all your heart and lean not on your own understanding; in all your ways acknowledge him, and he will direct your paths." Proverbs 3: 5-6

_____ 8. Do I encourage my students to please God rather than themselves and their selfish
lusts?

"Those controlled by the sinful nature cannot please God." Romans 8: 8

"And we pray this in order that you may live a life worthy of the Lord and may please him in every way: bearing fruit in every good work, growing in the knowledge of God." Colossians 1: 10

_____ 9. Is prayer integrated into the life of the classroom?

"Pray continuously." I Thessalonians 5: 17

_____ 10. Is humility promoted and pride discouraged in my classroom?

"Young men, in the same way be submissive to those who are older. All of you clothe yourselves with humility toward one another, because, 'God opposes the proud but gives grace to the humble.'" I Peter 5: 5

Biblical Integration and Worldview

_____ 1. Do I hold up the Bible as God's inerrant revelation to mankind?

"All Scripture is God-breathed and is useful for teaching, rebuking, correcting and training in righteousness." 2 Timothy 3: 16

_____ 2. Do I foster a familiarity and love for God's word?

"Oh, how I love your law! I meditate on it all day long" Psalm 119: 97

_____ 3. Do I teach the academic subjects within the Biblical metanarrative of God's creation,

man's fall, and Christ' redemption as opposed to secular humanism?

"See to it that no one takes you captive through hollow and deceptive philosophy, which depends on human tradition and the basic principles of this world rather than on Christ." Colossians 2: 8

_____ 4. Are Biblical principles applied to life situations?

"Do not merely listen to the word, and so deceive yourselves. Do what it says." James 1: 22

_____ 5. Is Biblical integration evident in my lesson plans and content?

"He is before all things, and in him all things hold together. And he is the head of the body, the church; he is the beginning and the firstborn from among the dead, so that in everything he might have the supremacy. For God was pleased to have all his fullness dwell in him, and through him to reconcile to himself all things, whether things on earth or things in heaven, by making peace through his blood, shed on the cross." Colossians 1: 17-20

_____ 6. Is a Christian worldview taught that provides a unified vision of how to view and relate

to the world around us?

"He is the image of the invisible God, the firstborn over all creation. For by him all things were created: things in heaven and on earth, visible and invisible, whether thrones or powers or rulers or authorities; all things were created by him and for him. He is before all things, and in him all things hold together. And he is the head of the body, the church; he is the beginning and the firstborn from among the dead, so that in everything he might have the supremacy." Colossians 1: 15-18

_____ 7. Do I look for opportunities to lead my students to a personal relationship with Christ?

"Therefore go and make disciples of all nations, baptizing them in the name of the Father and of the Son and of the Holy Spirit" Matthew 28: 19

_____ 8. Is discipleship to Jesus Christ evident in my classroom?

"This is to my Father's glory, that you bear much fruit, showing yourselves to be my disciples." John 15: 8

Love in Learning

_____ 1. Is the love of God evident in student and teacher interactions?

"By this all men will know that you are my disciples, if you love one another." John 13: 35

_____ 2. Is the love of God and neighbor reflected in the rules of my classroom?

"'Love the Lord your God with all your heart and with all your soul and with all your mind.' This is the first and greatest commandment. And the second is like it: 'Love your neighbor as yourself.'" Matthew 22: 37-39

_____ 3. Does the love of God manifest itself in action such as acts of kindness or compassion?

"Dear children, let us not love with words or tongue but with actions and in truth." I John 3:18

_____ 4. Does the love of God demonstrate itself in gratefulness and stewardship of what He has given us?

"Let the word of Christ dwell in you richly as you teach and admonish one another with all wisdom, and as you sing psalms, hymns and spiritual songs with gratitude in your hearts to God." Colossians 3: 16

Hospitality and Community

_____ 1. Do I provide a welcoming community by which the children can be a part of?

"And whoever welcomes a little child like this in my name welcomes me." Matthew 18: 5

_____ 2. Do I encourage healthy fellowship in all relationships--between teacher and student,

God and student, and student and student?

"And let us consider how we may spur one another on toward love and good deeds. Let us not give up meeting together, as some are in the habit of doing, but let us encourage one another – and all the more as you see the Day approaching." Hebrews 10: 24-25

_____ 3. Do I demonstrate a spirit of service?

". . .just as the Son of Man did not come to be served, but to serve, and to give his life as a ransom for many." Matthew 20: 28

_____ 4. Do my students demonstrate a spirit of service?

". . .just as the Son of Man did not come to be served, but to serve, and to give his life as a ransom for many." Matthew 20: 28

_____ 5. Is my classroom a place of healing?

"The tongue that brings healing is a tree of life, but a deceitful tongue crushes the spirit." Proverbs 15: 4

_____ 6. Do I provide a safe place where students let go of fear and anxiety in the learning

process?

"For God did not give us a spirit of timidity, but a spirit of power, of love and of self-discipline." 2 Timothy 1: 7

_____ 7. Is there a healthy balance of competition *and cooperation* in my classroom?

"I have fought the good fight, I have finished the race, I have kept the faith." 2 Timothy 4: 7
"Make every effort to keep the unity of the Spirit through the bond of peace." Ephesians 4: 3

Self-Knowledge and Reflection

_____ 1. Do I use questions that cause the students to reflect on God and on the relationship

between God and what they are learning?

"Jesus and his disciples went on to the villages around Caesarea Philippi. On the way he asked them, "Who do people say I am?" Mark 8: 27

_____ 2. Is self-knowledge encouraged through students' identity in Christ?

"Therefore, if anyone is in Christ, he is a new creation; the old has gone, the new has come!: 2 Corinthians 5: 17

_____ 3. Do I promote appropriate self-disclosure during the lesson that allows the students to

reflect on their own self-knowledge?

"I have revealed you to those whom you gave me out of the world. They were yours; you gave them to me and they have obeyed your word." John 17: 6

_____ 4. Do teachers and students show they are good listeners?

> *"My dear brothers, take note of this: Everyone should be quick to listen, slow to speak and slow to become angry." James 1: 19*

_____ 5. Through reflection and encouragement, are my students becoming aware of how God has gifted them to serve Him and are they encouraged to use that self-knowledge to make a lifetime commitment to serving God?

> *"For this reason I remind you to fan into flame the gift of God, which is in you through the laying on of my hands." 2 Timothy 1: 6*

Commendations:

Recommendations:

Goals for Professional Growth*
Completion Date

"I press on toward the goal to win the prize for which God has called me heavenward in Christ Jesus." Philippians 3:14

1.

2.

3.

*To be completed with your supervisor after comparison and discussion of evaluations.

Teacher's signature: _____ Date: _____

      Administrator's signature: _____Date: _____

CHINO VALLEY CHRISTIAN SCHOOLS
Job Description/Evaluation
Developing and nurturing children through excellence in Christ-Centered Education

Description: To prayerfully help students learn subject matter, skills, and attitudes that will contribute to their development as mature, able, and responsible Christian men and women to the praise and glory of God.

Qualifications: The teacher shall be one who has received Jesus Christ as Savior and Lord. The teacher shall be a member in good standing of an evangelical church and shall lead a mature Christian life. She/He shall be a person with spiritual, academic and leadership abilities that will allow him/her to "train up a child in the way he should go". The teacher shall reflect the purpose of the school to honor Christ in every class and in every activity. The teacher shall be a college graduate, certified by ACSI, and one who feels called of God to the teaching profession. Other qualifications may be added by the Board as deemed appropriate.

> **Note:** When using this form for evaluation, follow this rating scale:
>
> 5-with high consistency   2-inconsistently
> 4-with good consistency   1-rarely
> 3-with moderate consistency

Responsible to: Administrator

Supervises: Aides and volunteers

Responsibilities:

Developing and nurturing children through excellence in Christ-Centered Education

_____1. *Wisdom:* Wisdom comes only from God. Wisdom is a person (Jesus Christ). Searches and discusses scriptural truth. *James 1:5 If any of you lacks wisdom, he should ask God, who gives generously to all without finding fault, and it will be given to him.*

_____ 2. *Biblical Principles:* The Bible tells us who God is and how we should live our lives. Teaching and understanding what we should do with the Word of God: a) read it to receive a blessing and grow, b) study it to discern truth from error, c) keep it out of love for the Lord and d) sharing it with others. *Psalm 119:105 Thy word is a lamp unto my feet, and a light unto my path.*

_____ 3. *Worship:* Encourages worship of God in a variety of ways, well planned and executed. ***Colossians 3:16 Let the word of Christ dwell in you richly in all wisdom; teaching and admonishing one another in psalms and hymns and spiritual songs, singing with grace in your hearts to the Lord.***

_____ 4. *Submission and obedience:* Submission and obedience are things we do for our own good-not out of duty to someone else. When we are disobedient to authority, we are disobedient to God as well. Teaching and learning submission and obedience. ***2 John: 6 And this is love: that we walk in obedience to his commands. As you have heard from the beginning, his command is that you walk in love. I Peter 5:5 Young men, in the same way be submissive to those who are older. All of you, clothe yourselves with humility toward one another, because, "God opposes the proud but gives grace to the humble."***

_____5. *Humility:* God promises to teach us what we need to know if we are willing to listen. Developing humility vs. pride ***Proverbs 15:33 the fear of the Lord is the instruction of wisdom; and before honor is humility.***

_____6. *Service:* God uses men to show His power and love. Teaching and learning how to serve Him and others. ***Ephesians 6:7 Serve wholeheartedly, as if you were serving the Lord, not men, because you know that the Lord will reward everyone for whatever good he does...***

_____7. *Forgiveness:* We need to learn to forgive others when they wrong us. Teaching and learning about forgiveness. ***Ephesians 4:32 And be ye kind one to another, tenderhearted, forgiving one another, even as God for Christ's sake hath forgiven you.***

_____ 8. *Leading of the Holy Spirit:* Interventions and leadings and followings-allowing the Holy Spirit to make changes in daily life and attitude. ***Matthew 5:3-12 Blessed are the poor in spirit, for theirs is the kingdom of heaven...***

_____9. *Trust:* Teaching and learning to trust God because we know He will not change what He says. We can trust God to be with us through every circumstance. ***Proverbs 3:5 Trust in the Lord with all your heart and lean not on your own understanding; in all your ways acknowledge him and he will make your paths straight.***

Developing and *nurturing children* through excellence in Christ-Centered Education

_____1. Teaching and understanding what salvation is all about (creation, fall, repentance, and restoration) and encourages students to trust Christ as their Savior and grow in their faith. ***John 3:16 For God so loved the world that he gave his one and only Son, that whoever believes in him shall not perish but have eternal life.***

_____2. Emphasizes to students the reality of their self-worth in Christ. ***I Peter 3:4 Instead, it should be that of your inner self, the unfading beauty of a gentle and quiet spirit, which is of great worth in God's sight.***

_____3. Demonstrates and teaches the character qualities of the Fruits of the Spirit *Galatians 5:22-23 But the fruit of the Spirit is love, joy, peace, patience, kindness, goodness, faithfulness, gentleness, and self-control. Against such things there is no law.*

_____4. Demonstrates and evidence of the Beatitudes: *Matthew 5:3-10* **"Blessed are the poor in spirit"**-being emptied of self and filled with Christ; **"Blessed are they that mourn"**- a turning to God from sin; **"Blessed are the meek"**-learning to let the Holy Spirit lead; **"Blessed are the hungry and thirsty"**-seeking a right standing before God; **"Blessed are the merciful"**-understanding what forgiveness is and why it is important to forgive others; **"Blessed are the pure in heart"**-focusing on inner development rather than outward conformity; **"Blessed are the peacemakers"**-developing peace with God and with others as a pattern of life; **"Blessed are the persecuted"**-our willingness to stand for Christ under all circumstances

Developing and nurturing children through excellence in *Christ-Centered* Education

_____1. Seeks to role-model in speech, actions, and attitude, and a consistent daily walk with Jesus Christ. *I. Cor. 15:58 Always give yourselves fully to the work of the Lord, because you know that your labor in the Lord is not in vain.*

_____2. Sets an example of the importance of prayer, Scripture memorization and study, witnessing, and unity in Christian fellowship. *Phil.4:6-7 Be careful for nothing; but in every thing by prayer and supplication with thanksgiving let your requests be made known unto God. And the peace of God, which passeth all understanding, shall keep your hearts and minds through Christ Jesus.*

_____3. Implements "body-life" principles as they relate to the spiritual well being of students, and staff. *Romans 12:16 Be of the same mind one toward another.*

_____4. Follows the Matthew 18 principle in dealing with students, parents, staff, and administration. *Matt. 18:15-16 If your brother sins against you, go and show him his fault, just between the two of you. If he listens to you, you have won your brother over. But if he will not listen, take one or two others along, so that every matter may be established by the testimony of two or three witnesses.*

_____5. Shows support for the role of parents as primarily responsible before God for their child's education and assists them in the task. *Ephesians 6:1-3 Children, obey your parents in the Lord, for this is right. "Honor your father and mother"-which is the first commandment with a promise-"that it may go well with you and that you may enjoy long life on earth."*

_____6. Cooperates with the board and administration in implementing all policies, procedures, and directives governing the operation of the school. Submits respectfully and is loyal to authority. *Ephesians 6:7 Serve wholeheartedly, as if you were serving the Lord, not men, because you know that the Lord will reward everyone for whatever good he does...*

_____7. Seeks the counsel of the administrator, colleagues, and parents and is teachable. *Proverbs 11P:14 Where no counsel is, the people fall: but in the multitude of counselors there is safety.*

Developing and nurturing children through *excellence in Christ-Centered Education*

_____1. Integrates Biblical principles and the Christian philosophy of education throughout the curriculum. *II Timothy 3:16,17 All scripture is God-breathed and   is useful for teaching, rebuking, correcting and training in righteousness, so that the man of God may be thoroughly equipped for every good work.*

_____2. Employs a variety of instructional aids, methods, materials, and special activities that will provide for creative teaching to reach the whole child-spiritual, mental, physical, social, and emotional, challenging each to do his best work. *Proverbs 22:6 Train a child in the way he should go, and when he is old he will not turn from it.*

_____3. Assesses the learning of students on a regular basis and provides progress reports and report cards to meet the demands for a comprehensive understanding of each student's growth. *Proverbs 20:11 Even a child is known by his doings, whether his work be pure, and whether it be right.*

_____4. Keeps proper discipline in the classroom and on the school premises for a good teaching community. *Proverbs 3:11-12 ...do not despise the Lord's discipline and do not resent his rebuke, because the Lord disciplines those he loves, as a   father the son he delights in.*

_____

Teacher Signature

_____

Grade/Subject

_____

Administrator Signature

Philippians 4:9 Those things, which ye have both learned, and received, and heard, and seen in me, do: and the God of peace shall be with you.

Staff Spiritual Formation Assessment

Developing and nurturing children through excellence in Christ-centered education

And thou shalt love the Lord thy God with all thy heart, and with all thy soul, and with all thy mind, and with all thy strength: this is the first commandment.

Mark 12:30

(Please circle the number that applies to you)

HEART

My attitudes and actions towards others reflect God's love for them, not their benefit to me (II Cor. 5:16).

1-Never 2-Seldom 3-Sometimes 4-Usually 5-Always

I forgive others as Christ forgave me (Col. 3:13).

1-Never 2-Seldom 3-Sometimes 4-Usually 5-Always

My attitudes towards others reflect humility instead of pride (Phil. 2:3).

1-Never 2-Seldom 3-Sometimes 4-Usually 5-Always

I reflect Christ to my family members (Eph. 5:25).

1-Never 2-Seldom 3-Sometimes 4-Usually 5-Always

SOUL

I believe that the only way to have a personal relationship with God on earth and eternal life with Him in heaven is by faith in the death and resurrection of Jesus Christ and not by anything I do (Rom. 10:9).

1-Strongly Disagree 2-Disagree 3-Don't Know 4-Agree 5-Strongly Agree

I believe that I am forgiven because my sins were placed upon Jesus Christ on the cross, and His righteousness was credited to me (II Cor. 5:21).

1-Strongly Disagree 2-Disagree 3-Don't Know 4-Agree 5-Strongly Agree

I believe that salvation is not just a change in behavior, but through the power of the Holy Spirit I am a new person with a new future, hope and purpose (II Cor. 5:17).

1-Strongly Disagree 2-Disagree 3-Don't Know 4-Agree 5-Strongly Agree

I believe when I became a Christian, I turned from a life of sin and made Jesus Lord of my life (Acts 2:37-39).

1-Strongly Disagree 2-Disagree 3-Don't Know 4-Agree 5-Strongly Agree

I communicate with God and He communicates with me through prayer (Luke 1:13).

1-Never 2-Seldom 3-Sometimes 4-Usually 5-Always

I spend meaningful time in prayer every day (Dan. 6:10).
1-Never   2-Seldom   3-Sometimes   4-Usually   5-Always
I pray more for God's will to be done than for my needs to be met (Mt. 6:10; 26:39).
1-Never   2-Seldom   3-Sometimes   4-Usually   5-Always
I pray for others; even my enemies (Mt. 5:44; Col. 4:12).
1-Never   2-Seldom   3-Sometimes   4-Usually   5-Always
I believe that prayer changes things (James 5:13 -18).
1-Never   2-Seldom   3-Sometimes   4-Usually   5-Always
I worship God in every situation (Rev. 5:13-14).
1-Never   2-Seldom   3-Sometimes   4-Usually   5-Always
I worship God through a life that is fully committed to Him (Rom. 12:1).
1-Never   2-Seldom   3-Sometimes   4-Usually   5-Always
I have a thankful attitude for what God has done for me (Luke. 17:11 -19).
1-Never   2-Seldom   3-Sometimes   4-Usually   5-Always
I value God more than anything or anyone (Ex. 20:3-6).
1-Never   2-Seldom   3-Sometimes   4-Usually   5-Always

MIND

Since I became a Christian, there has been a change in my behavior and attitude that is noticeable to others (I Cor. 6:11).
1-Never   2-Seldom   3-Sometimes   4-Usually   5-Always
I guard what I see, hear and think so that I can be more like Jesus (Rom. 12:2).
1-Never   2-Seldom   3-Sometimes   4-Usually   5-Always
I practice self-control in every area of my life (Rom. 6:14 -16).
1-Never   2-Seldom   3-Sometimes   4-Usually   5-Always
I depend on the power of the Holy Spirit to act like Christ (Gal. 5:22 -25).
1-Never   2-Seldom   3-Sometimes   4-Usually   5-Always
I am an example of Jesus Christ to others through my actions (I Cor. 11:1).
1-Never   2-Seldom   3-Sometimes   4-Usually   5-Always
Every part of my life is dedicated to God and His purpose (Rom. 12:1).
1-Never   2-Seldom   3-Sometimes   4-Usually   5-Always
My actions resemble what the Bible teaches more than what my culture promotes (I Pet. 4:4).
1-Never   2-Seldom   3-Sometimes   4-Usually   5-Always
I read the Bible everyday (II Tim. 3:16).
1-Never   2-Seldom   3-Sometimes   4-Usually   5-Always

I try to obey everything I read in Scripture (James 1:22).
1-Never   2-Seldom   3-Sometimes   4-Usually   5-Always
I study the Bible enough for it to become a part of my thought process as a guard against sin (Ps. 119:11).
1-Never   2-Seldom   3-Sometimes   4-Usually   5-Always
I have a good understanding of the history and culture of the Bible (I Cor. 10:6).
1-Never   2-Seldom   3-Sometimes   4-Usually   5-Always

STRENGTH

I treat others like I want to be treated (Mt. 7:12).
1-Never   2-Seldom   3-Sometimes   4-Usually   5-Always
I display my love for God in the way I treat other people (Mt. 22:37 - 40).
1-Never   2-Seldom   3-Sometimes   4-Usually   5-Always
My actions reflect that everything I am or possess belongs to God and that I should use it as He would (I Tim. 6:17 -19).
1-Never   2-Seldom   3-Sometimes   4-Usually   5-Always
I am faithful in the little things so that God will entrust me with more (Mt. 25:21).
1-Never   2-Seldom   3-Sometimes   4-Usually   5-Always
My main goal in life is to serve others (Phil. 2:5-7).
1-Never   2-Seldom   3-Sometimes   4-Usually   5-Always
I encourage recognition of others over myself (Mt. 6:1).
1-Never   2-Seldom   3-Sometimes   4-Usually   5-Always
I believe that accomplishing God's will in the lives of others is more important than the specific role that I play (I Cor. 3:5-9).
1-Never   2-Seldom   3-Sometimes   4-Usually   5-Always
I know my talents and spiritual gifts and use them to serve the body of Christ (I Cor. 12:7).
1-Never   2-Seldom   3-Sometimes   4-Usually   5-Always
I share my faith with non-Christians (II Cor. 5:20).
1-Never   2-Seldom   3-Sometimes   4-Usually   5-Always
I try to live so that others will see Christ in me (Eph. 4:1).
1-Never   2-Seldom   3-Sometimes   4-Usually   5-Always
I pray for non-Christians to accept Jesus (Phil. 3:18).
1-Never   2-Seldom   3-Sometimes   4-Usually   5-Always

Classroom Observation Form

Developing and nurturing children through excellence in Christ-centered education

II Peter 1:4-7 "Now since you have become partakers of the divine nature, applying all diligence, in your faith supply moral excellence, and in your moral excellence, knowledge; and in your knowledge, self-control, and in your self-control, perseverance, and in your perseverance, godliness, and in your godliness, brotherly kindness, and in your brotherly kindness, love."

Teacher_____Grade____Date_____

No. of Students_____Length of

Visit_____Subject_____

Mark each item observed according to the following scale:

> 5-with high consistency   2-inconsistently
> 4-with good consistency   1-rarely
> 3-with moderate consistency   0-not observed

____ *Salvation:* Teaching and understanding what salvation is all about (creation, fall, repentance, and restoration) and challenging students to trust Christ as their Savior. *John 3:16 For God so loved the world that he gave his one and only Son, that whoever believes in him shall not perish but have eternal life.*

____*Bible:* The Bible tells us who God is and how we should live our lives. Teaching and understanding what we should do with the Word of God: a) read it to receive a blessing and grow, b) study it to discern truth from error, c) keep it out of love for the Lord and d) sharing it with others. *Psalm 119:105 Thy word is a lamp unto my feet, and a light unto my path.*

____*Prayer:* Prayer is focused on God-adoring Him, confessing sins to Him, thanking Him, and asking Him for things. Teaching, understanding, and demonstrating the importance of prayer. *Jeremiah 29:12-13 Then you will call upon me and come and pray to me, and I will listen to you. You will seek me and find me when you seek me with all your heart.*

____*Worship:* Encourages worship of God in a variety of ways, well planned and executed. *Colossians 3:16 Let the word of Christ dwell in you richly in all wisdom; teaching and admonishing one another in psalms and hymns and spiritual songs, singing with grace in your hearts to the Lord.*

___*Biblical principles:* A principle is an unchanging rule based on the character of God, by which we govern our lives. Biblical principles are stated, explained and applied. *Exodus 20:6 but showing love to a thousand generations of those who love me and keep* **my** *commandments.*

___*Fruits of the Spirit:* The fruit of the Spirit is the character of God. Teaching and developing the fruit of the Spirit *Galatians 5:22-23 But the fruit of the Spirit is love___, joy___, peace___, patience___, kindness___, goodness___, faithfulness___, gentleness___, and self-control___. Against such things there is no law.*

___*Wisdom:* Wisdom comes only from God. Wisdom is a person (Jesus Christ). Searching and discussing scriptural truth. *James 1:5 If any of you lacks wisdom, he should ask God, who gives generously to all without finding fault, and it will be given to him.*

___*Submission & Obedience:* Submission and obedience are things we do for our own good-not out of duty to someone else. When we are disobedient to authority, we are disobedient to God as well. Teaching and learning submission and obedience. *2 John: 6 And this is love: that we walk in obedience to his commands. As you have heard from the beginning, his command is that you walk in love. I Peter 5:5 Young men, in the same way be submissive to those who are older. All of you, clothe yourselves with humility toward one another, because, "God opposes the proud but gives grace to the humble."*

___*Humility:* God promises to teach us what we need to know if we are willing to listen. Developing humility vs. pride *Proverbs 15:33 The fear of the Lord is the instruction of wisdom; and before honor is humility.*

___*Service:* God uses men to show His power and love. Teaching and learning how to serve Him and others. *Ephesians 6:7 Serve wholeheartedly, as if you were serving the Lord, not men, because you know that the Lord will reward everyone for whatever good he does...*

___ *Trust:* Teaching and learning to trust God because we know He will not change what He says. We can trust God to be with us through every circumstance.   *Proverbs 3:5 Trust in the Lord with all your heart and lean not on your own   understanding; in all your ways acknowledge him and he will make your paths straight.*

___*Forgiveness:* We need to learn to forgive others when they wrong us. Teaching and learning about forgiveness. *Ephesians 4:32 And be ye kind one to another, tenderhearted, forgiving one another, even   as God for Christ's sake hath forgiven you.*

___*Encouragement:* God promises to be with us in the midst of our trials. He has given us the Holy Spirit as our guide. *Philippians 4:13 I can do all things through Christ which strengtheneth me.*

___*Leading of the Holy Spirit:* **Interventions and leadings and followings-allowing the Holy Spirit to make changes in students and my life and attitude.**

LEADERSHIP AND ADMINISTRATION SURVEY
WESTERN CHRISITAN SCHOOLS
CLAREMONT CAMPUS

Our Mission: *The mission of Western Christian Schools if to provide a Christ-centered community that integrates faith and quality education.*

Dear Teachers,

Please take some time to prayerfully reflect and score these statements regarding the performance of your administrative leadership team. Your input is extremely valuable to us as we seek to improve and ultimately bring glory to God in our service.

The following statements are based on the ACSI *Encyclopedia of Bible Truths for School Subjects* (Dr. Ruth Haycock, 1993)

Scale: (4) Outstanding   (3) Well Done   (2) Acceptable   (1) Poor

_____1.The leaders effectively set the pattern for the whole group (faculty).
> *Proverbs 28: 2 "…By a man of understanding and knowledge, right will be prolonged.*

_____2.The leaders delegate responsibility and include the authority to act with set limits.
> *Matthew 14:19 "He blessed and broke and gave the loaves to the disciples; and the disciples gave to the multitudes."*

_____3.The leaders show concern for the unity and well-being of the community.
> *I Corinthians 12:12 "For as the body is one and has many members, but all the members*
> *of that one body, being many, are one body, so also is Christ."*

_____4.The leaders are faithful in carrying out responsibilities and keeping promises.
> *Romans 12:8 "He who leads, let him do it with diligence."*

_____5.The leaders place God's honor above their own and model servanthood to the community.
> *Matthew 20:28 "…Just as the Son of Man did not come to be served, but to serve, and to*
> *give his life as a ransom for many."*

_____6.The leaders appreciate each member's unique gifts from God.
> *Romans 12:6 "Having then gifts differing according to the grace that is given to us, let us*
> *use them…"*

_____7.Job descriptions are clearly stated and fairly executed within the community.

Luke 10: 2 "The harvest is plentiful, but the workers are few. Ask the Lord of the harvest,

to send out workers into his harvest field."

____8.The leaders give adequate preparation for any major changes that occur.

Joshua 1:11 "Go through the camp and tell the people, 'Get your supplies ready. Three

days now you will cross the Jordan..."

____ 9.The leaders reflect godly and exemplary virtues.

Joshua 1:8 "This Book of Law shall not depart from your mouth, but you shall meditate

in it day and night, that you may observe to do all that is written in it."

____10.The decisions made by the administration are based upon Scripture and indicate God's

will.

Proverbs16:33 "The lot is cast into the lap; but its every decision is from the Lord."

Additional comments:

Culver City Christian School

Student Evaluation

Dear CCCS Student,

All of the teachers and staff here at CCCS are here to honor God and serve you as our students. Your thoughts and answers to the following questions are very important to us so that we can provide you the very best Christ-centered education possible. Take a moment to look at our mission statement (the reason our schools exists) and then answer the following questions below as best you can. We appreciate and thank you for your honest and helpful answers.

The mission of Culver City Christian School is to glorify God by means of educating children-spirit, soul, mind, and body by:

- *Leading students into a transforming relationship with Jesus Christ*

- *Instilling a Christian worldview*

- *Providing a community of academic excellence*

- *Cultivating a lifetime commitment of doing God's will*

Your Teacher's Name: -

_____Grade:_____

Purpose of evaluation: The purpose of this evaluation is to help your teacher make her/his class even better than it is right now.

Ratings: When using this form for evaluation, please follow this rating scale:

               5 = all the time, consistently   2 = a little bit
               4 = most of the time   1 = not at all
               3 = some of the time

1. The teacher shows love for God in word and action.

   _____

2. The teacher demonstrates a Godly love for me in word and action.

   _____

3. The teacher relates God's word to whatever we study.

_____

4. The teacher shows me how to apply God's word to everyday life.

   _____

5. The teacher talks often about his or her relationship to Christ.

   _____

6. The teacher talks and how I can have a relationship with Jesus.

   _____

7. The teacher talks to our class about how to grow as Christians and be more like Jesus.   _____

7. The teacher encourages us to pray in the classroom.

   _____

8. The teacher encourages us to trust God.

   _____

9. The teacher recognizes and encourages me to see the special abilities that I have. _____

10. The teacher asks our class questions so that we have to think things through on
our own.   _____

11. My teacher makes me feel welcome and comfortable in the classroom.

   _____

12. My teacher is fair in discipline.

   _____

13. My teacher expects me to do my best.

   _____

14. My teacher expects me to cooperate with my classmates.

   _____

15. My teacher encourages my class to serve God and others.

   _____

16. My teacher gives God praise and worship in class and encourages us to do the
same. _____
What do you like best about your teacher?

What is one thing that your teacher could improve on?

In what ways does your teacher show the fruits of the Spirit (love, joy, peace, patience, kindness, goodness, faithfulness, gentleness, and self-control)?

35024897R00160

Made in the USA
San Bernardino, CA
14 June 2016

WHAT YOU DON'T KNOW ABOUT THE

100

MOST IMPORTANT EVENTS IN
CHURCH HISTORY